Looking Around

Other Books by Witold Rybczynski

Paper Heroes

Taming the Tiger

Home

The Most Beautiful House in the World

Waiting for the Weekend

Witold
Rybczynski

Looking Around

A Journey Through
Architecture

Viking

VIKING
Published by the Penguin Group
Viking Penguin, a division of Penguin Books USA Inc.,
375 Hudson Street, New York, New York 10014, U.S.A.
Penguin Books Ltd, 27 Wrights Lane, London W8 5TZ, England
Penguin Books Australia Ltd, Ringwood, Victoria, Australia
Penguin Books Canada Ltd, 10 Alcorn Avenue, Suite 300, Toronto, Ontario, Canada M4V 3B2
Penguin Books (N.Z.) Ltd, 182–190 Wairau Road, Auckland 10, New Zealand

Penguin Books Ltd, Registered Offices: Harmondsworth, Middlesex, England

First published in 1993 by Viking Penguin, a division of Penguin Books USA Inc.

10 9 8 7 6 5 4 3 2 1

Most of the essays in this collection first appeared, some in slightly different form, in the following periodicals: *Architectural Record*, *Art & Antiques*, *The Atlantic*, *Domino*, *The Fifth Column*, *The Los Angeles Times Magazine*, *The New York Review of Books*, *The New York Times*, *Newsday*, *Quality*, *Saturday Night*, *Wigwag*, and *The Wilson Quarterly*.

A portion of "If a Chair Is a Work of Art, Can You Still Sit on It?" was originally published in the catalogue for the exhibition "Masterworks," Peter Joseph Gallery, and "Little Architects, Little Architecture" in the catalogue for the exhibition "Building in Boxes," Canadian Centre for Architecture.

Grateful acknowledgment is made for permission to reprint "A Place Map" from *McGill: A Celebration*, McGill–Queens University Press, Copyright 1991 by McGill–Queens University Press, and "Art Inside the Walls" from Mr. Rybczynski's monograph titled *A Place for Art*, National Gallery of Canada, Copyright by Her Majesty the Queen in Right of Canada (1992) as represented by the National Museums of Canada.

Illustration credits:
Part I: The Grow Home, Witold Rybczynski and Avi Friedman, Architects, Drawing by Susan Ross, reproduced courtesy of McGill University.
Part II: The Portland Building, View from Fifth Avenue, Michael Graves, Architect, reproduced courtesy of Michael Graves.
Part III: Portico Details of the Pantheon, Rome, from *I Quattro Libri dell'Architettura* by Andrea Palladio, published in Venice, 1570. Illustration taken from facsimile edition published by Casa Editrice Libraria Ulrico Hoepli SpA, Milan, Italy, 1980.

LIBRARY OF CONGRESS CATALOGING IN PUBLICATION DATA
Rybczynski, Witold. Looking around: a journey through architecture/Witold Rybczynski.
p. cm. ISBN 0-670-84421-7 1. Architecture—Themes, motives. I. Title. NA2550.R97
1992 720—dc20 92-14555

Printed in the United States of America • Set in Electra • Designed by Francesca Belanger

For my editors

Acknowledgments

Almost all these pieces, written between 1986 and 1991, first appeared in magazines and newspapers, and I must acknowledge the guidance of several editors, especially Lex Kaplen and Harriet Brown, with whom I worked so happily at *Wigwag*; Marilyn Minden at the *New York Times*; Bill Whitworth and Corby Kummer at the estimable *Atlantic*; Robert Silvers, always a stimulating editor, at the *New York Review of Books*; John Fraser and Barbara Moon at *Saturday Night*; Gene Stone at the *Los Angeles Times*; and Usher Caplan at the National Gallery of Canada.

"Home, Sweet Bungalow Home," "Our Town," "Airports," "At the Mall," "The Birthplace of Postmodernism," " 'But Is It Art?'," "How to Pick an Architect," and "Fame" appeared in *Wigwag*, where I was architecture critic from October 1989 until February 1991, when the magazine sadly ceased publication. "As American as Blue Jeans and Sweat Shirts," "Habitat Revisited," "Hot Housing Buttons," "If a Chair Is a Work of Art, Can You Still Sit on It?," "Curious Shrines," "Shaping Chicago's Future," "God Isn't in the Details, After All," and "Listen to the Melody" appeared in the Arts & Leisure section of the *New York Times*. "Living Smaller" and "Should Suburbs Be Designed?" were written for the *Atlantic*; "Good Housekeeping" and "Getting Away from It All" for the *New York Review of Books;* "A National Gallery" and "A National Billboard" for *Saturday Night*. "High Tech" appeared in *Domino*, "From Mao's House to Our House" in the *Los Angeles Times Magazine*, and "Low-Cost Classicism" in *The Fifth Column*, a Canadian architecture students' magazine.

Several pieces were the result of specific requests: "A Homemade House" was commissioned by *Art & Antiques*, "A Decade of Disorientation: 1910–19" by *Architectural Record*, "The Androgynous Home" by *Quality*, and "Looking Back to the Future" by *Newsday*. "Little Architects, Little Architecture" was written as a catalogue essay for the Canadian Centre for Architecture's exhibition "Buildings in Boxes"; "A Place Map" appeared in *McGill: A Celebration*, published by McGill–Queens University Press. "Art Inside the Walls" is part of a longer monograph titled *A Place for Art*, published by the National Gallery of Canada.

"Will the Real California Architecture Please Stand Up?" was the title of the Tenth Monterey Design Conference, organized by the California Council and the American Institute of Architects. I have shamelessly appropriated the title for my essay, which was originally presented in slightly different form as a lecture for this event. "If a Chair Is a Work of Art, Can You Still Sit on It?" was expanded by adding material that originally appeared in a catalogue essay commissioned by the Peter Joseph Gallery for the 1991 exhibition "Masterworks." In February 1991, I was invited to give the Teetzel Lectures by University College in Toronto; "The Art of Building, or the Building of Art?" was the result, and it later appeared in *The Wilson Quarterly*. My gratitude to professors Peter

Richardson and Lynd Forguson for their kindness in offering me this opportunity to put my thoughts in order.

In most cases, the original essays have been edited to eliminate redundancies and anomalies of grammar and punctuation; their sense remains unchanged. Thanks are due to Nan Graham at Viking for her sterling assistance and sage advice in editing, ordering, and culling this collection, to Eva Resnikova for copy-editing, and to Carl Brandt for his wise counsel.

W.R.

The Boathouse, October 1991

Contents

Introduction

I never expected to write architecture criticism. For one thing, it seemed unlikely that the opportunity would present itself; for another, I've always had reservations about the value of architecture critics. More than twenty years ago, my teacher Peter Collins pointed out the futility of reviewing buildings in the popular press. He reasoned that although the public reads reviews of plays, movies, and concerts in order to decide whether or not to attend them, the same could hardly be said of buildings, which would be inhabited—or used—irrespective of any positive or negative evaluation.

I found myself persuaded by his views. After all, Lincoln Center was poorly received by architecture critics, but that did not stop New Yorkers from going to the opera. The fact that the Lyndon B. Johnson Presidential Library was not praised by the architectural press appears to have had no effect on attendance (it is the most popular of all the presidential libraries); conversely, the Yale School of Architecture, which received accolades when it was built in 1963, proved to be unpopular with succeeding generations of students.

There are other difficulties with reviewing buildings. The press is typically invited to view the building before it is officially opened—that is, before it is actually put to use. How is it possible to formulate a considered judgment about what is really an empty shell, devoid of its inhabitants, often even unfurnished? The new Paris Opera, for example, was dismissed by architecture critics before they had an opportunity to experience performances in it. By the time a building is occupied and a critic might ask users their opinion of it, the architecture is old news.

But even if the critic were to postpone his review, the task of evaluating the success or failure of a building is not an easy one. A building succeeds—or fails—on many different levels: as a practical object as well as a beautiful one, as a work of art, but also as a setting for life. To complicate matters further, there are many vantage points from which to pass judgment on a building. A museum is experienced differently by passersby, visitors, scholars, and curators. The tourist (or the visiting critic) may be thrilled by the dramatic lobby, but what of the regular museumgoer, who after the seventh visit continues to be assaulted by the exciting forms? Buildings such as offices, houses, and schools are used day in and day out. How is one able to evaluate them on the basis of a lightning visit?

In the past, it was assumed that a new building would withstand the wear and tear of use and climate in a predictable way. All buildings aged, of course, but time only enhanced their original charms. However, as architects have set aside tried and true techniques of construction and have experimented with new materials and innovative forms, it can no longer be taken for granted that buildings will last. What appears to be an admirable and provocative architectural statement today may be shown with the passage of time to have been a misguided and flimsy attempt at novelty.

Oddly, architecture criticism is unaffected by such considerations. The dramatic cantilevers that gave Frank Lloyd Wright's prairie houses their visual impact have sagged severely. Has this reduced Wright's reputation? Not a bit. Many of Le Corbusier's technical inventions were inoperable from the beginning; some, like the famous *brises soleils*, or concrete sun shades, were climatic disasters. Indeed, Le Corbusier's buildings in India have proven to be considerably less climatically appropriate than those of a traditionalist such as Edwin Lutyens. Though Louis Kahn's Richards Medical Research Laboratories and James Stirling's Cambridge University History Building have experienced severe dysfunctions, both are held up as design achievements. On the other hand, the New York Public Library on 42nd Street, which incorporated numerous technical innovations, was scorned by modernist historians as a Beaux-Arts relic; it has functioned admirably since it opened in 1910.

For all these reasons, and although there were critics I did admire—Lewis Mumford, Reyner Banham, Martin Pawley—architecture criticism seemed to me an unsatisfactory occupation. Collins's objections ran even deeper: it was his harsh conclusion that architecture journalism served little purpose except as a public-relations arm of the architectural profession. If anything, the tendency of criticism to degenerate into hagiography has worsened of late, especially in architecture magazines, where reviews of new buildings read as if they were written by their designers' publicists. I had no interest in becoming yet another practitioner of the celebrity-blurb school of criticism.

So why, when Lex Kaplen asked me in December 1987 to be the architecture critic for *Wigwag*—a national, monthly, general-interest magazine he was launching—did I say yes without giving it a second thought? It was partly his openhandedness: he told me that I could write what I liked, as often as I liked. But it was also the chance to try to write about buildings in a different way—as places rather than objects, and as a part of a larger social and cultural context rather than as diverting works of art. (This was hardly original; Mumford, for one, had always written about architecture this way.) The importance of buildings, it seemed to me, was not what they said about the vision of individual architects, but how they reflected the values of the society of which they were a part. In that sense, architecture is always a mirror in which, if we look carefully, we can catch glimpses of our own aspirations and beliefs.

I. Homes and Houses

Home, Sweet Bungalow Home

One year, I asked my architecture students to design a small house. To help them, I pinned up drawings of several suburban cottages and bungalows built in the 1920s. These houses are of slight historical interest—their designers were not celebrated architects—but they do exhibit a modest and unaffected charm, as well as considerable ingenuity in combining many and varied rooms in small, convenient layouts. Despite the constraints of budget, their makers managed to bestow on these little houses all the requisite attributes of domesticity—inviting trellised porches, intimate bay windows, dining alcoves, and cozy fireplaces.

My young charges were not impressed. Surely I wasn't suggesting that they had something to learn from such ordinary buildings? After all, the tyros argued, they had elected to study Architecture—I could sense that the word was capitalized—and for them that meant flights of fancy and imagination, an escape from the mundane and conventional world represented by these prosaic buildings.

I was not altogether surprised by their reaction. As a student, I, too, had spurned the commonplace indigenous bungalow. There was a feeling that modern architecture—like sports cars, wine, and art films—was a European invention. The architects my classmates and I esteemed were Le Corbusier and the Finnish master, Alvar Aalto. Both men had designed family homes, but their domestic architecture could not be confused with suburban cottages. The houses of Le Corbusier were exciting white sculptures, unmarred by anything as trite as a screened porch; they had roof gardens instead of front lawns and expanses of glass instead of bow windows. Aalto's romantic villas were more recognizably domestic, but they appeared to be situated in sylvan surroundings, not cheek by jowl with suburban neighbors. These houses were filled with elegant chrome-and-leather furniture (or bentwood, in the case of Aalto)—not a plump chesterfield or a La-Z-Boy in sight. We likewise admired the work of the American architect Louis Kahn—precisely because his taut, flat-roofed houses with their unusual windows and spartan materials rejected traditional suburban values.

There had been one illustrious architect who had designed suburban homes, dozens of them—Frank Lloyd Wright. He called these houses "Usonian" (a term he coined to emphasize their native U.S. character) and in them he skillfully combined inexpensive materials, such as plywood and concrete, with extremely compact floor plans. In the 1950s, the last decade of his life, Wright promoted masonry building techniques that allowed owners to build houses themselves, without a contractor, thus further reducing costs. "I did it for the GIs," he said.

Although Wright's suburban designs were publicized in popular magazines such as *House and Home*, they were largely forgotten after his death in 1959, overshadowed by more extravagant residences like Wingspread, and by striking designs like the Johnson

Wax Building. In any case, the architectural profession was never interested in the problem of the "little house," which it left to the developer and the builder, whose popular and often unsophisticated designs were disdained and deplored. Architects-to-be, we scorned the suburban wasteland and looked down on the poor fools who were forced—or worse, had chosen—to live in such unimaginative buildings. The fact that for most of us the poor fools were also our parents was only grist for our sophomoric mills.

That was certainly true for me. Since the age of thirteen I had lived in a suburban bungalow. The one-story house, situated on a small plot, was surrounded by similar homes. That was in the 1950s and sixties, when the bungalow had evolved into its definitive form and had become the most common type of house on the North American continent, both in big-city suburbs and in small towns like the one in which my family lived.

I did not think about whether our house was ugly or plain, cozy or uncomfortable, or whether it looked like all the other houses on the street. (It did.) It had an empty front lawn, matching those of our neighbors, and a back garden with gooseberries, currants, a crab-apple tree, and the obligatory patio. I never thought of our house as something special; it was just the way we all lived, and I accepted this accoutrement of small-town life much the way, I suppose, an Inuit accepted his igloo or a Plains Indian his tepee.

Today I look back on my bungalow home with an affection that has caused me to reconsider my earlier prejudices. The house, which was built by a local builder (without architectural assistance), managed to provide a comfortable setting for family life in only 1,100 square feet. This postwar model was smaller than its 1920 antecedents and lacked refinements such as a dining room, but like most bungalows it provided privacy in several small bedrooms and a place for the family to congregate at the center of the house in the form of a living room with a picture window.

The picture window—a term already in common use by the early fifties—was important, because it was the single extravagance of houses contrived for convenience rather than architectural effect. The picture window usually faced a distinctly unpicturesque street, but it was designed less for viewing out than for viewing in. It was a place for displaying special objects, like lamps or Christmas decorations. The American architect Charles Moore has likened the votive function of the picture window to that of the traditional Japanese *tokonoma*, a place of honor in the home used to exhibit a favorite scroll or flowers in a vase.

The large window proclaimed probity and openness, as if the family had nothing to conceal from the outside world, but the suburban bungalow of the fifties had another, hidden face. Although half of the house was subdivided according to well-established domestic traditions into rooms for cooking, eating, and sleeping, the other half was a large, undenoted, and unfinished space that was concealed from public view and whose arrangement and use were left to the inclinations of the homeowners. I mean, of course, the basement. It was in the basement that the apparent conventionality of suburban living was suspended and the personal idiosyncrasies of the family were let loose—in private. Here was the den, playroom, family room, or rec room, often decorated with an individual exuberance that would not have been out of place during the Gilded Age.

Looking back, I think I spent most of my free time in this subterranean world. It was here that I had my train set, my model-making materials, and my puppet theater. Dodging behind the furnace and the hot-water heater, my brother and I played swashbucklers with a pair of aluminum foils, or gangsters with tommy guns made from wood and lead pipe. Part of the basement was "finished"; I can't remember what we called this room, and it seems to have had no single purpose. Sometimes it was a guest room, sometimes a place to look at my father's vacation slides, and sometimes a kind of party room. It was also where we watched television: "Have Gun, Will Travel," "Father Knows Best," and, every Sunday evening, the burlesque of Ed Sullivan.

The architectural pretensions of the suburban bungalow were modest; no wonder they have been largely overlooked, and even scorned. Picture windows and basement playrooms do not stir the soul of the art historian, or of the architecture student. Still, the bungalow was no mean achievement. A homegrown product, it has effectively accommodated family life for more than three-quarters of a century, and for a very large number of people. If the difficult conditions of the 1980s—exorbitant land costs, high interest rates, rising gas prices, changing family structures—seem to be overtaking the bungalow, that is not necessarily cause for celebration. Finding an equally successful solution to the current problem of the American family home will not prove easy.

Good Housekeeping

I recently was shown a house whose interior was in the process of being renovated. The house was in a prosperous part of Montreal, and I was curious to see what sorts of changes and alterations had been specified by owners with enough money to consider a wide range of choices. It was not the interior decoration itself that concerned me, although like most people I am a voyeur when it comes to the homes of strangers—especially rich strangers. Interior decoration is customarily thought of as merely an illustration of good or bad taste or of fashion; but it is more than that. The embellishment and arrangement of a home are a graphic (and sometimes symbolic) representation of public and private cultural attitudes toward domesticity and family life. More interesting, they are also an indication of how these attitudes are changing.

As we walked up the garden path I could hear the sounds of hammering and the whine of an electric saw. I enjoy visiting building sites. Unlike the ordered anonymity of office bureaucracy or the featureless regularity of a factory assembly line, a building site appears disorderly and chaotic. In fact, there is organization, but it is a loose orchestration of many separate tradesmen, working side by side but not necessarily together. In this aspect, a building site—especially a small one—has changed little since the Middle Ages. Journeymen still ply their separate trades, and work is still done largely by hand, or at least with hand-held tools—few company men here; no industrial robots, either.

Inside the house, carpenters, electricians, and plumbers were busily at work. Plywood covered the floor, and everything was shrouded in a thin film of white dust. A plasterer on a ladder was touching up a molding; an older man in overalls stood at a table saw, cutting strips of wood flooring; two other workers—electricians, to judge from the tool belts slung around their waists—were conferring over a set of blueprints spread out on a makeshift trestle table. A well-dressed woman—obviously the owner—surveyed this activity with what appeared to be a mixture of pride and trepidation.

Since a friend of mine lived in a matching house next door, I was surprised to see little evidence of the original structure in this one. The interior was being transformed—walls moved about, skylights added, new services installed. The ceilings were perforated with new recessed lamps, the windows had been replaced, and so had the front door. The scope of these changes suggested to me the need for a major reconstruction, as if the house were the survivor of some earlier, pretechnological period whose antiquated standards of comfort and convenience would no longer do. The exterior facade hardly suggested great age, however, and this impression was confirmed when my guide informed me that the house was barely twenty-five years old.

As I walked through the interior, my attention was caught by the enlarged bathroom adjacent to the master bedroom. Even though it was unfinished, I could see that this would be an impressive space. It contained not only a window but a new, large skylight. In the center of the room was a commodious and very elaborate bathtub; along the walls, pipes sticking out of the floor suggested an assortment of additional as-yet-uninstalled plumbing fixtures. The wall surfaces were to be entirely covered by mirrored glass and marble; the cost of the marble alone, I was told, was over twenty thousand dollars.

The kitchen was less sybaritic. Its cabinets and work counters were purposeful and businesslike but slightly bloated, and with just enough luxury to take the edge off the laboratory-like efficiency. It reminded me of the interior of an expensive German sedan. The similarity was not accidental; like most prestigious cars, stylish kitchen paraphernalia is largely European: German cabinets and appliances, French food processors and cooking pots, Italian espresso machines and pasta makers, and British porcelain. In the corner of this kitchen I saw a Swedish Aga stove, a complicated affair with round stainless-steel lids covering the cooking range. The sixty-year-old design had the frumpy chic of a Saab 93.

Much care and money had obviously been expended on these two rooms. Bathing and cooking are familiar domestic activities, but the degree of emphasis that had been given to them here—as in so many other, less expensive houses—is something new. In the past, even in grand houses, the bathroom was generally a utilitarian space. Often it was a converted closet or spare room. It was rarely adorned; indeed, a decorated bathroom was considered to be a decadent extravagance, and slightly sinful; that is why the luxury bath, filled with soap bubbles, was the customary setting for the Hollywood vamp.

Kitchens, too, were unadorned, but for a different reason. Rich people didn't cook; they had servants for that. Middle-class housewives spent a great deal of time in the kitchen, but, like the laundry, this room was considered backstage; proper people did not eat in the kitchen. Hence it was not a room that required decor; at best, the 1950s kitchen could be "cheerful." Serious interior decoration was reserved for the public parts of the house, especially the living room.

Just before leaving the house, I was shown the blueprints, and as I leaned over the trestle table to look at the plans, I realized that I was standing in what would be the living room. There was a small fireplace—a vestige of the family hearth—but otherwise the room exhibited no special architectural features, not even a picture window. There were no striking materials—no marble, no imported cabinetry. Although the furniture was absent, I could imagine that the finished room would resemble what used to be called a sitting room—it would be comfortable, but modest and unpretentious.

The extravagance or sparseness of decor is a barometer of the fortunes of different parts of the house—a sign of which rooms have increased in status and which have fallen. It was obvious that in this house the living room had a secondary position, both functionally and symbolically. This shift in size and degree of embellishment from the living room to other rooms is not unusual in new North American houses. It is difficult to say how far it will go. The living room may persist in a diminished form, just as the foyer is a reduced version of the once-spacious entrance hall. Or, in a decade or two, the living room may disappear altogether, replaced by a combination of kitchen and "eating area," by a "media room," or by some other sort of family room. The demise of the living room would not be an unprecedented occurrence;

rooms have come and gone before. Jane Austen's heroines chatted together in breakfast rooms, which were small spaces for morning entertaining; contemporaneous French ladies had intimate conversations in their boudoirs. They also had dressing rooms, which were small sitting rooms. We store clothes in walk-in closets, but during the nineteenth century, "closet" referred to a small private room, like a study. Georgian houses had one or two large drawing rooms, successors of the "withdrawing" room. In the early 1900s, smoking rooms were popular, and so were billiard rooms. Not long ago, most American homes had a TV room—sometimes called a "den"—which lasted only as long as there was but one set in the house. Suburban bungalows also had "rec rooms," but that was before Ping-Pong was replaced by Donkey Kong and other computer games.

The living room's fall from grace should come as no surprise, for this room is a relatively recent arrival, dating from the turn of the century. The living room has its roots in the Victorian parlor, as Katherine Grier makes clear in *Culture and Comfort: People, Parlors, and Upholstery, 1850–1930* (1988). This erudite study, which could have been subtitled "The Rise and Fall of the American Parlor," traces the fortunes of this room from its emergence in the mid-nineteenth century to its ascendancy, and concludes with the eventual replacement of the parlor by the modern living room. Grier pursues this analysis by examining many sources—literary, commercial, and photographic—but the particular focus of her study is upholstery: the loose textile furnishings of rooms, which includes not only furniture covering but also draperies, curtains, and carpets.

The notion of a historical study that concentrates on upholstery is compelling; after all, interior decorators were originally called "upholsterers," and textiles were important in the furnishing of Victorian parlors, which were crammed with brocade, chenille, plush, chintz, velvet, satin, and lace.

The parlor in a Victorian American home was always the "best" room in the house. It was where the family met on formal occasions and where visitors were entertained—functions that superficially resemble those of a modern living room. In another way, however, it was different, for the parlor also represented a social ideal, and it was one that originated outside the home. As Grier points out, domestic parlors were preceded by "public parlors"; we still speak of ice-cream parlors and parlor cars. Public parlors—including women's parlors and so-called family parlors—were a common feature of hotels, steamboats, and trains in the second half of the nineteenth century. These parlors had an important symbolic function: they were a sign of middle-class gentility and refinement. And of separateness—ordinary folk got their hair cut in barbershops, while proper ladies and gents went to tonsorial parlors. It was this sense of class division that the parlor was intended to convey.

Like home exercise machines or big-screen video, which first appeared in public establishments and later migrated to the home, the parlor was made to seem desirable by etiquette books and assorted domestic manuals—as well as by the promotional material of manufacturers and upholsterers, who encouraged new styles, such as French and Turkish, and less expensive, factory-made furniture. It would be a mistake, however, to judge the parlor as merely a commercial vehicle for a burgeoning industrial society.

What distinguished the domestic parlor from the earlier drawing room was not only the quantity of furnishings but their importance as symbols.

Furnished in the prescribed manner, the parlor conveyed a range of middle-class messages: probity, refinement, sensibility, beauty. Ideally, the parlor was to be used only for special occasions. Larger homes had two parlors: one at the front of the house and one at the back. The back parlor was a more casual sitting room for everyday use; the front parlor was opened only a few times a year. It's easy to make fun of the stuffy, unused parlor, but it was kept closed not out of Victorian parsimony but rather to emphasize its special character and to underline its isolation both from daily domestic life and from the outside, public world. In that sense, it resembled an infrequently visited religious shrine.

The cultural functions of the parlor required formality and decorum—what were called "parlor manners." This was not a place for fun and games—except, of course, parlor games. Women wore uncomfortable corsets and bustles; men wore stiff collars and waistcoats in all weather. (Gentility had its price.) At the same time, a countercurrent began to be evident in American life. The invention of inexpensive, spring-seat chairs, lounges, and sofas coincided with a growing relaxation in posture and general behavior. According to Grier, this preference for comfort, particularly in sitting furniture, epitomized an inherent conflict in American middle-class values that was played out in the parlor.

After the turn of the century, the parlor began to go out of fashion. Partly this was a result of the relaxation of manners and of methods of self-presentation in the home, and partly it was the result of functional necessity: as servants became scarcer, and houses and apartments became smaller, it was difficult to accommodate separate, formal parlors. As early as 1900, in a model house designed for the *Ladies' Home Journal*, Frank Lloyd Wright showed the public rooms separated only by wide, open doorways. This practice, which became common, encouraged a more unified decor, in which the rooms were all of a piece. It was the precursor of the "open plan" that combined all public functions into a single space—the living room.

The living room reflected a different sensibility. It was simpler, less cluttered, and more convenient for women, who now had an increasingly active life outside the home. It was also more personal than social. Grier suggests that growing car ownership had a part in the decline of the parlor, since the automobile served as a "portable facade" that publicly expressed social standing—a Chevrolet family or a Buick family. Cars and car travel also diverted time, attention, and money away from parlor life.

The mutation of parlor into living room occurred slowly, and it is by no means complete. Many homes in rural America and Canada still have a front room that is reserved for special occasions, such as weddings and funerals. The separation of casual family room and formal living room, the latter filled with slipcovered furniture, is also a continuation of the parlor tradition. Even the location of the living room, facing the street (the family room usually faces the backyard), is a reminder of the traditional front parlor.

It is Grier's intriguing and original thesis that the parlor exemplified a tension in the American psyche between an emerging consumer society and middle-class sensibilities. The parlor may have disappeared, but the tension persists. She writes in her concluding paragraph: "Being middle class—having that state of mind both compelled and repelled by consumption as a form of rhetoric, seeking a balance between culture and comfort—may be a fundamental component in a dynamic consumer society."

The house that I visited represented this state of mind in different but recognizable ways. The preference for a more casual and relaxed comfort had continued—hence the devaluation of the living room and the shift to the informal kitchen and eating space. At the same time, the locale for self-presentation had changed. Kitchen appliances were the new carriers of domestic status—German cabinets rather than Turkish upholstery, granite counters instead of lace antimacassars.

Just as the parlor manuals counseled aspiring Victorian cosmopolites, a modern primer such as Terence Conran's *Kitchen Book* proposes a variety of kitchen styles—country house or farmhouse, modernistic or traditional—to suit the owners' self-image. Much of what constitutes the fashionable kitchen does not necessarily have anything to do with cooking or food preparation per se, and, as in the parlor, the tension between culture and comfort continues. The stylish gadgets are not always a convenience, the prestigious decor can interfere with the work going on. A sensible working kitchen, such as that of Julia Child, does not resemble the interior of an expensive automobile; it is more like the jumble of my local mechanic's garage, with tools conveniently at hand and neat visual effects disturbed by the complex choreography required of a good cook.

Perhaps the most significant shift has taken place in the luxuriously appointed bathroom, which could be called a "bathing parlor," for it, too, appears to be a shrine. But a shrine to what? Is the emphasis on more relaxed bathing a reflection of the charged schedules of working couples? Is the hot tub the place where they meet? Or is the personal bathing parlor another sign of the further privatization of the home? One thing appears certain: in the bathing parlor, the tension between culture and comfort, restraint and desire, appears to have been temporarily resolved, emphatically in favor of the latter. It is truly a place for self-presentation—of oneself, to oneself. A fitting sign of the self-absorbed, individualistic 1980s.

The Androgynous Home

I remember a photograph of Jayne Mansfield in her bathroom. The bathtub was heart-shaped and overflowing with soap bubbles; the room itself was frilly and pink, a walk-in Valentine card. To a young boy it appeared inaccessibly exotic. In the health-conscious 1980s, the peignoir has been replaced by the sweat suit, and the atmosphere, like the decor, has changed. It is the nature of the change that is revealing. Jayne's ultrafeminine seraglio reflected the dream world of Hollywood, to be sure, but it also recalled another time, when the bathroom—and, indeed, the entire home, whether it belonged to a movie star or to a housewife, proclaimed the woman's dominion.

The feminization of the home began during the seventeenth century, when Dutch women asserted their domestic sovereignty and demanded that their menfolk leave their muddy shoes on the stoop. The next hundred years were characterized by a series of small but binding annexations. It was a British tradition that after dinner, the ladies retired to a small parlor, while the gentlemen stayed in the dining room with the port and the cigars, letting down their hair, and sometimes their trousers—there was a chamber pot provided for this purpose in the corner. Safe in their boozy camaraderie, the men did not notice that outside the closed door, the ladies' "withdrawing" room was growing in size and importance until the drawing room was the dominant space in the house. Cut flowers, antimacassars, gathered window draperies, skirted furniture, and delicate wallpapers appeared, like boundary stakes, to demarcate the growing feminine presence.

Over the years, men learned to leave more than their shoes at the door; they learned gentility. In the postwar home, father knew best; but, among the chintz and the china, he was an immigrant, no longer the master. The mistress of the house, on the other hand, found herself cast in a new role. Since the feminization of the home coincided with another social phenomenon of equal significance, the gradual disappearance of hired domestic help, it was now the so-called homemaker who attended to the household duties (note the word of obligation) and spent almost all her time in the home.

During the 1960s and seventies, the nature of the American family, and of the home, changed: women reentered the work force. In short, women began abandoning the territory that had been the site of so many hard-fought domestic campaigns. When women decided that their place was no longer in the home—or, at least, not exclusively so—the home also ceased to be "a woman's place."

If the home is no longer a woman's place, whose place is it? Will it become an impersonal consumer product, a symbol of status, to be used and then discarded as one moves up the career ladder or from one life-style to another? It might; but I think it is more likely that the instability of our lives will make us work even harder to create permanence and stability in our homes.

Surveys indicate that families spend less time together in the home than they did in the past. When the family does get together, it is usually for a meal, and it is to this part of the house that the center of gravity is shifting. We no longer need or want even the descendant of the parlor—a room to be adorned, not used. A working woman, after all, derives her status from career achievements, not from doilies and porcelain figurines; and most men have always preferred less decorous surroundings.

The dining room could become a new type of family room—a real living room, with a fireplace and large, cushioned chairs, in which we can relax together around the dining table. As for the television and our other electronic toys, they could be accommodated in smaller, more intimate rooms, to be enjoyed in cozy comfort—and auditory privacy.

The dining room no longer needs to be isolated from the kitchen. In the past, after the supper dishes had been put away, the housewife liked to be able to close the door; after all, who wanted to be reminded of the endless series of meals yet to be cooked? Today we eat out more frequently, daycare provides lunches, and home delivery relieves us of the obligation of preparing three meals a day. The modern kitchen seems in danger of becoming an empty status symbol—a latter-day parlor—replete with polished granite and hardwood trim but devoid of practicality. Cooking can be fun, but it is also work. We need to rediscover the utility, and the pleasure, of the country kitchen, where utensils and work spaces were pragmatically arranged to permit easy use, just as eating and cooking were done side by side in unostentatious familiarity.

We can learn from the past, but we cannot go back. The androgynous home is here to stay. This should not dismay us, nor is it cause for alarm. As before, we can create a sense of well-being in our homes. Only now, we—women, men, and children—must share in the making.

Looking Back to the Future

What's going on? Today's dream house is looking more and more like the house of a hundred years ago. A visit to a model home is like a tour of a house restored by a historical preservation society. The open plan of the 1950s and sixties has disappeared. Instead of "spaces," with room dividers that never quite reach the ceiling, we find traditional rooms. Wall-to-wall glass has been replaced by honest-to-goodness windows, and instead of gaping picture windows we look through delicately mullioned oriels, bows, and bays. Fluted Doric columns have supplanted the slender steel pipes that were so favored by modern designers. Screened porches are back, as are various traditional roof shapes, on which cupolas and lanterns have replaced rudimentary skylights.

Real estate advertising shows recently built Victorian-looking houses with protruding porticoes, and ornamented gables in turn-of-the-century clapboard houses. An exclusive housing development on Shelter Island, for example, offered the prospective buyer a choice of houses in what appears to be the Shingle style, patterned after the shingle houses built on Long Island's North Shore at the end of the nineteenth century.

"Historical" is a word commonly associated with such architecture. Indeed, its traditional appearance has become a potent marketing tool. But appearances, like fiberglass columns and polyurethane moldings, can be deceiving. When we look at these comfortable and handsome houses, we see the surface of history—the footprint, not the foot—and it's easy to forget how much separates us from the past.

The home of one hundred years ago meant something totally different to its inhabitants, and it contained a way of life unlike our own. To begin with, a mid-nineteenth-century middle-class house was large by today's standards; a renovated Victorian house can easily be subdivided into three or four modern dwellings. Families themselves were considerably bigger than they are today. Not only were there more children, but the household often included grandparents, unmarried sisters, visiting relatives and friends, and live-in servants.

This was a world without public entertainment, without professional sports and vaudeville, and, of course, without movies. The automobile was yet to be invented. The attractions of the theme park were unimagined. In short, people stayed home. And leisure—of which the middle class had a plenitude—meant, above all, domestic leisure.

It was the age of parlor games and cards, of home theatricals and musical soirees. Varying degrees of intimacy and formality characterized Victorian social life, and a proper home included not only a parlor (sometimes two) but also a drawing room, a library, and a sitting room. Etiquette also required the separation of the sexes—women received their friends in the morning room; men had smoking rooms and studies. The dining room was neutral territory until the end of dinner, when it became the men's domain.

These public rooms contained a bewildering array of stuff: furniture, bric-a-brac, paintings—not just on the walls but on easels—vases, statuettes, urns, flowers, and plants. Unlike the elegant but bare decor of the eighteenth century, this proliferation of objects was intended to express the personality of its owners—particularly that of the woman of the house, who took the main responsibility for its running and arrangement. Just as we might try to make a room "comfortable" or "tasteful," the Victorians strove for the "artistic," which meant a wealth of visual, usually exotic, detail, the more picturesque the better. Since the Victorians were also great collectors, these houses sometimes resembled crowded museums.

If the nineteenth-century interior was organized like a theater setting, full of props and painted backdrops, this was not inappropriate, because it also had a backstage. Behind the scenes, in the passages and backstairs, in the dark basements and drafty attics, lived another family—the servants.

Domestics were an essential ingredient of middle-class life. Plumbing was rudimentary. There were sometimes water closets, but it was servants who carried hot water up to the portable bathtub, which usually stood in a corner of the bedroom or dressing room, and carried the dirty water back down again. It was backbreaking work.

This was also a world without processed food, and the large assortment of rooms associated with the kitchen—pantry, scullery, larder—are a reminder of the effort that went into food preparation and preservation. Cooking in an open hearth, only slightly improved by that newfangled gadget the cast-iron range, was taxing and unpleasant. So was scrubbing the laundry and cleaning the house.

And housecleaning consumed a great deal of time. There were all those gimcracks and bibelots to dust. Candles and oil lamps produced little light but a great deal of soot, which settled on the walls, ceilings, carpets, furniture, and aspidistra plants. Some urban houses had gaslight, which was brighter but not much cleaner. However, the greatest source of dirt was the emotional and spiritual center of the Victorian home—the family hearth. Stoves were considered inelegant and low-class, and in a wealthy home every room contained an open fireplace. This produced smoke and a great deal of work for the servants but, unfortunately for the occupants, relatively little heat.

The labor of domestics slightly compensated for the lack of material comforts, but for most people, who were without servants, life was hard indeed. This was so especially during the winter, because even the grandest houses were uninsulated and lacked double glazing. To save fuel, the less prosperous families gathered in the single heated parlor, trying to derive some warmth from the ornamental but ineffective fireplace. The water froze in the wash basin, wine froze in the glass, and winter evenings dragged on in the forced intimacy of crowded and dimly lit rooms.

Only the fittest survived such rigors. Visit a restored nineteenth-century house and you will usually find a small bedroom on the ground floor. This was not a guest room; it was reserved for illness, which, before antibiotics, was common. Recuperation was a lengthy affair, and the sickroom was rarely unoccupied. Death, particularly of young children, was a common family occurrence, and in that unhappy event the front parlor would be opened for an extended wake.

Which is not to say that the Victorian home was an unhappy or desolate place; far from it. The family was the center of people's lives, and the home was probably the single most important social institution of the age. John Ruskin called it "a sacred place, a vestal temple." That may have been an exaggeration, but the care that its owners lavished on interior and exterior decoration was evidence of the esteem in which the home and the family were held by rich and poor alike. It is an appreciation for our forebears' fond attachment to the idea of home that explains, I think, the current appeal of nineteenth-century domestic styles and our wistful nostalgia for shaded porches, window seats, and cozy inglenooks.

In the 1950s and sixties we tried to domesticate the public place, but we soon found that the delights of domesticity were absent in the public realm. You can't live in a shopping mall—only a teenager would want to—and for most of us, only the home can nurture a sense of individual belonging.

This revival of traditional forms is more than an architectural revival or a frivolous, temporary fad. The original meaning of "nostalgia," after all, was "homesickness," and while we undoubtedly shun the chilly ambience and sooty ceiling of the Victorian parlor, we are attracted, as our grandparents were, by the bourgeois domestic traditions that it represented. The revival of traditional architectural forms is also evidence of a longing for the bourgeois ideals that the Victorian home represented: stability, continuity, and domesticity. This nostalgia raises questions—so much has changed, after all. Architects have proved skillful in reproducing the forms of the past and adapting them to present circumstances and to our desire for modern conveniences. The values that these forms represented, however, may prove more difficult to resurrect.

If a Chair Is a Work of Art, Can You Still Sit on It?

When is a chair not a chair? When it is a work of art. That, at least, is the assumption of a growing number of collectors, critics, museum curators, gallery owners, and furniture makers who form the vanguard of the growing studio-furniture movement. Furniture galleries now represent furniture makers, much as art galleries represent painters and sculptors. Collectors are paying higher and higher prices for contemporary handcrafted pieces, secure in the knowledge that their value will increase. And—the final cachet—art museums, which previously exhibited only antique furniture, are beginning to acquire, and even to commission, contemporary works for their collections.

It was in the eighteenth century that the art of furniture making—and hence, the individual furniture maker—came to the fore. André Charles Boulle, who served both Louis XIV and Louis XV, was the first cabinetmaker to achieve fame and personal recognition. This put Boulle on an equal footing with the best-known painters and sculptors, and, like them, the famous *ébéniste* was considered an artist as well as a craftsman. Like paintings and sculptures, beautiful furniture was then made individually, painstakingly, and slowly. When J. F. Oeben and Jean Henri Riesener were commissioned to build a writing desk for Louis XV, the task took them nine years.

Boulle relied on royal patronage (he lived at Versailles), but later celebrated furniture makers, especially in England, produced work for a larger clientele. George Hepplewhite and Thomas Chippendale started as cabinetmakers, but they became, in the spirit of the age, entrepreneurs. Although their pieces were sometimes signed, we know that they were made by employees who worked in what amounted to small factories. (These factories continued in operation for many years after their owners' deaths, just as some designer-label manufacturers do today.) Making furniture was still a craft, but selling furniture had become a business.

By the third quarter of the nineteenth century, thanks to industrialization, handicraft had been displaced by machinery, and craftsmen by workers: the furniture factory had become an assembly line. But if mass-produced furniture was cheaper, most of it was also of inferior quality and poor design. One antidote to machine-age mediocrity was a revival of craftsmanship—or, at least, so taught Henry Cole (an art critic) and Owen Jones (an interior decorator). Their ideas formed the basis for the British Arts and Crafts movement, led by the masterly William Morris. Morris inspired such architects and designers as Charles Rennie Mackintosh, Arthur Mackmurdo, and C. F. A. Voysey, and, in the United States, Gustave Stickley. Their furniture designs reflected a new sensibility, which relied less on decoration than on a straightforward use of materials, on a direct ("honest") expression of utility, and, above all, on craftsmanship.

Studio furniture—or art furniture, as it is sometimes called—can be traced to the Arts and Crafts movement, but it found its main impetus in the United States in the work of such postwar craftsmen as Wharton Esherick, George Nakashima, and Sam Maloof. What distinguished these furniture makers from contemporaneous furniture designers such as Charles Eames and George Nelson was their firm rejection of industrial techniques and mass production (they built the furniture themselves, by hand), as well as of industrial materials (they worked almost exclusively in wood). The growth of handcrafted furniture making in the 1950s is sometimes called a revival, but it was a revival of skills, not of forms: Nakashima's and Maloof's work has spare lines, and no ornament, and makes few references to the past. It is a curious amalgam of pre-industrial craftsmanship and modernist aesthetics.

One of the chief attributes—and attractions—of traditional crafts is their avoidance of fashion and novelty; they evolve slowly and embody a sense of permanence. This is natural. A traditional craft is, by definition, the craft of a traditional society, and it reflects the stability of its social and technological surroundings. In dynamic, changing societies, however, the stationary quality of craft is threatened. Either the craft must embrace a hermetic and artificial existence, holding fast to old orthodoxies and reiterating old ways, or it must accept change.

One way in which American crafts have been changing is in the direction of art, placing more emphasis on the creativity of the individual furniture maker; this has been visible in glassblowing and ceramics for some time. In the case of furniture, this evolution raises some fascinating questions about the relationship between craft and art, between furniture as functional object and as a means of personal expression, between utility and art. Does one plump down into a studio chair, or merely admire it? If it is a work of art, is it still a chair?

The studio-furniture movement appears to be divided on these issues. On one side are furniture makers who wish to be considered artists. The work of these men and women is moving clearly in the direction of sculpture, in which function takes second place to formal invention, and craft is no longer an end in itself but is at the service of an artistic idea. The original and most prominent exponent of this approach is undoubtedly Wendell Castle, whose retrospective exhibition ended a tour of five museums at the American Craft Museum in New York in the fall of 1991. Castle's work combines superb craftsmanship and expensive, exotic materials with forms and ideas borrowed from surrealism, abstract expressionism, deconstructivism, and postmodernism. It is meant to be avant-garde. In most cases, the utility of the furniture is ingeniously disguised, so that the effect is not of, say, a cabinet that looks like a sculpture, but rather a sculpture that mysteriously reveals itself to have drawers and hinged panels. You can sit in a Castle chair—utility is never banished outright—but it is not the first thing that comes to mind.

A different approach is evident in the work of John Dunnigan, a young furniture maker from Rhode Island, who was the subject of a one-man show at the Peter Joseph Gallery in New York in 1991. There were a dozen new pieces on display, mostly sitting furniture, as well as a small selection of earlier works, produced since 1976, when Dunnigan opened his own workshop.

Anyone looking for furniture that shocks, startles, or thrills would have been disappointed. In the studio-furniture world, Dunnigan, like Timothy Philbrick and Richard Scott Newman, is a traditionalist. His chairs not only look like chairs, but are versions of specific types of chairs: dining chairs, slipper chairs, armchairs, fauteuils. Their very familiarity challenges our idea of creative invention.

And unlike those furniture makers who assign expressive titles to individual pieces (as if to underline their "artistic" function), Dunnigan calls his daybed "Daybed" and his settee "Settee." What you see is what you get.

Well, not quite. The settee is at first glance an unremarkable object, albeit beautifully made, until one begins to appreciate the delicate proportions, the contrasting textures of wood and fabric, the lascivious back (whose curves suggest a mouth), and the plump asymmetry. The last hints that this sensuous piece is really a love seat—"his" side being slightly more ample than "hers"—and a wickedly suggestive one, in which decorous sitting will soon give way to reclining. This fanciful set of conjectures does not occur at first glance, of course. Like all good sitting furniture, Dunnigan's must be not only looked at but sat on (or lounged on, in the case of a languorous daybed), slouched in, fingered, touched, stroked, caressed (which is why photographs reveal so little of furniture's multifaceted personality), and looked at again.

This is stylish, urban furniture that often recalls Empire and Biedermeier, or the confections of the French *ébénistes* of the art deco period. Like the latter, it often has an air of decadence, which sets it apart from the prim, woodsy, Scandinavian-influenced furniture of the earlier generation of craftsmen. The seductive fabrics are rich, and there are sumptuous touches: wool tufts, tassels, decorative fabric buttons, pleated skirts. The tiny drawers of an ebony cabinet are lined with silk; the top is upholstered in pale peach fabric. Two armchairs are covered in leather (hand-tooled by Jennifer Wahl) that is as soft and indulgent as the seats of a British luxury sedan.

John Dunnigan's sitting furniture is extremely comfortable. This is the result not only of his careful adherence to age-old dimensional conventions but also to his skill as an upholsterer. The craft of upholstery, which originated in the eighteenth century, is not generally associated with studio furniture—or with designer furniture in general, which tends to rely on flat cushions and thinly padded seats rather than fully sprung upholstery. Its re-emergence here is a reminder that truly comfortable sitting furniture is impossible without carefully considered upholstery, and that providing support for the body, as well as pleasure for the eye, remains at the center of the furniture maker's art.

The three pleasures of furniture—practical, visual, and intellectual—call to mind the Vitruvian triad of commodity, firmness, and delight, which the ancient Roman author held to be the requisite condition of all successful architecture. Utility, solidity, and beauty resurfaced in the writings of Renaissance architects such as Alberti and Palladio. "That work therefore cannot be called perfect which should be useful and not durable," Palladio wrote, "or durable and not useful, or having both these should be without beauty." It is noteworthy that Palladio did not consider that beauty was merely the result of accommodating utility (form did not blindly follow function), nor did he suggest that practicality was secondary to aesthetics. On the contrary, perfection demanded that equal attention be paid to all three qualities.

Of course, Palladio was describing the art of building, not of furniture making, but surely his point applies equally well. Like the architect—and unlike the sculptor or the painter—the furniture maker is governed by both utility and aesthetics: by how furniture is used as well as how it is made, by what sentiments it evokes (formality, casualness) as well as how beautiful it looks and how comfortable it feels. These concerns are not always compatible, and it goes without saying that contradictions may arise between them—between beauty and comfort, say, or between the limitations of a particular material and the functional requirement of a piece, or between social and aesthetic demands. Herein lies the fascination of studio furniture, for different furniture makers react differently to the demands of utility—some, like Dunnigan, embracing it; others appearing to shun such mundane constraints. So, too, with craftsmanship, which for so long appeared to be the foundation of studio furniture. While some furniture makers celebrate technical virtuosity, others place it firmly in the background. Nevertheless, utility, visual pleasure, and meaning finally must be brought into a state of equilibrium; and in that sense, the art of the furniture maker could be said to consist in a considered search for balance.

Getting Away from It All

Every American city is surrounded by its counterpart: cottage country. Each Friday evening, people make their way to their rustic retreats; on Sunday, the exodus is reversed. The precise magnitude of this periodic emigration remains undocumented, but if one includes not only beach houses, mountain lodges, lakeside cabins, and ski chalets but also trailer parks, permanent campgrounds, hunting camps, ice-fishing houses, marinas, and houseboats, the number of second homes is vast. The well-to-do go to Kennebunkport, the Hamptons, or the Cape; the less affluent make do with less scenic, or merely less desirable, locations. The destinations vary, but the aim is the same: take a break, get away, get out of the city.

This desire is nothing new, for as James Ackerman points out in his 1990 book *The Villa: Form and Ideology of Country Houses*, which traces the evolution of the villa since antiquity, people have been building country places for more than two thousand years. What is a villa? "A building in the country designed for its owner's enjoyment and relaxation," he writes. To complete the definition, one need add only that the owner is almost always a city dweller, for the villa exists because of, and as a counterpoint to, the city. The great periods of the villa and the country house—sixteenth-century Italy, Georgian England, between 1890 and 1940 in the United States—have always coincided with times of vigorous metropolitan growth. Indeed, Ackerman identifies only two periods in Western history when thriving urban cultures did not build themselves country retreats: the burgeoning of the communes of central Europe and Italy between 1000 and 1400, and the heyday of the republican city-states of ancient Greece. The reason for these two exceptions is unclear—most likely, life outside the protection of city walls was simply too perilous.

The villa was a Roman invention, and in many ways all subsequent country houses—whether belonging to Florentine merchant princes, English aristocrats, Tidewater planters, or New York City tycoons—were merely variations on this Roman theme. What binds all these buildings together—and I would include the humble lakeside cottage and beach shack in this prestigious company—is the city dweller's idealization of rural life and his establishment of an architecture that encompasses and expresses this ideal.

The urban ideal of country life is, of course, a fantasy, and herein lies the interest of the villa as an architectural type: its unchanging program. "The villa has remained substantially the same," writes Ackerman, "because it fills a need that never alters, a need which, because it is not material but psychological and ideological, is not subject to the influences of evolving societies and technologies." When Pliny the Younger described the pleasures of lazing about on his seaside terrace, or of getting out of a toga and into some comfortable clothes, we know exactly what he was talking about. Petrarch, who reawakened Italians' appreciation for the pleasures of country life, wrote, "I came to the villa at Careggi to cultivate not my field but my soul"; it is a sentiment that every weekend cottager shares.

The ancient Roman villa began as a rural version of the typical town house. The rooms were arranged around two courtyards—an atrium near the entrance and an inner peristyle surrounded by a colonnade—and looked into these courts rather than out at the countryside. After the first century A.D., this scheme was turned inside out. Rooms were planned so as to take advantage of the best views. Instead of courts, there were porticoes that looked out at the surrounding countryside; and instead of being a compact cube, the villa acquired wings that extended into the landscape. These later villas, of which only excavated ruins remain, appear to have been added to over time, enlarged and altered. Their irregular and picturesque appearance reflected the informal way of life they contained. We don't know the extent of the gardens around these houses, but if we can judge from Pliny's descriptions of his own villas, views of the agrarian landscape were the most appreciated, especially as the Roman villa was often, though by no means always, at the center of a working estate.

The villa reappeared in fifteenth-century Italy, although by then the only evidence that remained of Roman villas was in literature, and the earliest Renaissance villas derived their form from medieval castles. Like their military forebears, although for different reasons, these villas were often built on heights, with commanding views of their owners' extensive landholdings. Eventually, villas lost their medieval features, but there was a curious indecision about what new style should prevail. On the one hand, there was Cosimo de' Medici's villa at Fiesole, designed by Michelozzo, which resembled a rather grand farmhouse—informal, undecorated, and, to a surprising degree (the result of artificial terracing), a part of the hillside on which it stood. Thirty years later, when Cosimo's grandson Lorenzo the Magnificent designed a villa at Poggio a Caiano, he made it formal, grand, classically ornamented, and palatial in appearance—clearly a beautiful object *in* the landscape, not of it.

Enter the sixteenth-century genius Andrea Palladio, who brought the two Renaissance strands together and established the definitive form for the villa—a form that would last for several centuries and reappears occasionally today. The twenty or so villas designed by Palladio, most of which are still standing, are intended to be experienced as objects in the landscape. Yet they are also a part of the countryside—not only because of their siting and their explicit response to view and vista, but also because of their design, which combines classical pediments and columns with an almost rustic simplicity in forms and materials. Palladio knew nothing of the appearance of the villas of antiquity, but there is a Roman pragmatism in his plain stuccoed surfaces and his sparing use of ornament; indeed, in terms of building techniques, not much had changed in the intervening sixteen hundred years. These were not, strictly speaking, places for leisure, but the Venetian gentlemen farmers for whom they were built were certainly city folk, whose urban culture—and urban wealth—demanded more than mere functionality. "The particular aim of the Palladian country house," writes Ackerman, "was to give magnificence to the once humble agricultural complex, symbolically joining the substructure of work to the superstructure of consumption."

The Palladian idea of a country house re-emerged in another urban culture—eighteenth-century England. English country houses were bigger and grander, partly because their owners were wealthier, and partly because they used their country estates to entertain vast numbers of guests. These palatial homes, which Mark Girouard has called "power houses," divested themselves of any agricultural associations, and though they owed their architectural form to Palladio's *Four Books of Architecture*, their relationship to the countryside was altogether different. The vistas they favored were not cultivated fields, but what Ackerman calls "England's most influential and enduring contribution to the visual arts," the landscape garden.

This innovation, which Horace Walpole credited to the painter and landscape gardener William Kent, represented a reversal of the tradition of the Italian and French gardens. Instead of treating the landscape as a huge formal garden, the English created gardens that resembled a natural landscape. Natural, in this context, did not mean rough or rustic, however. Sheep were sometimes allowed to graze in a pasture, but only as an ornamental accessory. The purpose of the landscape garden was to be scenic, romantic, and, above all, evocative of the classical past. To that end, it incorporated Grecian temples, statuary, grottoes, waterfalls, bridges, and a variety of architectural fragments that Kent called "eye-catchers." These structures were arranged to give the observer an orchestrated sequence of views and experiences as he walked or rode through the garden.

The landscape garden was a conscious re-creation of the sort of scene that appeared in the paintings of Claude Lorrain and Nicolas Poussin, and was thus described as "picturesque." It was inevitable that a taste for informality and the picturesque would eventually influence the design of the villa itself, and in mid-nineteenth-century America it did so, thanks largely to the writings of Andrew

Jackson Downing. Downing was a horticulturalist, not an architect, but his books on the design of gardens, cottages, and country residences had great success with the public and were extremely influential. Downing was addressing an upper-middle class that had the means, and the inclination, to build retreats outside the city, and he wrote at a time when railroads and steamboats were making suburban living a practical possibility.

The type of suburban villa that Downing advocated—and which architects such as A. J. Davis built on the banks of the Hudson—was influenced by a landscape that only recently had been wilderness. Unlike their classical European antecedents, these houses often were built of wood rather than stone. They incorporated features such as board-and-batten siding, scrollwork ornament, and steep roofs, and something that would become a characteristic feature of the American country house—porches. They were picturesque houses in a picturesque setting.

Ackerman closes his engaging narrative on the villa with a juxtaposition of two twentieth-century architects whose country houses neatly embody the two contrasting ideologies of the villa: Frank Lloyd Wright and Le Corbusier. Wright's own country house, Taliesin, in Spring Green, Wisconsin, begun in 1911, was in many ways a replay of the early Tuscan villa. (He had spent the previous year—his year of social exile from Chicago—in Italy, principally in Fiesole.) As in his later masterpiece, Fallingwater—a weekend retreat built for a Pittsburgh department store millionaire in 1935—Wright carried Downing's conception of the picturesque to its full artistic fruition. Not only did the house evoke the forms of its natural settings, but because of its irregular composition and use of rough masonry, it actually seemed to be a part of the landscape—a landscape that, at least in the case of Fallingwater, was left in its original, untouched state.

This natural quality, which Wright called "organic," was also an affirmation of his growing rejection (literal, in the case of his move from suburban Chicago to rural Wisconsin) of the city. Whereas the villas of Palladio brought urbanity to the Veneto countryside, Wright's country residences, with their great hearths and expansive plans, were imbued with the age-old American ethos of returning to the land.

As Colin Rowe pointed out in 1947 in his famous essay "The Mathematics of the Ideal Villa," the suburban houses that Le Corbusier built in the vicinity of Paris during the 1920s and thirties were an explicit reinterpretation of the plans of Palladio's villas such as the Malcontenta and the Villa Rotonda. They were a reaffirmation of the villa as an urban artifact deposited in nature, but distinct from it. Le Corbusier considered himself an urban man, and his country houses did not sentimentalize the move to the country. The nautical imagery that he adopted in the Villa Savoye (pipe railings, ramps, funnel shapes, expansive roof decks) gave the occupants the impression that they were passengers steaming through the landscape.

Like most works of art history, Ackerman's *Villa* is based on the assumption that it is possible to make a clear distinction between buildings that are works of art and those that are merely functional. "What distinguishes a villa from a farmhouse or a country cottage," writes Ackerman, "is the intense, programmatic investment of ideological goals." This sounds reasonable, but one wonders how exactly to judge the "intensity" of a villa builder's architectural goals. The remains of ancient Roman villas, for example, suggest that these houses grew by addition over time, and their rambling plans often appear more pragmatic than ideological.

Ackerman maintains that what also distinguishes the villa from the farmhouse is that the villa is the product of an architect's imagination. Here, too, the Roman villa raises doubts. We don't know who designed these houses, or, indeed, if architects were always involved; Pliny's letters imply that at least some parts of his seaside villa may have been planned by himself. Still, there is no doubt that, beginning in the Renaissance, a distinction arose between formally designed buildings and popular construction. Architects confined themselves to designing expensive, monumental buildings, chiefly churches and palaces—and in their heyday, villas—and the history of architecture of this period is easily construed as a chronicle of the evolution of these few building types.

After the eighteenth century, however, the architectural profession grew more numerous in its membership, and it began to be involved in a greater variety of buildings. Offices, commercial buildings, and even private houses, which had previously been left to builders and craftsmen, were now designed by architects. Some of these buildings were just as grand and monumental as churches and royal residences. But there were also many buildings in which practical and functional considerations were often more important than architectural ideology, and which were characterized by (hidden) technological devices rather than by the formal manipulation of their facades. Such buildings were designed by architects, but they provided little to interest the art historian.

To identify which buildings would be included in the canon of architecture, the art historian had to acquire a new role: that of critic. He had to pick and choose. Inevitably, the choice reflected personal bias, so much so that in the case of some art historians—one thinks of Siegfried Giedion's championing of modern architecture, or Vincent Scully's more recent promotion of postmodernism—it is hard to distinguish history from advocacy.

Ackerman purposely avoids discussing contemporary developments. "No historian," he writes, "can see his own time clearly because he cannot stand back from it sufficiently to distinguish its truths from its ideologies." Nevertheless, he, too, is selective. He devotes much space to a discussion of Fallingwater, for example, which he obviously admires. But how important was the influence of this unusual house on the evolution of the ideology of the villa in America? Certainly less than the English-style country houses of William Adams Delano on Long Island or the ranches and haciendas of G. W. Smith in California. But the work of these and other society architects, who were Wright's contemporaries, receives no mention at all in *The Villa*. Indeed, a single, disparaging reference to "the bombastic Beaux-Arts style mansions" that the rich were building for themselves in places such as Newport and on the shores of the Hudson River is the only allusion to what was probably the single greatest burst of villa building in history.

The period in question, which began in the late 1860s and lasted approximately until the Second World War, coincided with the industrialization of the United States and with the rise of great family fortunes. In the popular imagination, the architecture of the American country house is typified by the palatial extravagances built by millionaires such as George Washington Vanderbilt (Biltmore in North Carolina), James Deering (Villa Vizcaya in Florida), and William Randolph Hearst (San Simeon in California). These are the largest and most dramatic examples, but there were thousands of imposing country houses built during this time all across the nation.

These country homes were obviously built for their owners' enjoyment and pleasure. They also reflected a specific ideology, which was derived from Europe but developed its own, peculiarly American, manifestation. Like Palladio, who modeled himself on antiquity, and the English gentlemen architects, who studied Palladio, the American country-house designer looked to the past. The English country house, Tudor or Georgian, provided an obvious model, but not the only one. At Biltmore, the architect Richard Morris Hunt took his inspiration from the châteaus of the French Renaissance; the style of Louis XIV was also popular, especially for grand mansions. In Florida and California, the inspiration was often Mediterranean—Italian at Villa Vizcaya, Spanish at San Simeon. In the Adirondacks, where New York architects designed romantic log camps (more than two thousand of them), the influence was Swiss.

Just as Palladio freely interpreted the past to suit the needs of his sixteenth-century patrons, American architects adapted the European models to suit their clients. This meant an emphasis on comfort, informality, and outdoor living, and the use of modern building techniques (both San Simeon and Villa Vizcaya are built of reinforced concrete). Of course, these modern plans and modern technologies were clothed in historical dress, for the American country-house architects were traditionalists, not formal innovators. They refused to accept the modernist creed that a new age required a new architecture. But they were also eclectics. If a client wanted Colonial Revival or Moorish or Jacobean, they were pleased to oblige. This obviously gained them commissions, but it didn't impress the modern art historians, who were more interested in artistic consistency—and originality—and who were uncomfortable with an architectural ideology that was so accommodating and so malleable.

The result is that the period of the American country house—"the bombastic Beaux-Arts style mansions"—has been ignored and belittled by art historians, at least until the last decade. Happily, Mark Alan Hewitt has produced a comprehensive study that goes a long way in filling the gap. Hewitt is not a historian but a practicing architect, and as his title suggests, *The Architect and the American Country House* (1990) deals not only with the houses but with the men and women who designed them.

Hewitt lists three generations of architects—over eighty individuals—who were involved in country-house work. They include not only people who specialized in country homes for the well-to-do, such as Horace Trumbauer and Charles Adams Platt, but also virtually all the foremost architects of the day: Richard Morris Hunt (whom Hewitt credits as the role model for the society architect), John Russell Pope (who also designed the Jefferson Memorial and the National Gallery), Thomas Hastings (who, with John Carrère, was responsible for the New York Public Library), and the New York firm of McKim, Mead & White, where many of these architects served their apprenticeships. This diverse group included architects such as Julia Morgan (the designer of San Simeon), Royal Barry Wills, who also specialized in middle-class homes, and Grosvenor Atterbury, who designed the pioneering suburb of Forest Hills Gardens, in Queens, New York.

The American country-house movement took its architectural inspiration from Europe, but the idea of building a grand house in the countryside had an American history, too—in Virginia, Maryland, and the Carolinas. Colonial planters built masterpieces such as Shirley and Mount Airy in Virginia, Drayton Hall near Charleston, and, probably the greatest of the architectural achievements of the period, Stratford Hall on the Potomac River in Virginia. There were also neoclassical villas built by Philadelphia patricians along the Schuylkill River during the second half of the eighteenth century. More modest in scale than either plantation mansions or the later constructions of the Gilded Age, these elegant, exquisite houses represent an architectural high point in the evolution of the American country house.

The country-house movement is well worth a second look—not only because the 1980s introduced a resurgence in the building of large country retreats and a revival of interest in architectural eclecticism, but because, as the handsome illustrations in *The Architect and the American Country House* amply demonstrate, many of these houses are outstanding works of architecture. My favorite is Hill-Stead, in Farmington, Connecticut, built for a Cleveland industrialist, Alfred Atmore Pope, in 1898–1902. It was designed by Pope's daughter, Theodate, working together with McKim, Mead & White. The sprawling house is part of a complex of attached barns and outbuildings, whose informality recalls that of a Roman villa—or would, if the Romans had built with wood. The beautiful white clapboard house, with its Mount Vernon porch and dormered roofs, was one of the earliest examples of the Colonial Revival style, and its merging of stylish forms with traditional New England building techniques is masterful. Henry James, who visited Hill-Stead in 1910, wrote that the house "made everything else shrivel and fade: it was like the sudden trill of a nightingale."

Hill-Stead was the product of the fruitful combination of the artistic discrimination of its owners (the Popes had an excellent collection of impressionist paintings); the talent of its chief designer, Theodate Pope; and the historical knowledge and proficiency of its architects (both McKim and White were leaders in the Colonial Revival). But its sense of restraint and moderation and its avoidance of the grand architectural gesture were not typical of American country houses, which were generally designed to be more striking, more dramatic, more opulent. The Popes were defying a long tradition of conspicuous indulgence. When the Roman patricians went to their country estates, they expected to have all the comforts of their city homes: banqueting halls, hot baths, ball courts. They may have removed their togas, but they were hardly roughing it.

The function of a villa has always been to provide a luxurious setting for leisure, and rarely was luxury so celebrated as in the country houses built by the American rich during this period. This was not what Andrew Jackson Downing had hoped for. He deplored ostentation and complained that "the indulgence of one's taste and pride in the erection of a country-seat of great size and cost is becoming a favorite mode of expending wealth." Little did he know that when he wrote this, in 1850, the ideology of the villa—or rather, of the American villa—would produce a new and more modest representative. I am not referring to the eclectic country house, which was firmly in the European mold, or to the Wrightian organic house, which while modern in appearance followed essentially the same program. The original American contribution to the villa tradition was the weekend cottage.

The weekend cottage was the product of several interlocking circumstances: middle-class affluence, universal car ownership, good roads, a national inclination for outdoor recreation, plentiful rural land, and the widespread availability of weekend leisure time. Although it took many forms, the cottage owed more to Downing than to Pliny or Palladio. It was small and informal, usually built by the owner rather than designed by an architect, and often expressing the personality of its occupants in its form and decoration. Though it was no less ideological than its grand antecedents, its sources of inspiration were different—usually vernacular: the pioneer cabin, the fisherman's shack, the mountain chalet.

The weekend cottage was not an architectural milestone, but it represented a prodigious achievement. For the first time in history, the possibility of owning a country retreat was extended beyond the well-to-do. So potent was the ideology of the villa that even in this miniaturized form, its chief elements remained visible: one's own plot of land, a view, an opportunity for rural relaxation, a setting for informal behavior, a retreat from urban ways.

One peculiarly original variation on the weekend or vacation cottage—probably inevitable, given American mobility—was the travel trailer. The evolution of the trailer is traced by Allan D. Wallis in *Wheel Estate*, a 1991 history of the mobile home. During the 1920s and thirties, tens of thousands of Americans took to the road. These "tin can tourists" traveled in wheeled homes manufactured by companies with evocative names like Covered Wagon and Prairie Schooner; there were also luxury models like Glen Curtiss's Aerocar. By 1937, the industry was producing one hundred thousand trailers annually. These really were "machines for living," and while Le Corbusier was designing his landlocked nautical villas, Norman Wolfe and Wally Byam were manufacturing streamlined trailers like the Silver Dome and the Airstream.

Although travel trailers began to be used as permanent homes by migrant laborers during the Depression, and by the government to house workers at defense plants during the Second World War, their chief function was as a temporary country home. Like the cottage, the villa-on-wheels was an object in the landscape, but it was an object in a variety of settings—the Grand Canyon one week, the Florida Keys the next. This detachment and self-sufficiency had a curious effect on the occupants. The landscape was now something to be controlled, chosen to suit whim and fancy. Wallis recounts that in 1938, Walt Disney Studios released a cartoon titled *Mickey's Trailer.* The famous mouse was shown living in a country cottage surrounded by a lawn and picket fence. When Mickey pulled a large lever, the saddle roof, porch, picket fence, and lawn all folded up and disappeared into compartments, and the cottage, revealed now to be a trailer, was towed away. In Mickey's villa, the dichotomy of house and landscape was resolved at last.

As American as Blue Jeans and Sweat Shirts

Strolling down a Key West street lined with porches can feel a bit like domestic window-shopping. There are moody porches with silent old men in rocking chairs, and gaudy porches whose sole occupant is a squawking parrot in a cage. There are grand porches with elegant wicker furniture and overhead fans, and sagging porches with cracked car seats and plants in old tin tubs. A cascade of bougainvillea can turn the most ordinary porch into a magical arbor. Some porches are primly restored but obviously unused; others have the comfortable, slightly grimy appearance of old, well-worn clothes. There are bohemian porches with wind chimes, yuppie porches with twelve-speed mountain bikes, and proletarian porches with old, vinyl-covered armchairs. There are even eccentric porches, like the one built by Octavio Castillo in 1941 with V-for-Victory-shaped windows.

Porches here come in a variety of shapes and sizes. Classical Revival porches with carefully proportioned moldings and elegant pedimented fronts stand beside nondescript metal-roofed porches of a type that is ubiquitous in the South. The eyebrow house, said to be unique to Key West, derives its name from the roof overhang that extends above the second-story windows and creates a tall porch over the entire facade. Recessed apron porches, similar to those found in Creole cottages in the Louisiana bayous, contrast with generous, Bahamian verandas that are wrapped around the entire second floor.

The Hemingway house (probably the most visited on the island) has a surrounding gallery supported by ornamental cast-iron columns with ornate railings, which gives it the slightly dissipated appearance of a New Orleans bordello. Some porches are open to the street; others are mysteriously shrouded in wooden jalousies. Victorian houses are draped with porches whose gingerbread filagree and delicate fretwork recall antimacassars and old lace. Even the little shotgun houses in Old Town, originally built for Cuban cigarmakers, have tiny porches, just big enough for a hammock or a couple of easy chairs.

The ubiquitous porch in south Florida undoubtedly owes its popularity to the lack of air conditioning in that climate, but porches are just as popular in the Midwest as in the South, in New England as in California. The most famous American porch was built by George Washington, who added it to his house at Mount Vernon in 1772. Many of the early plantation houses had similar porches and galleries.

The original impetus for these additions may have come from the landscape as much as the climate. These new Americans were accustomed to the cultivated landscapes of Europe, not the wilderness outside their doors, and a porch frames—hence, tames—a rugged view, acting as a mediator between the house and its surroundings. Eventually the porch migrated to towns and villages, where it fulfilled a similar role, providing a space that existed in the margin between private and public life.

Since then, there have been not only front porches and verandas but back porches, screened porches, sleeping porches, galleries, breezeways, and what used to be called piazzas. The latest version, which originated in California but is now found attached to the back of suburban houses across the nation, is the sun deck.

It may be stretching things to call a deck a porch, for a true porch, unlike a terrace or a patio, is always a partially enclosed outdoor room. But it is much more than simply an architectural feature. Because it is not really in the house but rather attached to it, the porch provides an occasion for different behavior. Most rooms are associated with particular activities; the charm of the porch is that it serves no precise function—except, perhaps, idleness. The porch signifies leisure: work done, the day complete. It usually does not put on airs. It is a place for old furniture and old clothes, for watching the world pass by, or for dozing off with the Sunday paper.

The porch is the architectural equivalent of two other American inventions: blue jeans and sweat shirts. It is probably this characteristic atmosphere of informality and relaxation that explains the popularity of the porch and has made it a distinctive feature of American houses, and of American domestic life. The current interest in nineteenth-century domestic architecture has seen a revival in the construction of bay windows, roof turrets, and front porches. More often than not, this fashion is a reflection of aesthetic interest, or of nostalgia. Still, it would be nice to think that it might also encourage a revival of porch life. Sitting on the porch in the evening used to be an invitation to the passerby to stop and say hello. This sociable custom is no longer as common as it used to be, although in Key West, as in many small Southern towns, it has not altogether died out. But even an empty porch gives a house an affable demeanor and conveys an agreeable sense of welcome. It is nice to see porches again, even if they only serve as reminders of an earlier, friendlier time.

From Mao's House to Our House

It was my first visit to a modern home in mainland China, where I had been invited to lecture on housing at Shanghai's Tongji University in the summer of 1986. We stood in a small hallway that also served as a dining room; it held a tiny table and three folding chairs. The kitchen nearby was not much larger than a walk-in closet. A single tap protruded from the wall over an enameled cast-iron sink. Beside the sink were a small counter and a hot plate. I could see outside the kitchen a shallow balcony, whose main function seemed to be to dry clothes. Off the hallway was the bathroom; unabashedly, I looked in. It contained a squatting-type toilet and a sink, but no shower or bath; a metal tub hung on a hook on the wall. As our host showed us around, he told us that he considered himself lucky to have such a modern apartment. He worked as an environmental engineer for the municipality; his wife was a teacher at a daycare center. Since it was a holiday, they were both at home. Their daughter was visiting friends.

"Let's have some tea," he said, inviting us into an adjacent room, which was small and crowded, serving not only as a living room but also as the family's bedroom. Most of the space was taken up by the two beds, a double and a single. The room also contained a small desk, a bookshelf, and a cupboard squeezed into the corner. There is a traditional Chinese saying: "A beautiful room need not be large, and fragrant flowers need not be many"; but one would have to be a skillful interior decorator indeed to create beauty out of such cramped surroundings. The whole flat occupied by this family of three was considerably smaller than the average American motel unit.

The room was neat and clean but lacked warmth; utility, not beauty, seemed to be its occupants' main concern. The white walls were bare except for two unframed drawings and a calendar. We sat on uncomfortable folding chairs drinking jasmine tea; outside, the spring rain beat gently against the windowpane. It was cool in the apartment; I looked for a radiator, but there didn't seem to be one. My host explained that the Chinese authorities had decreed that to conserve fuel, home heating was not permitted south of the thirty-fifth parallel. I was glad that I was not in this uninsulated building in January, when temperatures regularly fell below freezing.

The small flat, though not exactly cozy, did at least have the basic amenities. There was electricity, running water (albeit only cold), and gas for cooking. Of course, to us these are ordinary and unremarkable things, everyday conveniences that hardly bear mention. Wall posters in Beijing and student demonstrations in Shanghai, not indoor plumbing, are what make headlines in the American media, and it's easy to forget what a novelty such domestic comforts represent to the majority of Chinese.

Sixty years ago, when more than 60 percent of American homes had electricity (and more than half of those homes already contained electric irons and vacuum cleaners), most Chinese families lived in the sort of wretched conditions described by the novelist Yu Dafu in his 1923 short story "Nights of Spring Fever." His protagonist lives in a one-room garret in Shanghai's International Settlement. His room lacks even a window, let alone facilities for washing or cooking. He eats cold food—bread and bananas—and once a month treats himself to the public bath. His only possessions are his books—he is a writer—and a padded gown. His neighbor, a factory girl, is slightly better off: her room has a window. How these two would have admired the tiny flat I had just seen—its fresh air and sunlight, its electric lamps, its plumbing. How they would have relished the achievements of a domestic revolution—a change as significant as, and probably more lasting than, Mao's ill-fated attempt at cultural reform.

A domestic revolution is under way in China, but it is hardly complete. Walking through the narrow lanes lined with tiny hovels, I could see that for many people, not so much had changed in the last sixty years. We were stopped by a man who invited us into his house, a room about ten feet square where he lived with his wife and child. We exchanged cigarettes and smoked, sitting on the bed; there was no other furniture except a table, and a dresser on which was balanced a large, improbable cassette player. The family shared, with a dozen neighbors, a privy, outdoors in the yard, where they also collected water from an outdoor tap and where they did their washing. Cooking was done on the stoop, and as we left, I noticed a small brazier and a pile of briquettes of compressed coal dust outside the door.

Li Dehua, the director of the Shanghai Architectural Society, told me that more than a third of the city's population is still living in overcrowded, pre-Liberation housing. Although the official planning norm for new housing is sixty square feet of living space per inhabitant, in the old neighborhoods of Shanghai the actual amount of living space was half that. (A single bed takes up at least eighteen square feet.)

The continued presence of urban slums highlights the problems facing the Chinese authorities. Socialism has promised shelter for everyone, but who is to pay for this new housing? Rents are so low—typically about three or four dollars a month—that they don't even begin to cover the cost of construction. "The rents we collect are only one-third of our *maintenance* costs," complained an exasperated housing official in Tianjin, an industrial city near Beijing. "We get the second third from the central government."

"What about the rest?" I asked. He shrugged his shoulders. And what was the solution? Not Karl Marx, but Adam Smith. "We have to recover our investment," said Luan Quanxun, the director of the Tianjin Housing and Estate Research Institute. "We must raise rents. We are even considering privatizing home ownership and offering houses for sale to those that can afford them."

It is a daring suggestion, and in the busy street markets, signs of a growing prosperity indicate that some people can afford to buy a house. The privately owned shops I visited stocked a large variety of products that had previously been available only to a select few in the hard-currency Friendship Stores. Now anyone with cash can purchase a bicycle, moped, radio, cassette player, television, stove, small refrigerator, or washing machine. The washing machine, the first large electric appliance to appear in America (in 1909), is a barometer of domestic change. It signals the presence not only of citywide electric supply but of disposable income. It also suggests two possibilities—either that servants are no longer available for tub washing (which was the case in turn-of-the-century

America), or that the woman of the household has less time available for housework.

In China, both conditions are now true. The number of women who work outside the home is probably greater than it is in the United States (where more than half of all women over sixteen now have jobs) and has produced similar effects. Daycare centers provide babysitting services. Fast-food outlets have sprung up in Chinese cities, and people eat less frequently at home, though this phenomenon may be as much the result of tiny apartments as of working mothers.

The growing independence of women has encouraged another change in family life: elderly parents rarely live with their grown-up children, as they continue to do in many other Asian countries, but live instead in their own homes. Which means, of course, that even more apartments are needed. As for domestic servants, since the advent of Communist rule, they have disappeared altogether. They may be returning, however, in another guise: the *China Daily* has suggested that, with so many working mothers, there is now a need for "home-maintenance workers."

As in America, all these changes have profoundly affected the domestic atmosphere. And also as in America, there is questioning of some of the effects of modernization. A recent editorial in the Beijing *Wanbao*, an evening paper, criticized the anonymity and impersonality of high-rise housing and suggested that life in modern housing developments strains the relations within families and affects "the physical and mental health and the intellectual development" of old people and children in particular. The writer went on to praise the more traditional type of courtyard houses, "which have unique social functions. They form a social network, which centers on courtyards and neighborhoods . . . and represents an important tool for social stability."

Courtyard houses are a common feature of most cities. From the window of my room in the Overseas Chinese Building in Beijing I could see that although tall, modern buildings lined the main streets, behind them the inner blocks consisted of clay-tile roofs that gave the appearance of villages in the middle of the city. The large, one-story courtyard houses, which date from as early as the Ming dynasty and belonged to prosperous families, are now subdivided, and their crowded interiors provide even less space than the modern apartment blocks. Nevertheless, the quiet quadrangles, which are entered from the street through heavy wooden gates, afford a sense of neighborliness and domestic privacy that is a welcome respite from the busy surrounding city.

I visited one of these courtyard houses in the old Chinese quarter of Tianjin. The quadrangle had originally been intended for a single household but now was occupied by seven or eight families. It was a Saturday evening, and many people were at home. A middle-aged lady invited us in; her family of four shared two rooms. I could see vestiges of what had been an elegant interior: dark, wood-paneled walls; round wood columns burnished with age; a Biedermeier dresser. It reminded me that China before Mao had not only consisted of coolies and mandarins but had included a flourishing bourgeoisie. According to the lady—a bank employee and a longtime resident—the building had not always been so crowded. A large influx of strangers had occurred during the "Disaster," as most Chinese call the Cultural Revolution. Overcrowding was not the only legacy of that troubled period. I noticed that every single ornament in the carved brick gateway and around the still-graceful courtyard had been systematically chipped and defaced.

More than the facades of Chinese homes had been scarred by that neurotic decade of unrest. In many households I felt a sense of newness, as if people were still in the process of unpacking and setting up house. That was literally true for professionals and university professors, since they had been relocated to the countryside and had had to reassemble their lives—and their homes—upon returning. It was not just a lack of continuity, however, that explained the underlying feeling of improvisation and temporariness in many of the homes. It was as if people were ready to move on, as if they didn't really believe in the permanence of their situation. I felt that it would be many years before the Chinese home recovered its sense of stability and security.

Habitat Revisited

Montreal has several outstanding buildings, new and old, but unlike any other Canadian city, it also contains at least one work of architecture that has become known internationally and whose place in the history of architecture is assured. I am referring to Habitat, which was designed by Moshe Safdie and built as part of Expo, the world's fair hosted by the city in 1967. The fame garnered by this unusual housing experiment was based both on the building itself and on the ideas it represented. Almost a quarter century later, it is time to examine how both have fared.

The building first. Habitat consists of 354 concrete boxes (158 apartments) stacked one on top of the other to form an elongated pyramid eleven stories high. Because the boxes step back as they rise, each lower roof provides a garden-terrace for the apartment above. This image of a child's pile of toy blocks—albeit in concrete—is familiar to many, since more than seven million people visited Habitat during Expo, and pictures of the building were widely published in newspapers and popular magazines. However, like all architectural photographs, these were taken when the building was brand-new, pristine, and unlived in.

Buildings age in different ways. Ancient stone buildings—medieval cathedrals, for example—are weather-beaten and scarred, but this merely makes them more impressive. The sag and tilt of an old barn is charming rather than sad. Some modern buildings, like the Seagram tower on Park Avenue in Manhattan, are eerily ageless—the bronze curtain-wall looks exactly the same today as it did when it was built thirty-five years ago. Others, like the Centre Pompidou in Paris, are less fortunate: the effect of peeling paint and scratched surfaces is tatty and undermines the architects' intentions.

Sometimes—rarely—a building improves with age, like an adolescent growing into adulthood. Habitat is such a building. The Montreal climate is hard on concrete, and the surfaces, once so crisp and machinelike, are pleasantly weathered; in several cases, ivy has begun to cover the walls. Large trees shade much of the building; on the terraces, smaller trees, bushes, and plants cast a green blanket over the building. Safdie titled one of his books *For Everyone a Garden*, and in Habitat everyone does get at least one garden, sometimes two. Unlike apartment balconies, which frequently become places for storing bicycles and winter firewood, the large Habitat terraces are used as outdoor living spaces, judging from the evidence of the canvas awnings and garden furniture.

Sunrooms have been built on several of the terraces. I saw at least one case where skylights had been cut into the flat roof of a box, and one maverick inhabitant of a top-floor apartment has installed a fireplace—and a masonry chimney. The effect of these modifications is not disturbing, however; the appearance of Habitat is enlivened by such idiosyncratic additions.

People have been living in Habitat since 1967, when the building was used to house visiting dignitaries and Expo officials. After the world's fair, the owner—the Canadian government—decided to lease the units on the open market. There was some difficulty in attracting tenants: the building was unusual, and the federal bureaucrats were used to managing public housing, not marketing commercial projects. It took two years for people to discover the attractions of an advantageous location—on a spit of land between the port and the St. Lawrence River, and conveniently close to downtown. When the unrealistically high rents were lowered and amenities added, the building quickly filled up; soon there was a long waiting list for vacant apartments. In 1985, the tenants, some of whom had been there since the world's fair, formed a limited partnership and bought the building.

Pierre Teasdale, a professor at the University of Montreal, has been living in Habitat for seven years. "Like many Montrealers, I had been critical of the building when it was built," he says, "but after visiting friends and seeing the apartments on the inside, I was totally seduced. It's a very nice place to live. It has many qualities that you don't find in apartments: windows on all sides, complete acoustical privacy, and rooms on two floors. It's very much like a house."

Habitat is a building, but it is also a demonstration of an idea. It was intended as a hybrid of two common forms of North American housing, the urban apartment building and the suburban bungalow. Habitat improves on apartment living by providing each home with an exterior front door, a variety of views, and a large outdoor terrace—for everyone, a penthouse—and it counters suburban sprawl by stacking houses one on top of another. Safdie (who himself owns an apartment in Habitat, although he has not lived there since 1979, when he moved his office to Boston) continues to believe in the environmental advantages of this housing form.

"What you are left with in Habitat that is really significant," he reflects, "is a way of living in a high-rise building."

Habitat was also an experiment in prefabrication and mass production—or, as Safdie put it, "houses from factories." The idea of manufacturing entire houses is hardly original. Thomas Edison devised a monolithic cast-concrete house as early as 1908, although he eventually abandoned the idea—the cast-iron forms proved too expensive. Le Corbusier proposed that the individual apartments of a building that he was designing in Marseilles in 1946 be manufactured in a factory and placed in a superstructure, like shoeboxes on a shelf—or, in his more colorful Gallic metaphor, "like bottles in a wine rack." However, he encountered practical problems and resorted to more conventional building methods. With Habitat, the old ideal became a reality. "It obviously represents . . . an important direction that housing will take," announced a 1967 article in *Progressive Architecture*, an influential professional journal.

Safdie certainly believed so. He spent the decade after Expo designing versions of Habitat—for Washington, New York, Rochester, Baltimore, Jerusalem, and San Juan. Only the last project managed to get off the drawing table, and then only the foundations were built before it, too, was abandoned. The problem with industrialized housing was the size of the investments required for factory equipment and for technical research. "The seventies were, for me, a series of disappointments," reflects Safdie. The gap between actual building practice and his dream of a factory-made home proved too great, and finally he had to admit defeat.

"Our technological ideas were naive," he admits today. "The mistake in Habitat was the idea of a closed system in which everything was to be made in the same factory." In that sense, Habitat was a technological dead end, not because it suggested using industrialization but because it failed to foresee that the future of manufacturing—whether of cars, computers, or homes—lay in so-called open systems: assemblies that were unrestricted and flexible, and in which parts from different manufacturers could be interchanged.

Although Safdie continues to be involved with housing in Israel, where he is currently planning the new town of Modiin, about halfway between Tel Aviv and Jerusalem, he is now best known as a designer of prestigious public buildings, such as the recently completed National Gallery of Canada in Ottawa and the forthcoming campus of the Hebrew Union College in Los Angeles. This career shift is symptomatic of a general loss of interest in housing by prominent architects, both in America and, to a lesser extent, in Europe. Frank Gehry, Richard Meier, I. M. Pei, and Michael Graves in the United States represent very different approaches to the art of building, but all have one thing in common: their reputations—and their architectural ideas—are based on public and corporate buildings, and sometimes on private residences, but not at all on mainstream housing. This is in marked contrast to an earlier generation of architects—Le Corbusier, Walter Gropius, Mies van der Rohe, even that "nineteenth-century" master Frank Lloyd Wright—who showed us not only how we might work and play but also how, as a society, we might live.

Of course, many architects continue to be involved in designing mass housing, but where once the subject was at the center of architectural discussion, now it has been relegated to the status of a specialization on the fringe of the profession. Judging from the work being done in schools of architecture today, this situation is not likely to change soon. Graduation projects are freely chosen and hence are a good barometer of what interests the students. Recently these have included a wide array of building types, ranging from the arcane (I have come across monasteries, cemeteries, and planetariums) to the commemorative (museums, embassies, city halls). The drawings and models are uncommonly well made, and the designs wildly imaginative—deconstructivism is the current fad—but they reflect a curious vision of a world composed entirely of public and private monuments.

Why this loss of interest in ordinary housing? Certainly the problem of housing—especially affordable housing—is as urgent as it ever was. But architects need clients, and the virtual withdrawal of public agencies from the field of housing during the Nixon and Reagan years has deprived architects of government patronage, while the large commercial homebuilders have never been known for seeking out architectural talent. The students may also be taking the lead from their mentors. Most leading architects and architectural theoreticians, whose interest is in formal manipulation rather than environmental issues, have ceased to concern themselves with housing. Safdie conjectures, "I think that they feel—maybe rightly so—that apart from a luxury project, housing offers no latitude for architectural exploration, at least at the level that they are interested in." Put another way, housing may be too real to serve as a vehicle for the current narrow aesthetic concerns of the most acclaimed architects—concerns that no longer include a social and ethical commitment to the broader physical environment. It is a sad comment that the presence of this commitment, more than an optimistic faith in technology, should be what dates Habitat most of all.

Hot Housing Buttons

It's the architecture of the large and expensive new buildings—the glass-roofed museums, the granite-faced office towers, the glamorous hotels—that catches the media's, and the public's, attention. But all the institutional, commercial, and industrial buildings put together account for less than half of the money spent on new buildings every year. The rest is spent on a single category: residential construction. And more than two-thirds of this category consists of a building type that's so ordinary it's almost invisible: the single-family house.

About one million new single-family houses are built annually across the country, the vast majority by merchant builders. Although there are currently about 120,000 individual builders in the United States, American housing is marked by uniformity rather than diversity. This fact was brought home to me when I took part in judging the 1991 Builder's Choice Design and Planning Awards, an annual event organized by *Builder*, the leading magazine of the American home-building industry. In reviewing several hundred submissions, I was struck by the frequency with which similar designs cropped up. The homogeneity of American housing is due in part to similar building codes and standardized technology, and in part to the mobility of consumers, but it's also the result of an industry that is increasingly driven by trends and fashions—what merchandisers call pushing the hot buttons.

What were the hot buttons in 1991? Huge, well-appointed master bedrooms, for one. Even without counting the now-obligatory private bathroom, dressing room, and his-and-hers walk-in closets, the master bedroom has become easily the largest room in the house, taking up most of the second floor and often including such features as balconies, fireplaces, and skylights. The modern master bedroom recalls the vast bedchambers of prerevolutionary France, often used by the aristocrats for social as well as private functions. It makes one wonder if the custom of the morning *levée*, which turned getting out of bed into a public spectacle, is about to return.

The expansion of the master bedroom is often at the cost of the living room, which has shrunk to the extent that in many houses it resembles a sort of waiting room, with just enough space for a sofa and a couple of chairs. Instead of the living room it's the so-called great room that now takes center stage. Despite its medieval-sounding name, the great room combines the roles of the Georgian library, the Victorian drawing room, and the 1950s rec room; it marks another step in the evolution of the family room, which began with the basement playroom, a transparently improvised location for the television set.

Although the architectural style of new housing remains firmly traditional (Spanish Colonial in the West and Southwest, American Colonial in the Northeast), the interior arrangement of most houses has been affected by the modernistic notion of the open plan. Consequently, the living room, dining room, kitchen, and great room are conceived as part of one single, flowing space. This provides visual excitement as well as a feeling of roominess (American home buyers apparently love wide-open spaces), but it does create difficulties with noise. A recent solution to the problem of noisy teenagers is the enticingly titled "bonus room," which is a spare room on the bedroom floor that can be used as a den or a television room or a guest room.

Whatever the style of the exterior architecture, one rule appears to hold true: the facade along the street must be sprinkled with bay windows, recesses, protrusions, overhangs, and uneven rooflines. This architectural articulation provides the maximum of what homebuilders call "curb appeal." Paradoxically, the part of the house facing the garden, which is where most people spend the majority of their leisure time, is drab, flat, and unadorned.

This manner of building, in which an entrepreneur erects houses and offers them for sale, is hardly unique to the United States, but in no other country has housing become so dominated by the concerns of the marketplace; in America, the house may be a home, but it is first a consumer product. Hence the preponderance of hyperactive street facades, dazzling hallways with lofty staircases, and sparkling bathrooms, which all help to sell a house but do not necessarily make living in it more convenient or comfortable.

The design of the consumer house has been dramatically altered by the growth of car ownership, which has increased from an average of one, to two or three per family; the problem is where to put them. The conventional solution is simply to enlarge the garage. A single-car garage is only twelve feet wide, but a three-car garage is thirty-six feet wide; on a narrow lot this barely leaves space for the front door. Even with the best intentions, it is difficult for a builder to avoid giving the impression that the house is really a converted service station or car wash. The effect of a row of such houses can be deadly. The front lawns are replaced by almost continuous driveway paving, and the line of garage doors flanking the sidewalk hardly creates congenial streets.

There are ways to solve these problems, but they require rethinking some basic assumptions about how single-family neighborhoods are planned. One alternative, which has been tried successfully in new developments like Kentlands, in Maryland, is to provide rear service lanes and parking behind the houses. Another is to follow the pattern of Radburn, in Fairlawn, New Jersey, a 1920s development that kept automobiles on the periphery and provided landscaped pathways for pedestrians. Still another alternative would be to allow a certain amount of parking on the street rather than to require that all cars be kept on the lot.

A different challenge to the traditional single-family house is posed by the contradictory demands of consumers who want larger and larger houses (a recent survey by the National Association of Home Builders found that the median desired house size was 2,356 square feet, almost one-third larger than the median size of the respondents' present houses) and the high cost of land, which dictates smaller and smaller lots. This has produced housing developments that resemble parking lots filled with stretch limousines; no matter how attractive the individual houses, the overall effect is slightly ridiculous. It might be time to reconsider the single-family house: either we content ourselves with smaller houses, or we will be obliged to look at alternatives like patio houses and row houses, and to resurrect such earlier housing types as the California bungalow court and the Georgian housing terrace.

Perhaps the most disappointing revelation of the Builder's Choice jury was the scant evidence that the industry was responding seriously to the chief concern of many young Americans: housing affordability. Instead of pioneering innovations in construction, design, and planning that would reduce selling prices and enlarge the size of the first-time buyers' market, most builders prefer to cater to the prosperous second- and third-time buyer. The button that is labeled "Small and Cheap" remains largely unpushed. Too bad.

Living Smaller

In June 1990, my colleagues and I built a demonstration house on the campus of McGill University, in downtown Montreal, to test a thesis: if people considering a move could experience the advantages of high-quality, smaller, more flexible, and more adaptable houses, they might actually choose smaller rather than larger quarters. The Grow Home was small (1,000 square feet); it included unpartitioned spaces; it was adaptable to different households, it used good-quality finishes and materials, and it was a row house, only fourteen feet wide. The construction cost was about $35,000, which meant that the selling price in Montreal, including land and all development costs, would have been less than $60,000—about half the price of an average single-family home in Montreal at the time. (All prices are in U.S. dollars.)

The house was fully furnished (by a Swedish manufacturer of do-it-yourself furniture), and it was open to the public for three weeks. Each day a stream of people made its way up the stairs to the porch and through the space. As they approached the house, their first reaction was usually "Isn't it tiny." And the Grow Home *was* tiny—fourteen feet is unusually narrow for a row house. Its small size was exaggerated by its site: it stood alone, like a slice of bread removed from a loaf, surrounded by large university buildings. The Grow Home resembled a doll's house, albeit an elegant one, since the facade was designed in a traditional manner.

Once people got inside—the first room was the kitchen—the common reaction was surprise at the amount of space: "It's much bigger than I expected; it doesn't feel small at all." Fourteen feet is narrow for a house, but it's not narrow for a room, and an eat-in kitchen fourteen feet square is spacious, requiring no compromise in layout or counter space. The feeling of roominess continued in a short corridor, which was wider than usual in order to accommodate bookshelves or shallow cupboards. Immediately behind the kitchen (and sharing its plumbing) was the bathroom, which was large enough to include a full-size washer and dryer. At the rear of the house was a small sitting room with French doors leading outside to a pergola-covered deck. Like many of the features in the house, the pergola and the deck were part of a list of options that could be added according to the owner's wishes; one might choose a deck ($610), a wood-strip floor ($545), or varnished oak stairs ($800).

The staircase led to a second floor—an unexpectedly large space without interior walls, extending from the front of the house to the rear. Part of this loft was furnished as a baby's room; the other end was the parents' bedroom, with large doors leading to a balcony overlooking the front garden. Movable cupboards replaced built-in closets. It would be possible in the future to create a separate children's bedroom, and there was also enough space for a second bathroom.

About ten thousand people visited the Grow Home. A questionnaire was made available at the door, and although the 636 responses turned in do not represent a scientific sample, the results were nevertheless revealing.

Understandably, the Grow Home attracted people with modest incomes: half the respondents said that their household incomes were in the range of $15,000 to $35,000. Also understandably, these were relatively young households: three-quarters of the respondents were under forty-five. Just over one-third were single, and about one-third had children; almost 40 percent indicated that they were looking to buy their first house. Asked if they would be ready to live in a house smaller than 1,000 square feet, three-quarters answered yes. An overwhelming 93 percent approved the idea of a second floor that could be completed according to their personal needs. As for the quality of the materials and the finishes, 66 percent found it to be good or excellent, 32 percent checked off "Acceptable, considering the house price," and only 3 percent indicated "Disappointing." Did they think that the Grow Home was a good buy at about $60,000, including land? Sixty-nine percent said yes. The traditional appearance of the Grow Home appealed to 94 percent of the respondents.

The experience of the Grow Home suggests that our thesis about small houses may well be correct.* The urge to be a homeowner remains strong in Canada, as it does in the United States, and young, first-time house buyers obviously understand that they will have to show flexibility and make some compromises in their dreams of a home.

* In the following two years, more than eight hundred Grow Homes were built in the Montreal area by commercial developers. The selling price and the enthusiastic response of the public were as we predicted.

Housing Shocks

It is not really surprising that the Grow Home met with popular acceptance: over the last thirty years, the market and the economy have changed in ways that will make everyone compromise and be more flexible. The first of three seismic shocks that altered how Americans live—and how they will think about buying houses in the future—started as an undetected rumble in the early 1960s, just after the golden age of American housing. Almost three-quarters of present existing U.S. houses were built after 1940, many in the twenty years following the end of the Second World War. The overwhelming majority followed the same model: single houses for single families. The best-known example, which became a symbol of homeownership throughout the 1950s, was devised by the developer William Levitt. The house was small and uncomplicated, but it had a fully equipped kitchen, the lot was big enough for a garden, and at $7,990—no down payment and $65 a month—it was a bargain in 1949. Homecoming GIs, impatient to get on with their lives, saw this little cottage as just what they needed.

If such houses were uniform, it was not necessarily the result of a lack of imagination; rather, it was a reflection of a remarkable homogeneity in the size and composition of American households. In 1940, the typical number of occupants in the home was four: husband, wife, and two children. Their roles were predictable: Dad worked at the factory or office; Mom stayed home, kept house, and took care of the kids, who played in the yard.

The composition of the family changed in the early 1960s. In 1956, the median age at first marriage had been 22.5 years for men and 20.1 years for women, a historic low. Now young people started waiting longer before getting married, which, together with more reliable birth control (the pill was first marketed in 1960), affected reproduction rates: people had fewer children, and had them later. The size of households shrank accordingly, and by 1989 the average number of occupants in a house had dropped to 2.6.

Households were not only smaller, but different. Starting in the 1960s, for a variety of reasons, more women began to work outside the home, and by the 1970s they were entering the work force in unprecedented numbers; today, in more than half of all families, both parents work outside the home. At the same time, divorce rates have risen—it is now estimated that half of all marriages will end in divorce. Hence the increased number of single-parent families, most of them headed by women. More people are living alone, and single-person households now account for almost a quarter of the total, up from 17 percent twenty years ago; during the same period, married-couple households went down, from 71 percent to about 55 percent. The typical family in the Levittown cottage—a married couple with young children—is not typical anymore. Indeed, it is now called the "traditional" family and makes up less than a third of all households.

The second event that changed the American home involved ownership. Homeownership is important to Americans, about two-thirds of whom own their homes—twice the rate in France, Germany, and Great Britain. Throughout the postwar period the amount of money that the median-income family could afford to spend on buying a house exceeded the median price of a new house by several thousand dollars—a situation that persisted even though the average price of a new house increased to $16,000 in 1955 and to about $55,000 in 1978. Houses grew more expensive partly because of increased land values and inflation; but as long as family incomes also grew, the rate of homeownership continued to increase steadily. The rising numbers suggested that eventually all gainfully employed people could become homeowners if they wished.

During the late 1970s, house prices continued to climb as before, while family incomes rose more slowly, and inflation and higher interest rates reduced affordability. A graph of the chronological progress of median house price and median affordability would show that until the late 1960s, the two lines climbed side by side, affordability above and price below. Then they began to converge, until finally, at the end of the decade, they crossed, and began moving apart. The median price of a new house began to exceed what a median-income family could afford.

As a result, the percentage of Americans who owned their homes started to decline. The decline was small, but it was the first decline in fifty years. Throughout the 1980s the rate fluctuated, which led some observers to discount the significance of the change. Nevertheless, after an all-time peak of 65.6 percent around 1980, ownership had fallen to 63.8 percent by 1988, and among twenty-five- to twenty-nine-year-olds, the group traditionally associated with buying a first home, the percentage dropped eight points, to 35.4, in the eighties. For this group, the American dream of homeownership has been severely compromised.

The third and most important event was the October 1973 energy crisis, with an aftershock during the 1980s. The streetcar, the elevated train, the commuter railroad, and the automobile had made inexpensive suburban land available to housing developers, and the rapid postwar proliferation of single-family houses on large individual plots had been possible only because the rate of car ownership in the United States had been high ever since the 1920s. But for a short time during the winter of 1973 the world seemed to be turned upside down, and there was much talk of moving back to the city and of the benefits of energy conservation and mass transit. Eventually cars became smaller and cheaper to operate, home insulation retrofitting suddenly became a lucrative small industry, and energy efficiency became a selling feature of new houses, though residential development continued to depend on the automobile just as much as before. Then fuel prices declined, and things returned to normal.

The aftershock came in the form of a series of scientific disclosures about the deteriorating state of the physical environment, particularly global warming. Family cars, as well as power plants, were among the chief sources of carbon dioxide emissions, so dependence on the automobile was seen as a problem once again. The more general issues of conservation of energy, physical resources, and land were also again raised, and critics were quick to point out that the suburban house lavishly consumed all three. The abundant resources that accounted for the success of the large single-family suburban house—unlimited land, cheap transportation, and plentiful energy—can no longer be taken for granted.

When Houses Bulked Out

A short history of the American house since 1950 would have to include a chapter called "Bigger and Better." The Levittown house had two bedrooms, one small bathroom, and an eat-in kitchen; all of its rooms were arranged on a concrete slab whose dimensions were twenty-five by thirty feet (an unfinished attic was often converted into additional living space). William Levitt's strategy becomes apparent if one compares his house with earlier designs for modestly priced houses, such as those included in *Homes of Character*, a pattern book published in 1923 by the Boston architect Robert L. Stevenson. The porches, vestibules, entry halls, and dining rooms (or at least dining alcoves) that were standard domestic amenities in the 1920s were absent from the Levittown house, which lacked even a basement. It was bare-bones living.

The prosperity of the next two decades was an opportunity to recover some of the lost space. Not surprisingly, new houses increased in size. And they continued to grow. In 1963 the average new house had 1,450 square feet (the Levittown house had 750 square feet), and over the next decade another 200 square feet—the equivalent of two bedrooms—was added. According to the National Association of Home Builders, the average finished area of a new single-family house in 1989 was about 2,000 square feet, and thousands of houses were even bigger, often 3,000 to 4,000 square feet.

Houses became bigger in the 1960s and seventies both because rooms were larger and because there were more of them. Appliances such as dishwashers, food processors, and microwave ovens required larger, more elaborate kitchens with more counter space. Bathrooms proliferated throughout the house: powder rooms, guest bathrooms, private bathrooms attached to bedrooms and equipped with whirlpool baths and separate shower stalls. By 1972, half of all new houses contained two or more bathrooms. Ten years later, nearly three-quarters did. It became customary for each child to have his or her own bedroom, and for the parents' room to be larger than the others (in Stevenson's plans, there were no "master" bedrooms—all the bedrooms were roughly the same size). During the sixties, most homes augmented the traditional living room with a family room, or rec room. This allowed greater informality in living arrangements—a place for children to play and a place to put the television. The rec room was also a sign of the growing privatization of family life, which was a reaction to the disintegration of the public realm. The home was becoming the chief locale for family leisure, as it had been in Victorian times.

In a consumer society, homes not only shelter people but are also warehouses full of furniture, clothes, toys, sports equipment, and gadgets. It is a measure of the growth of consumerism that one of the things that immediately dates a house of the 1920s is how little storage space it has. In the 1920s, a bedroom cupboard three feet wide was considered sufficient; today, most bedrooms have a wall-to-wall closet, and master bedrooms are incomplete if they do not have an extended walk-in closet, often grandiloquently called a dressing room. There may be fewer people in the American house of the nineties, but there are a lot more things.

There is a price to be paid for this expansion, however. Bigger homes mean more time and money spent on cleaning and maintenance—work traditionally performed by women. Betty Friedan characterized the single-family suburban house as a "domestic trap." Even if one maintains that house-proud homemakers are satisfied to trade their free time for extra housework, what about the many women who also work outside the home? In *The Second Shift* (1989), Arlie Hochschild studied working couples and found that, on average, women performed three-quarters of the housework. She estimated that during the 1960s and seventies, housework and child care accounted for roughly fifteen hours a week of extra work for the working woman. As the house grows, so does the time spent on housework. Obviously, working women are ill served by the larger house.

The growth in the size of houses is also at odds with the shrinkage in the size of households. Why do families that are on average smaller require twice as much space? To some extent the expanding American house reflects a crude, bigger-is-better mentality. Homeownership is a sign of social accomplishment and status, and just as the most prestigious cars were once the Cadillac and the Continental, which served as models for cheaper (but equally bloated) Fords and Chevrolets, the houses of the wealthy—in particular Hollywood celebrities, whose sprawling Beverly Hills villas were prominently featured in fan magazines—were what the average tract house strove to imitate.

The increase in the size of the average new house, and in the level of amenities it contained, naturally cost money, and prices rose accordingly. Of course, the homebuilding industry was propelled by the same economic imperatives that drove the automobile industry and found it profitable to furnish the market with more expensive houses. And also like the automobile manufacturers, builders resisted reducing the size of their product dramatically, even when inflation, higher interest rates, and low household incomes (especially of single-parent families headed by women) suggested that it might be reasonable to do so.

When land prices, labor costs, or commercial interest rates rise, the builder passes on the increase to the buyer and raises the selling price of the house. If car prices rise too steeply, a prospective buyer has the choice of spending less and buying secondhand. But houses are not cars. Not only do older houses not depreciate in value, but their selling price is affected by the general housing market. If new houses cost more, then so do old houses, even though they were built years before, with less expensive labor, less expensive materials, and cheaper money. Hence, the higher the cost of new housing, the more difficult it is to become a homeowner, and also the more beneficial it is to be one already. Expensive housing means that a few people lose, but a lot of people gain.

Theoretically, prices should eventually drop as a result of reduced demand. However, unlike car prices, over time house prices have so far proved remarkably resistant to declines in demand. (A theory newly gaining prominence holds that house prices will never again be impervious to the rest of the economy.) Many homeowners who are selling a house prefer to wait rather than to reduce their asking price significantly. The nature of the homebuilding industry is also a factor. Large merchant builders have diversified into related fields, such as property development and commercial and industrial building. When housing demand falters, they are more likely to shift the focus of their construction activities than to lower prices. Small builders (more than half of all the residential builders in the United States build fewer than ten houses a year) are similarly immune to reduced demand. They operate with low overhead and few, if any, permanent employees; when prices soften, it is easy for them to cut back and wait until things improve, or simply to take a vacation.

The American dream of becoming a homeowner is so compelling that for a long time rising prices were slow to discourage demand; and as prices rose, banks and savings and loan companies made it easier to borrow money. The rule of thumb traditionally used by lenders to evaluate the financial capabilities of prospective home buyers was that housing costs (mortgage payments, taxes, and utilities) should not consume more than 25 percent of the household's income. By the 1980s, as house prices began to rise faster than incomes and this trend began to encourage borrowing, the percentage was adjusted upward—first to 30 percent, then to 35 percent, and sometimes to almost as high as 40 percent.

The rationale was that higher housing prices were being offset by the appreciation in the resale value of the property. This view had some validity, since houses were rapidly increasing in value; but it was a profit on paper, available only in the future, when the house was sold. In the meantime, the homeowner was obliged to tighten his belt and spend less—on recreation, travel, education, entertainment, books. Many people simply borrowed to make up the difference. No wonder credit cards became so popular, and so widely abused. Homeownership was being maintained, more or less, but at what price?

The House That Worked

The development of communities composed of freestanding houses surrounded by gardens was entirely American. Before 1840, American cities and towns followed the European model: attached, or row, houses were built side by side, on narrow lots, facing the street. This type of house first appeared in walled European towns in the Middle Ages, and it survived in various forms for the next five hundred years: seventeenth-century Dutch towns, Baroque Paris, Georgian London, and the Victorian industrial city were all composed almost exclusively of row houses. It was simply the way that towns—and villages, too—were made.

The row house proved remarkably adaptable to various social circumstances. The lower floor of a medieval row house was devoted to commerce or manufacturing; the upper floors, to domestic life. Rich people lived in large, wide houses; the poor lived in smaller, narrower ones. Sometimes the two classes shared the same house; in Regency terraces, the basement was given over to kitchens and servants' quarters, and the owners lived above. The Parisian town house carried social stratification further: the ground floor was usually a shop; the first floor contained a grand apartment; the upper floors contained less expensive lodgings, with lower ceilings; and at the top of the stairs, in the garret, were the cheapest rooms.

A similar adaptability was evident in the American row house, which was where people lived in all the Eastern Seaboard cities. The so-called Philadelphia bandbox was a tiny row house, ten to sixteen feet wide, built for renting to recent immigrants; on fashionable Society Hill, the houses were wider and grander but were also built in rows. The standard American city lot was about twenty-five feet wide, a dimension that could conveniently accommodate a living room and a hallway on the lower floor, and two bedrooms above. New York had its brownstones; Boston, the town houses of Beacon Hill; and Baltimore, rows of modest brick houses. As in Europe, the row house was not found only in cities. The Colonial Delaware town of New Castle, for example, was scarcely more than a large village, but many of the houses were row houses, which even today gives the historic district an urban—and an urbane—air.

America adopted the narrow row house not out of a concern for security, as in medieval Europe, or because of urban crowding. It is true that the row house kept walking distances short, but, more important, it defined city life in a congenial and satisfying way. One has the impression that just as people enjoyed the bustle of the city streets and squares, they also liked the gregariousness of living in relatively close proximity in compact, well-defined neighborhoods.

As the Columbia University historian Kenneth T. Jackson recounts in his 1985 history of the suburbs, *Crabgrass Frontier*, the freestanding house began to supplant the row house as the preferred American housing type sometime between 1840 and 1870. Cities were becoming noisy and congested. Immigration from Europe was on the increase: Italians, Poles, and Russians, ethnically and religiously different and usually poorer, crowded into the cities, and so did blacks from the South. Horse-drawn vehicles jammed the streets. Poor sanitation—there were no sewers—produced periodic outbreaks of cholera. Coal-fired industrialization produced eye-watering pollution. One remedy, if you could afford it, was to escape to the suburbs.

The move to the suburbs was not merely reactionary, however. It had also to do with a new appreciation for the outdoors and a desire to live in a more natural setting—or, more specifically, as Jackson says, to live in a house with a yard. Remember that the traditional row house was built either directly on the sidewalk or a few feet behind it—there was no room for a front lawn. Nor was there really a backyard. The small space behind the house was taken up with stables, service buildings, and privies; since there was no garbage collection, it was also a place to dump refuse. Even where land was available, city gardens were rare. When people wanted to be outdoors, they didn't go into a garden; they went into the street, or they promenaded in a public park.

In contrast, the yard reflected a desire for private leisure space (croquet and lawn tennis became favorite pastimes in the mid-nineteenth century) and a wish to isolate domestic life from the public world. Instead of stoops, which were really a part of the street, the early suburban houses had porches, which were definitely a part of the home and were separated from the sidewalk by expanses of lawn.

The British country house had provided the landed gentry with a garden setting for several centuries. What was new in America was the provision of such homes to large numbers of people—at first members of the upper-middle class, and then average working families. The earliest planned suburbs, such as Riverside (1869) outside Chicago and Forest Hills Gardens (1913) in Queens, nine miles from Manhattan, were so-called streetcar suburbs, linked to the city by railroad or streetcar lines. Since people were expected to walk home from the station, distances had to be kept short, and these new communities were thus relatively compact. They housed more than thirty people per acre, which was a population density a third that of the crowded city. The later automobile suburb had no such constraints and so could be more expansive. Broad streets and large lots with generous setbacks all reduced densities. Levittown, despite its small houses, accommodated only about fifteen people per acre. As houses and plots increased in size during the postwar period, densities dropped lower and lower. A typical suburban density today is rarely higher than ten people per acre, and is often even lower.

Downtown land costs more than it did in the past, of course, because there is a limited supply and an increasing demand. It is less obvious why peripheral land, the supply of which increases as the city grows, should cost more. One explanation is that the cheapest land in convenient locations was bought up first, and now that it is no longer available, developers are obliged to acquire higher-quality real estate. Another explanation is a change in the way land improvements are financed. In the past, the cost of building new roads and sewers came out of a municipality's general revenues—that is, it was absorbed by all taxpayers. Today the increasingly prevalent practice is for a municipality to levy development charges directly on the developer, who must pay these costs before starting construction. In some cases development charges also contain additional payments ("impact fees"), which are, in effect, an entrance tax. All these extra charges, and the cost of financing them, are passed directly on to the buyer in the form of a higher land price, and so is the cost of what is now a large number of necessary permits and the time expended in acquiring them. In 1949, the cost of land typically represented about 11 percent of the selling price of a new house; in 1988, though houses were much larger and better appointed, land cost accounted for more than a quarter of the selling price.

My point is not that land is being "wasted" but rather that the low density of suburban housing has produced some undesirable effects. Inevitably, a community of sprawling houses on large lots is going to mean a lot of driving. Shops, schools, libraries, swimming pools, and daycare centers are spread out; to reach them requires not only a car but time. As long as women stayed home and functioned as chauffeurs, this liability could be overcome.

The typical suburban home is a house of a unique type that emerged in response to a particular need, which it fulfilled in exemplary fashion. But there is no reason to believe that it has the versatility to adapt to different circumstances. It is ill suited, for example, to smaller and more heterogeneous households. Does a working single parent really want a large lawn? Does a couple without children require a playroom, and if both work, do they have the time to clean and maintain a large house?

It isn't clear what will happen to the large suburban houses of the 1960s and seventies as families shrink and heating and transportation costs rise. Basements with separate entries sometimes contain small apartments, but ranch houses are not easily converted from single to multiple occupancy. The row house, in contrast, has shown itself to be extremely versatile. A Philadelphia bandbox once inhabited by three families is now home to one; a Boston Back Bay row house on Commonwealth Avenue that once housed one large family now houses three professional couples. Family row houses in Manhattan have been subdivided into small apartments and are also used as offices and shops.

Today the row house could be an ingredient in a new and different type of housing development: more compact, more urbane, more neighborly. Such a development would have a variety of houses for different households: family homes, cottages, row houses, walk-up apartments. Considerably denser than current suburban developments (though not necessarily denser than the first streetcar suburbs) and incorporating many features associated with traditional American towns—commercial space as well as residential, public greens, well-defined streets—such communities would be characterized by social and economic mixing rather than homogeneity. They would be scaled to the pedestrian rather than to the driver, reducing, though not eliminating, dependence on the automobile. They also would reflect the variety of American families and would provide a wider range of economic choices than the present single, uniform housing solution.

The Advantages of the Small House

The simplest way to build less expensive houses is to build them smaller, not differently. That means fewer bathrooms; smaller kitchens with less cabinetwork, which is expensive; and fewer and smaller rooms. The cost of construction is almost directly proportional to the floor area ("almost," because certain costs, such as electrical hookup charges and building-permit and legal fees, remain constant). Because construction time is also proportionately reduced, the contractor's overhead—and profit—per house likewise go down. Smaller houses have the added advantage of being cheaper to heat and cool and easier to maintain. They also mean less housework, which should appeal to working couples and single parents.

How much smaller? Melanie Taylor, a New Haven architect, has designed several compact family houses intended for year-round living, some of them as small as 575 square feet. A modestly priced house designed for a new town near Gulf Shores, Alabama, combines two small bedrooms, a sleeping loft, an open living space, an eat-in kitchen, and a bathroom in only 1,100 square feet; additional space is provided by a front porch. Other Taylor houses, many of which have a faintly Victorian air, were featured in several national magazines and proved so popular that the architect was obliged to prepare stock plans for national distribution. In San Francisco, the architect Donald MacDonald has successfully built and marketed tiny row houses from 600 to 960 square feet, which includes a garage. These urban cottages, inexpensive by San Francisco standards (about $165,000), challenge what MacDonald calls "the mythology of space," compensating for their small size by incorporating oversized windows, skylights, fireplaces, soundproofing, and gardens. Last summer the architect unveiled an even smaller house, intended for a single person or a single parent with a small child. It contained only 240 square feet of space but included a fireplace, a sleeping loft, a tiny bathroom, and a fully equipped kitchen with dishwasher.

The MacDonald house represents the extreme limit—the housing equivalent of the micro-car. A less radical departure is a compact house like the Grow Home: about 1,000 square feet, within which it is possible to accommodate two or three bedrooms, one and a half bathrooms, and a basement that permits rooms to be added later. Such a house is about half the size and construction cost of the average new single-family house built in 1990, although it is still larger than Levitt's 750-square-foot Cape Cod model. Considering that the latter often accommodated a family of five, 1,000 square feet for two or three people seems adequate—by the standards of most European countries, it is even generous. Such smaller houses, sometimes called starter homes, would appeal to singles, couples, young families, and also older couples whose children have moved away from home—altogether a large market.

Reducing the floor area does not mean forsaking modern standards of comfort and convenience. There will have to be more and better-appointed bathrooms than in the small bungalows of the past, and ingenious, space-saving storage systems. The miniaturization that has been accomplished in electronics (smaller televisions, smaller audio equipment, smaller appliances) makes it easier to achieve high levels of domestic amenity in small spaces. If home automation—whereby a single electrical cable provides power, audio, television, security, telephone, and thermostat—becomes common, as seems likely, it will further increase domestic convenience, regardless of space. Like the Japanese car, the small house may start as an economic measure and finish as a luxury product.

Attempts at Industrialization

Rather than making houses smaller, wouldn't it be preferable simply to build them more efficiently and cheaply by industrializing the building process? This was the rationale for Operation Breakthrough, which was announced by the Nixon administration in 1969. Its aim was to enlist large corporations such as General Electric and TRW in a national effort to develop radically new ways of building housing using industrial methods, mass production, and innovative materials. Surely a nation that could put a man on the moon could improve upon traditional stick-built houses. By 1974, however, Operation Breakthrough had collapsed, partly as a result of a lack of political will but chiefly because the industrial giants were unable to produce a markedly better house at a lower price.

Independent of government efforts, an industrialized housing industry has developed, and it includes precut, panelized, and modular homes. Although these forms of building have been in existence for several decades, they have been unable to capture more than about 10 to 15 percent of the new-housing market, according to figures released by the National Association of Home Builders. Industrialized housing can be erected quickly, and it is usually of high quality. But industrialization has not significantly reduced the construction cost of the house. One problem is the investment in plant and equipment, which must be added to the selling price of the house, and the cost of weathering the ups and downs that are a characteristic of the homebuilding industry. Other reasons that conventional construction predominates include the low cost of on-site labor in many areas of the country and the paperwork required by a multitude of state and local building codes and regulations when manufacturers ship prefabricated components.

One type of factory-made housing has been consistently successful in reducing production costs: the mobile home. During the early 1970s, mobile homes made up a third of all new single-family homes, although this figure has now dropped to about half that. Mobile homes are small (usually less than 1,000 square feet), traditionally have used inexpensive interior and exterior materials, and are entirely produced in a factory (primarily by nonunion labor). The need to transport the product from factory to site imposes severe restrictions on its height and width, however, and a mobile home inevitably resembles a long shoebox. It is not a shape that can be happily integrated into most traditional neighborhoods. About two-thirds of mobile homes are located on rented land, the majority in commercial parks. While the separation of homeownership from landownership is part of what makes the mobile home affordable, it is also a disadvantage. In contrast to a conventional house, a mobile home usually does not appreciate rapidly in value—a fact that in the long run offsets its lower selling price.

Industrialized housing was prominent in postwar Europe and in countries such as the Soviet Union and Sweden, but it made little headway in the United States. The chief reason was, and continues to be, that the lightweight wood-frame house (which in its present form is unique to North America) is already a highly industrialized product. Indeed, it is much more industrialized than the often crude concrete building systems of Eastern Europe. Conventional American houses consist almost exclusively of bits and pieces that have been manufactured in factories and are quickly assembled on the site. The extent of this industrialization can be shown by a short list of the technical innovations that have become commonplace during the postwar period: factory-made wooden roof trusses (introduced in 1952), prehung doors and windows, gypsum wallboard, aluminum and vinyl siding, plywood, plastic plumbing, fiberglass insulation bats, rigid-foam insulation sheathing, sealed glazing units and low-emissivity glass, plastic vapor barriers and moisture barriers in wide rolls, and ready-mix concrete, and also laborsaving devices such as paint rollers, power tools, power staplers and nailing guns, small cranes, and forklifts. The most recent changes include metal and wood-composite substitutes for traditional solid-wood studs and joists.

The result of these improvements is apparent in both a higher quality of construction and a reduced amount of on-site labor, whose cost now accounts for only a small fraction of the selling price of a new house—about 15 percent, compared with 30 percent in 1949. Thus, the potential for reducing cost by increasing automation is small. Does industrialization produce less expensive houses? Yes. The difficulty in proposing industrialization as a strategy for reducing housing costs is that to a large degree it has already happened.

Less Land, More Do-It-Yourself

One advantage of smaller houses is that they can be placed on smaller lots. A modest one-story tract house typically needs a sixty-foot-wide lot—that is, every house requires sixty feet of sidewalk, roadway, sewer and water line, and storm sewer. A narrower two-story cottage can be built on a forty-foot-wide lot, immediately reducing these costs by a third. A semidetached house requires even less frontage—thirty feet. Such housing incorporates all the desired features of suburban life—individual houses, gardens, decks, natural surroundings—but on a reduced scale. Row houses, which can be built on twenty-foot-wide lots, have a more dramatic impact on land cost and density; infrastructure cost is reduced by two-thirds. With more people living closer together it is possible to plan neighborhoods with local stores, and walking rather than driving becomes a real option.

When affordability is a priority, it is possible to consider extremely narrow lots, less than twenty feet wide. In Victorian London, row houses were classified into four types, depending on lot width: twenty feet, eighteen feet, sixteen feet, and fifteen feet. In the famous Weissenhof Housing Exhibition, held in Stuttgart in 1927, the Dutch architect J. J. P. Oud built a row of houses each eighteen feet wide. Le Corbusier designed several projects with extremely narrow houses, and some of his ideas are visible in a Swiss housing cooperative, Siedlung Halen, built outside Bern in 1961; there the row houses are only sixteen feet wide.

Denser neighborhoods have a considerable impact on the environment: less automobile travel would mean fewer roadways and less energy invested in community infrastructure. Row houses, which share walls with their neighbors, provide savings in building materials because only the narrow front and back facades are exposed to the weather. A two-story row house has only about one-third the exterior wall area of a bungalow, and about one-half the roof area, and so heating and air-conditioning costs are reduced accordingly.

Smaller lots would also mean more-compact communities. Not only would these encourage walking, but the higher concentration of people would make possible more local services, such as day-care centers and shops. Many of the advantages of nineteenth-century town life could be recovered. Higher-density housing would provide a range of choices and opportunities for face-to-face contact between people.

The present housing market is characterized by many types of households. Home buyers include single people—unmarried or between marriages, with or without children—as well as couples—married or unmarried, childless or with young children, or, as is becoming increasingly common, with grown-up children who are living at home. All these different groups have different needs, resources, and priorities. The small but growing number of people who work at home need offices or workrooms; people with small children need playrooms; people with elderly parents need a guest room, preferably on the ground floor; childless couples may prefer large, open spaces; parents with noisy teenagers need separate rooms.

One way to accommodate this diversity is to leave part of the house unpartitioned—in effect, to create a loft space. An unpartitioned second floor is an idea that worked when William Levitt introduced the unfinished attic in his Cape Cod models, and it is still useful in reducing the initial construction cost of a house. Future bathroom connections can easily be provided for. The homeowner can choose to use the loft as a single open space or build partitions as required and as financial resources permit.

Most American males—and, increasingly, females as well—grow up learning rudimentary carpentry skills as a matter of course. Although we take these abilities for granted, they represent a national trait that is shared by few societies. The growth in the number of home-improvement centers attests to the popularity of the do-it-yourself movement. These stores sell a variety of tools, building materials, and electrical and plumbing supplies. Many of these products—such as adhesive floor tiles, plastic water pipes, and preassembled doors and windows—are specifically designed for home installation. In addition, there are shelves of plans, handbooks, and step-by-step manuals that cover every aspect of building construction. Traditionally the basement has served as the place for do-it-yourself additions and modifications to the home, and the use of flexible space has a long and tested history.

In 1961, John Habraken, a young Dutch architect, published a small book in which he proposed an approach to mass housing based on a separation of what became known as supports and infill. Habraken's proposal called for support structures to be built by contractors and for the infill—which includes interior partitions, bathrooms, kitchens, closets, and sometimes even exterior walls—to be bought separately by the occupant, much as furniture is bought, to suit the buyer's personal taste and pocketbook. This strategy, which was developed with multistory buildings in mind but was also applied in practice to row houses, attracted international attention and brought Habraken to the Massachusetts Institute of Technology as the head of the architecture department. Although a small number of housing projects derived from the support-infill model were built in Holland, the idea never really caught on. The chief drawback was that there was simply not a wide enough range of infill products, such as demountable walls and relocatable plumbing systems, available on the market.

Habraken's proposal was ambitious and complicated, requiring the development of too many new products at once. It also required that architects exert less control over the design process. Nevertheless, something like the support-infill approach could produce housing that is both more adaptable and affordable. It would be possible to provide houses without built-in kitchen cabinets and closets, for example, as has long been the custom in Europe. This would leave the homeowner free to choose how much and what type to install—big or little, fancy or plain, expensive or cheap.

This freedom of choice would have several benefits. First, the quality of finish carpentry and cabinetwork, which can vary considerably, would be left to the discretion of the homeowner. He or she could choose an inexpensive kitchen, for example, and replace it later with something better. Or a few high-quality cabinets could be bought initially and added to as more money became available. A handyman might decide to do the work himself. A large number of home-furnishings outlets, like Conran's-Habitat, sell knocked-down or partly assembled modular furniture; some, like IKEA, even sell kitchen cabinets and counters in a wide variety of styles, materials, and finishes.

Couples could install two sinks in the bathroom; working couples who eat out a lot could install small kitchens. Clotheshorses could put in more closets; readers could have more bookshelves. It would be possible to use space more efficiently in small houses by placing storage elements only where they were required—small closets in the guest room, toy chests in the playroom—and moving them as family needs changed.

Finally, there is the benefit of removing the cost of cabinetwork from the construction cost of the house. Finish work is time-consuming and costly for the contractor, and often causes delays and customer dissatisfaction. The efficiency of construction would be increased by cutting out finish work from the building process; the size of the down payment and of monthly mortgage payments would be reduced accordingly.

The chief obstacle to smaller houses on smaller lots is not the consumer, nor is it the homebuilding industry. It is those of us who already own our homes. Municipalities, reflecting the attitude of homeowners, have staunchly resisted the idea of modifying zoning regulations to permit the construction of smaller houses or to allow the subdivision of land into smaller plots. The chief reason is, sadly, selfish: smaller, less expensive houses are perceived as a threat to property values and to community status, even though housing in the $50,000 to $80,000 range, "less expensive" by today's standards, is still accessible only to solid middle-class citizens.

Despite the heightened awareness of environmental issues and wide opposition to nuclear power, the environmental advantages of more-compact neighborhoods have yet to enter the public consciousness. Many of the same people who extol the virtues of bicycling and of composting lawn clippings are up in arms whenever denser development is proposed. The institution of no-growth legislation by many towns exacerbates the housing problem, because it places quotas on the number of new houses that can be built each year and effectively guarantees that developers will build only large, luxurious houses.

Exclusionary zoning regulations create economically and demographically skewed neighborhoods. There are already signs that at least some communities are realizing that restrictive zoning may not in the long run be in their interests. First-time buyers eventually become second-time buyers, and towns that do not provide starter houses risk losing young families who would otherwise establish roots in the community. The lack of housing choices also has other negative consequences, as when, for example, public employees like firemen and policemen can no longer afford to live where they work, or when schoolteachers, nurses, and other valuable but low-paid professionals must commute long distances.

One can only hope that a more generous attitude will prevail—an attitude that recognizes that a new and different generation of prospective homeowners, faced with higher interest rates, energy costs, and land prices, is obliged to consider housing solutions different from those that were available to their parents. This is no cause for alarm. It may be an opportunity to build better—and more livable—towns and cities.

Should Suburbs Be Designed?

I recently conducted a graduate seminar on the subject of housing. If things got dull, as they sometimes did, I knew that I could always animate the discussion by introducing the subject of suburbia—or, rather, by insinuating that suburban housing had some merit. I might just as well have been defending male chauvinism or global warming. On this one subject, at least, my architecture students were unanimous: the suburbs, like fast food, big business, and Styrofoam cups, were bad, beneath contempt, certainly beneath study. One would never have guessed from their spirited condemnations that most of these young men and women had grown up in suburban surroundings and would probably return there someday to raise their families.

My students' reaction is hardly surprising. Ever since the 1950s, when David Riesman's *The Lonely Crowd* and William H. Whyte, Jr.'s, *The Organization Man* appeared, the suburbs have been associated with middle-class alienation and white-collar conformity. Resolutely middlebrow, suburbs incorporated none of the traditional virtues of the city; moreover, the rise of the postwar suburbs coincided with the decline of the city center. Even Lewis

Mumford, an earlier advocate of garden cities, came to see the growth of suburbs as an ominous sign of the disintegration of the traditional city and a symptom of the deterioration of civilized life. (Mumford spent the last fifty years of his life living outside New York City.)

These critics were reacting to the postwar suburbs exemplified by Levittown, but the idea of living outside the city was much older than that. The first modern suburbs were built on the outskirts of London in the late eighteenth century, reversing the tradition according to which the middle class lived in the center of the city and the poor on the edges. Although Continental cities resisted suburbanization (Vienna and Paris were ringed by dense working-class neighborhoods), in America the British model prevailed; the first "villa park," Llewellyn Park, was built on the outskirts of New York City in 1857. The long history of the American suburb demonstrates the resiliency of this urban form, which underwent many changes as it accommodated various types of families (first the rich, then the middle class, then everyone else), ways of life, and modes of transportation: the railroad, the streetcar, and finally the automobile.

In 1970, for the first time, there were more suburbanites in the United States than people living in cities or rural areas. The 1990 census showed that 46.2 percent of the U.S. population lived in metropolitan areas outside central cities—that is, in suburbs. Almost all city growth now takes place in suburbs, not in central cities. (From 1950 to 1960, the population of central cities in large metropolitan areas grew by a national average of only 1.5 percent; the population of suburbs increased by 53.9 percent.) The so-called back-to-the-city movement of the 1970s fizzled out; high rents, high prices, and high crime have continued to drive young families to the suburbs. Clearly, in one form or another, suburbs are here to stay.

According to Kenneth T. Jackson, a professor of history at Columbia University, "Suburbia has become the quintessential physical achievement of the United States." Why, then, the antipathy of my students—and of most intellectuals—to the suburbs? One reason, I think, is that suburbs have become a stereotype. To most people, suburbs conjure up images of uniformity and monotonous sprawl; of white, middle-class exclusivity; and of bedroom communities composed of self-satisfied lawn rakers and smug backyard barbecuers.

The reality is much more complicated. There are hundred-year-old suburbs that are now considered a part of the city and far-flung raw tracts where the lawns have barely had time to grow in. And suburbs are no longer as economically and racially homogeneous as they once were. There are rich suburbs and poor suburbs, and although it is true that inner cities are frequently minority ghettos, the suburbs are beginning to show considerable diversity. (During the 1970s, for example, the suburban black population increased by nearly 40 percent.) Critics point out that individual suburban enclaves often exhibit ethnic homogeneity (Chicano, black, Italian, Jewish), but that is often a mirror image of traditional city neighborhoods. The conventional view of suburbs as consisting exclusively of single-family houses is no longer valid; suburbs are just as likely to contain high-rise apartments, condominiums, and attached town houses.

Nor is it any longer correct to describe suburbs as chiefly residential. As Joel Garreau points out in his 1991 book *Edge City*, the nature of current suburban growth has changed. There is now far more office space on the outskirts of New York City than in

Manhattan; across the country, corporations are relocating their offices outside the city, to peripheral areas like Houston's Galleria, San Francisco's Silicon Valley, and Boston's Burlington Mall. These new suburban areas are no longer dependent on the metropolis for employment, shopping, or entertainment. They have become self-sufficient cities in their own right. Indeed, they have even spawned their own suburbs, or "sub-suburbs," which are half-rural communities surrounded by countryside.

Postwar planners and architects, influenced by the largely European ideology of modern architecture, preferred to turn a blind eye to what was happening in the suburbs during the 1960s and focused their attention on urban renewal and downtown rehabilitation. It is only in the last two decades that some postmodern designers, such as Robert Venturi and Robert A. M. Stern, and town planners, like Denise Scott Brown, Andres Duany, and Elizabeth Plater-Zyberk, have begun to take the suburban environment seriously. Stern, in particular, has mounted a spirited defense of the suburban enclave.

The physical character of American suburban development is the subject of *Making a Middle Landscape* (1991), by Peter G. Rowe, a professor of architecture and urban design at Harvard. In an attempt to break down the suburban stereotype, Rowe has coined the term "middle landscape" (between city and country), and he devotes a good deal of his book to an interesting examination of the evolution of the four chief cultural artifacts that have shaped it: houses, shopping places, workplaces, and highways.

The suburban house has gone through several transformations, from the picturesque cottages that Alexander Jackson Davis designed for Llewellyn Park to the postwar Cape Cod houses that

William Levitt built in Long Island potato fields. The turn-of-the-century Chicago bungalow, which became the predominant type in California in the 1920s, was supplanted by the Western-inspired ranch house, which is still being built across the United States and Canada. The Colonial Revival house became another popular model. After 1975, according to Rowe, the Colonial and the ranch were merged in a house that included a compact two-story facade and a less formal, more open room arrangement inside.

The shopping center is a suburban fixture that is usually taken for granted, but it, too, underwent many changes before assuming its present form. The earliest suburbs were explicitly promoted as purely residential and contained no shops whatsoever; express companies delivered all goods (usually by rail) from the city. Eventually, commercial strips grew up along the major streets, following the lines of electric streetcars. The first so-called shopping village, consisting of a grouping of stores interspersed with parking lots, was built outside Kansas City, Missouri, in 1908. In 1929, the developers of Shaker Heights, a famous planned community in the Cleveland suburbs, built a shopping center that included retail stores, a bank, and a theater. During the 1950s, shopping centers began to be replaced by shopping malls that were increasingly self-contained, often enclosed, and completely dependent on the automobile—though oriented to the pedestrian, once the car had been parked. The latest malls are best described as bazaars. They contain not only shops but also hotels and offices, as well as community, entertainment, and leisure facilities. Increasingly, their architectural form, too, is richer, often evocative of traditional town markets.

The first American suburbs were inspired by British examples, but American builders were soon developing their own ideas, and what emerges strikingly from Rowe's historical review is the degree of architectural innovation that went into making the suburban landscape. This involved not only inventing new house types and new forms for the commercial center but also refining the iconography of roadside buildings—everything from gas stations to restaurants and, although Rowe does not include them, movie theaters and even churches. More elegant were the office campuses and corporate estates, often in parklike settings. Tying it all together were a system of expressways and parkways (the first begun in 1906) and an elaborate network of boulevards, streets, looped roads, and culs-de-sac.

While Rowe admirably describes the evolution of these neglected building types, he betrays a dissatisfaction with the appearance of the suburban environment; as the final section of the book makes clear, Rowe's ambitious proposal is to refashion the American suburb to make it more aesthetically acceptable. The results, mainly illustrated by the projects of Harvard graduate students, are not convincing. Rowe criticizes the suburban environment's tendency toward conservatism, nostalgia, and sentimentality, and would replace these with a warmed-over abstract modernism (itself rapidly becoming a form of nostalgia, at least among some architects). He calls for a "modern pastoralism," which appears to consist of monumental buildings juxtaposed with untouched nature. Le Corbusier meets Kmart—an odd coupling indeed.

It is unlikely that Rowe's proposal for a "poetic of the middle landscape" will have much impact on the bumptious developments going up at Tysons Corner, outside Washington, D.C., or on the mammoth shopping mall recently built on the outskirts of Minneapolis. The sort of visual order and coherence that Rowe calls for is at odds with the dynamic and individualistic urges impelling suburban development today, whether in the mall or in the housing neighborhood.

The contemporary suburb appears to be driven almost wholly by market forces, and its development is not tempered, as the first villa parks were, by any intellectual ideal, except perhaps that of individual freedom. Some kind of considered architectural response to the way the majority of Americans want to live might be a good thing. I say "might," because the intervention of design professionals has not always had a salutary effect on the built environment. One thinks of the sterile British new towns, like Milton Keynes, or of the dampening effect of architectural stylistic uniformity on suburbs like Irvine, California. Nor is it altogether clear which of several possible directions designers ought to take: modern architecture in the park, as Rowe suggests; a return to the tradition of the villa park; or a sort of habitable theme park. Given the catholicism of the marketplace, the likelihood is some combination of all three.

Our Town

Seaside, on the Florida Panhandle, facing the Gulf of Mexico, is only eight years old, and when it is completed it will have a population of fewer than two thousand persons, many of them seasonal residents. Nevertheless, this tiny place—despite its civic pretensions, it's really a beach community—was described by Philip Langdon, in a 1988 *Atlantic* article, as "the most celebrated new American town of the decade," because it represents a shift in sensibility, from the suburban to what has been called the post-suburban. In 1972, three architects—Robert Venturi, Denise Scott Brown, and Steven Izenour—published a collection of essays that lauded the suburban strip, titled *Learning from Las Vegas*. If someone were to write a book about Seaside, it might be called *Learning from Siena*.

Seaside and Siena—a mellifluous combination, but what possible connection could there be between this beach town, on what is known locally as the Redneck Riviera, and the venerable Tuscan city? Obviously, not what meets the eye, for the pastel clapboard houses of Seaside are nothing like the brick walls and tile roofs of the Italian city, which is characterized by the rich, reddish-brown color that bears its name.

"The city is the image of the soul," wrote Saint Catherine of Siena, "the surrounding walls being the frontier between the outward and inward life. The gates are the faculties or senses connecting the life of the soul with the outward world. . . . And in the center, where beats the heart, stands the holy sanctuary." Her native Siena really has two hearts, one religious and one civil—the Piazza del Duomo and the Campo—but I shouldn't quibble with her lovely metaphor.

Catherine lived in the second half of the fourteenth century, when Siena was an important city-state that only recently had ceded to Florence its position as the banking and trade capital of Italy. Siena was famous for its artists: not only painters, but sculptors, goldsmiths, stonemasons, and master builders. The chief product of their creative endeavors was the town itself.

Medieval Siena has survived intact and unspoiled. The narrow, curving streets, lined with brick and stucco houses, are encircled by a defensive wall pierced by eight gates. The clay-tiled roofs form a variegated, horizontal backdrop for the spires and towers of the Gothic and Romanesque churches, and for the beautiful black-and-white-striped marble campanile of the cathedral. At the geometric center is the Campo, an unusual fan-shaped, sloping piazza, ringed by palazzi, houses, cafés, and shops, and in the shadow of a graceful brick tower, which was completed in 1348, when Catherine was one year old, to commemorate the deliverance of the city from the Black Death.

The idea of the city as the image of the soul is not one that would carry much weight with urban planners of the last several decades. During the 1950s, planning theory was dominated by the monumentalism of Le Corbusier and produced capitals such as Chandigarh and Brasilia—cities not as images of the soul but of the all-powerful state. The sixties saw the emergence of a different idea: the megastructure, in which the entire city resembled one enormous building. Mercifully, none was built, and the mechanistic visions conveyed by the conceptual sketches of visionary architects have survived mainly in the form of settings for films—*Blade Runner* and *Batman*, for example, and some of George Lucas's science-fiction fantasies.

Other architects turned their attention from the future to the past. They reread Camillo Sitte, a Viennese city planner who, in 1889, had published a book advocating a return to town building based on visual and aesthetic principles. He drew his ideas from traditional European cities, particularly older ones like Salzburg, Bruges, and Siena, admiring especially their small size. Before Siena was decimated by the Black Death, it is estimated to have housed about 50,000 inhabitants; even today, the population is only 65,000. Since the buildings were close together, it was a compact city, epitomizing what architects now call "human scale." From the Campo, in any direction, it is less than a ten-minute walk to the encircling wall.

The ten-minute walk—a comfortable distance of about half a mile—has become a canon for modern designers of so-called traditional towns. Seaside, for example, has been laid out explicitly in accordance with the ten-minute walk: it is almost a mile across. As in Siena, there is a large space at the center—not a paved Campo but a grassy village green. When Seaside is finished, the green will be surrounded by arcaded shops and commercial buildings; as in many older towns, there will be offices and apartments above the stores.

A town laid out on a human scale makes walking possible, but the particular attraction of Siena is that walking is also pleasant. This is a result of two different elements: the spatial variety of the streets and squares, and the architectural coherence of the buildings that line them. Precisely the reverse is true of most modern towns, in which a confusing assortment of buildings is contained in a highly standardized system of identical blocks and streets. One feature of Seaside that has attracted the attention of architects and planners is that it has tried, with considerable success, to return to the Sienese model. There are streets of different widths—boulevards as well as lanes and narrow footpaths. To avoid monotony, the streets are not long, and they usually terminate in an interesting focus—a house, a small square, or a beach pavilion.

Seaside is probably best known, however, for its architecture. The houses, of which more than 150 have been built so far, exhibit the familiar vernacular of small Southern towns: screened porches, tin roofs, clapboard siding, and white picket fences. Stylistic uniformity (Colonial, Spanish, Tudor) is a common feature of many formally planned communities, but Seaside is coherent rather than uniform, because the buildings are not the work of one architect, or even of a like-minded group of architects. Instead, the planners of Seaside, Andres Duany and Elizabeth Plater-Zyberk, wrote an "urban code": a simple set of regulations, only one page long, that all builders—owners, contractors, and architects—must follow. For example: "The porch and window openings shall be square or in vertical proportion not less than 1 to 1½." And: "The principal roof shall be a gable or hip with a slope of 8 in 12." Although the result is often vaguely Victorian, some elegant houses recall Charleston; others, more casual, reminded me of Key West.

Despite the fact that the code does not mention architectural style, the first builders at Seaside adhered strictly to a traditional idiom. The result was charming, but a trifle cloying; the town was becoming a kind of architectural theme park. Happily, later construction has taken a slightly different turn. There have been several distinctly untraditional interpretations of the urban code, and the first phase of the arcaded town center is a large gray stucco building that recalls the unsentimental designs of the early modern architect Adolf Loos. Camillo Sitte, who deplored the tedium of repetitive, identical buildings, whatever their style, would have approved this variety.

Time described Seaside as a "down-home utopia," but it's a curious utopia, the product of neither political idealism nor bureaucratic planning but rather of a combination of entrepreneurship and private enterprise. Seaside's financial success, owing in part to its architectural celebrity, has been a mixed blessing. Building plots, initially around $25,000, have tripled in value, and homes built on them are considerably more luxurious than the original small cottages. The number of seasonal residents is larger than anticipated, since many homes are rented for part of the year; and it's likely that the permanent population of Seaside will never be large. These effects have surprised the planners. "Success may destroy the idea of Seaside," says Duany. It would be a cruel paradox if he were right.

Nevertheless, there are architectural lessons to be learned from Seaside. A visitor walking its narrow streets at dusk can just make out the broken outlines of pitched roofs, balconies, and lookout towers against the sky. Light from the porches spills out and illuminates the brick pavement. The night stillness is interrupted by the unmistakable murmur of domestic life: the clink of glasses, conversation, a sudden laugh. It is easy to imagine that one has been transported to the town of Thornton Wilder's imagination. And, in a way, Seaside *is* our town. Not our town as it exists today, but as we want it to be: small, comfortable, safe, friendly.

II. Special Places

A Place Map

About a dozen years ago, I started playing squash with a friend at the Sir Arthur Currie Gym at McGill University. In truth, it was not the game that attracted me; I am not what Americans call a jock, or even what the French call a *sportif*. What I did enjoy was the ritual of the Saturday-morning event, the highlight of which was a postgame beer at the Pines Tavern. I also liked the gymnasium, the cavernous locker room (an unselfconscious male preserve), and the curious architecture of the courts—their dark exterior passages, midget doors, and reverberatory acoustics. The word "gymnasium" is derived from the Greek and means "training naked," and the freedom to stroll unclothed to the showers was also part of the pleasure of this ancient institution.

All grown men who indulge in sports are, to a greater or lesser extent, reliving their boyhood. This was doubly true in my case, since I had attended McGill as an undergraduate, and the Currie Gym was a familiar, if not a cherished, place. Familiar, most of all, because it was the first building at the university in which I had set foot. Like all incoming students, I was obliged to line up with crowds of other eager freshmen on registration day, to await my turn to fill out innumerable forms on one of the hundred or so card tables that had been set up in the main basketball courts.

I would return to this building in a few weeks to participate in two sports, which was then a requirement for first-year students. I chose badminton—it seemed like an innocuous enough game—and swimming. Later, I also made an effort to join the Rifle Club. I had never owned a gun—which, I suppose, explained the attraction; several sessions in the dark and noisy firing range cured me.

Other than for the obligatory athletics, I rarely went to the gym—except to take exams. Every spring, the same card tables reappeared, and the basketball court was turned into a vast examination room. As the invigilators glided silently between the tables, we hunched over our exam books, an anxious eye on the passing time. I sweated a lot more then than when I was swinging at the badminton bird.

The gym was "up the hill," at the top of University Street, that cheerful gauntlet of dissolution, fraternity row. The gym marked the northernmost edge of my campus world, just as Joe's Steak House circumscribed it to the south. The latter does not appear on the official map of the university, but each of us carries mental place maps within us—maps that often bear little resemblance to reality. Like the New Yorker's view of the world in Saul Steinberg's famous drawing, which appeared on a cover of the *New Yorker* magazine in March 1976, showing everything beyond the Hudson River and a narrow strip labeled "New Jersey" as a featureless desert. These imagined maps are distortions, yet for the individual they arc truer depictions than those of cartographers.

Looming large in my own place map was the nondescript wing of the McConnell Engineering Building, which housed the School of Architecture, where I spent my days, and many of my nights. Appended to the school—that is how it appears on my map—was the rest of the engineering faculty: a rabbit warren of anonymous classrooms and steeply sloping lecture halls, peopled by boisterous young men with slide rules dangling from their belts. This was where I was inducted, more or less, into the mysteries of calculus, surveying, and soil mechanics.

The American architect Christopher Alexander maintains that every building, or group of buildings, has a heart; when you enter that place, you know you have reached the center of things. For me, the heart of McGill was unquestionably Moyse Hall. This had partly to do with its location, behind the Doric porch of the stately Arts Building and at the head of the main symbolic axis of the campus—what would be the *decamanus* of a Roman town. And partly it had to do with the building's communal and convivial function. It was in Moyse Hall that I saw the revue *My Fur Lady* and the theatrical productions of the English Department. This was where eminent visitors to the university spoke. One evening, Brendan Behan gave a reading; the Irish poet arrived late, obviously drunk; he read a few verses, made suggestive comments about a girl in the front row, and nearly fell off the stage. Such occurrences were memorable enough, but what made a greater impression was that it was in Moyse Hall that I had my first experience of a great teacher. Economics 100 was a required course for all first-year students, and several hundred of us sat rapt in the large, classically decorated auditorium as Cyril James nimbly led us through the giddy sweep of economic history, from ancient times to today.

It was because of this course, which had a long reading list, that I was introduced to the pleasures of the library. If Moyse Hall was the heart of the university, the Redpath Library was its brain, or at least its memory. I always had liked libraries, but this one was many times larger than the one-room high school library where I had devoured G. A. Henty and Edgar Rice Burroughs. The first time I entered the stacks, a peculiar space with glass-block floors and low ceilings, I was overwhelmed by the sheer quantity of knowledge—and by the smell of old paper, which I enjoy still. Another pleasure of the library was the vast and silent reading room—Tyndale Hall, since lost in the course of renovations and additions—with its polished cork floor and stylized murals. Outside, the sunny terrace—happily, still in place—provided a sort of academic corniche, fronting the campus green instead of the ocean. For a student from the outland of the engineering faculty, going to the library was also an opportunity to observe, sometimes even to meet, girls.

The place where I spent much time during my first three years at the university was the Student Union, now the McCord Museum. This most civilized of buildings, designed by Percy Nobbs in 1905, stood outside the campus proper, but that accorded well with its function, and with its autonomy. The classroom clearly belonged to the teacher; the library was a sort of no-man's-land, neutral and accessible to all; but the Union was our own—I never remember seeing a professor there—neither of the city, nor quite yet of the university.

Although the Union building had been designed for use as a student center, it was patterned on a nineteenth-century men's club and incorporated the solid comforts of that institution. On the ground floor was a cafeteria, which served indifferent but inexpensive food. A grand stair led up to the upper floors, which contained the ballroom and several meeting rooms, but the real action was in the basement, which housed the offices of several student societies. I belonged to the Players Club, whose pokey quarters were across the corridor from the noisy newsroom of the *Daily*. Twice a year we put on plays—I recall *Under Milk Wood* and *Fando and Lis*—moments of great excitement, even for someone who worked backstage, as I did.

I mentioned Joe's Steak House—my culinary education lagged behind my formal one—which marked the southernmost extremity of my mental map. Joe's was part of a cluster of extra-academic institutions along Metcalfe Street, which included Ben's—apostrophe still in place—and a second-floor jazz club where I spent many Friday and Saturday nights. There were a few other such places—the Three Kings Studio in the Prince of Wales Terrace, the Vienna Pastry shop across the street, the Hungarian restaurants on Stanley Street—which drew me out of the campus but were really an integral part of my university world.

At this point, if I were drawing my place map, I would get out my green Prismacolor pencil and shade in all the spaces between the buildings. That is how I remember it: greystone buildings surrounded by grass and trees, and the sheltering flank of Mount Royal. Even Sherbrooke Street was green, for the great elms had not yet been struck down. That would complete my drawing, since there was not much to show beyond the green island of learning. Perhaps I would include, on the distant horizon, a country labeled "The Outside World"; but probably not. Like the mnemonic constructions that medieval scholars used as aids in retaining information, my place map is a repository of memory, and the outside world was something to which I gave little thought at the time.

Art Inside the Walls

You want to see a real panda, you go to the zoo; you want to look at a real Picasso, you go to an art museum. Although more people view reproductions of art in picture books and on television than they do the actual objects, these are not successful surrogates. Despite the advanced technology of color printing, reproductions are always too small, television images too fuzzy. In art nothing can take the place of the real thing. And for most of us, museums offer the main opportunity for a satisfying firsthand experience of great art. Happily, most North American cities have an art museum. Like the public library, the theater, and the concert hall, the art museum is a cultural institution we've come to take for granted. It seems natural to us that there should be places where we can go on a Sunday afternoon to look at paintings, or where groups of schoolchildren will be taken to see their artistic heritage. At least once a year there will be a major exhibition assembling works from around the world, or presenting a great artist's lifework, or bringing us treasures from ancient cultures. Even if we aren't regular museumgoers, it's comforting to know there's a place where art is on display for all to see.

Special Places

Most of our urban cultural institutions have a long history. There have been libraries, for instance, since ancient times—archaeologists have found examples in Assyria and Egypt as early as 1200 B.C. Western drama traces its development from the open-air theater of Dionysus in Athens; during the Renaissance, theaters were common features in European cities. The antecedents of the concert hall were the music rooms built over London taverns in the late seventeenth century; by Mozart's time, Vienna had many public buildings in which popular musical theater, concerts, and opera were performed. But if one were to ask a contemporary of Mozart's, say, the way to the art museum, the response might be unexpected: "The art museum? What's that?"

The idea that works of art could be publicly displayed in a special building is not much more than two hundred years old. Art, of course, is much older than that, and buildings housing private art collections existed even in ancient Greece and Rome. But before the development of the museum, art was not something that ordinary people went to one place to look at. Art was experienced in the course of daily life: in the sculptured metopes in the Parthenon frieze, Trajan's Column in the Forum, the mosaics of Sant' Apollinare Nuovo in Ravenna, the great stained-glass windows of Lincoln Cathedral, the doors of the baptistery in Florence, or the statue of *David* in the Piazza della Signoria. For most people, art was experienced as part of an ensemble; there were few "individual" works of art, at least not as we understand the concept today.

All art, religious as well as secular, embodied meaning, and its meaning was often more important than its formal qualities. When we admire Michelangelo's *David*, we think of the genius of its maker; to the sixteenth-century Florentine, however, the statue was also a political symbol commemorating the victory of republicanism over tyranny. This is still the way we experience war monuments: first, as symbols (of military heroism and personal sacrifice); second, as civic landmarks; and last, as works of art.

Before the rise of the museum, works of art could be seen in homes, at least in the homes of the wealthy, but until the seventeenth century it would have been rare to find an assortment of paintings hanging on the walls of most grand houses. The ancient Romans engaged mural painters to decorate their homes, and for a long time this was the most common form of domestic art. In the case of the Villa Barbaro, designed by Palladio in 1556, art and decor were one: the painter, Veronese, worked right on the walls and ceiling. Later it became common for the architect to design the interior paneling and leave space, especially over the mantelpiece and on the ceiling, for paintings; wall niches were provided for sculptures. Tapestries and carpets were created for specific rooms. Such art—often on a theme requested by the client—was integrated into the decoration of the room and, like much of the furniture, was never moved.

By the late sixteenth century, easel painting was firmly established, and art began to be divorced from its surroundings; in *Henry VI*, Shakespeare mentions pictures hanging in a "gallery." In large houses, the gallery, which resembled an arcade, was a long corridor, usually with windows on one side and entrances to interior rooms on the other. Later, the gallery, still long and narrow, became a fully enclosed room, usually the grandest room in the house, where the family riches—silver plate, furniture, and sometimes works of art—were displayed. (By the nineteenth century, these private museums housed not only paintings and sculptures but also collections of curios and antiquities.) Smaller houses did not have galleries. Seventeenth-century Dutch burghers hung large numbers of individual paintings about the house—just as often in the bedroom or the kitchen as in the front room, sharing wall space with framed mirrors, maps, china, brassware, and musical instruments.

Throughout Europe, the rich collected art on a grand scale—big paintings and many of them—but the way in which pictures were hung suggests that the appreciation of individual works was secondary to the decorative effect of the overall display. Paintings were arranged side by side and one above the other, from floor level to ceiling. They were usually grouped symmetrically according to shape and size, not according to who had painted them. The effect of these "picture cabinets" could be overwhelming: the one in the royal castle in Prague, for example, which was itself the subject of a 1702 painting by Johann Bretschneider, was so full of paintings that it resembled a crazy quilt or a page in a child's stamp album.

The gallery and the picture cabinet were the precursors of the art museum, with one vital difference: they were not accessible to the general public. Although there were a few early public galleries (such as the Oxford Ashmolean, which opened in 1683), private art museums housing royal collections began—tentatively and very selectively—to open their doors to the public only at the end of the eighteenth century. The Public Art Gallery was inaugurated in Vienna in 1792; the Vatican collection opened to the public the following year. In America, art museums arrived about a hundred years later.

The chief impetus for what the British writer Paul Johnson has called the "democratization of art" was the French Revolution.

Not only was the Louvre opened to the public in 1793—it had been the private domain of the monarch—but it also became a repository for art that the victorious Republican armies sent back from the Italian states. The royal museum was transformed into a national museum. Nor was the public museum restricted to France. Napoleon Bonaparte was instrumental in establishing museums across Europe: the Accademia in Venice, the Rijksmuseum in Amsterdam, and the Brera in Milan. Eventually, Bonaparte fell, but the notion of sharing art with the public remained.

The public art museum came into its own during the early nineteenth century. It had two main purposes: it provided a home for what was coming to be seen as a national, or at least a cultural, heritage, and it exemplified the sort of high-minded civilizing mission evident in other Victorian institutions, like public libraries, science museums, botanical gardens, and, yes, municipal zoos. From its conception, the public art museum had a pedagogical role. The founders of these first museums believed that making great art available to the public would elevate the national soul. The museum was not merely a public building like a post office; it was a civic monument.

The museum made it possible for ordinary people to see the masterworks that had previously been hidden in the houses of the rich. In that sense, art had returned to the public sphere. But the museum had another, less evident effect, as André Malraux noted in the introduction to *The Voices of Silence*: It imposed on the spectator a wholly new attitude toward the work of art. Isolated in the museum, the painting or sculpture was no longer part of a larger context; it was now experienced as an individual artifact. Malraux maintained that this estrangement of art from its original context altered—if it did not altogether remove—the original meanings of the works themselves. The Elgin marbles in the British Museum are seen at eye level as isolated sculptures; that is very different from seeing the figures reclining high in the pediments of the Parthenon and as an integral part of the experience of that remarkable building. And not only public art was changed. A portrait by Thomas Gainsborough, for example, hanging in an English country house had been a representation of a revered ancestor; on the museum wall, the subject matter receded in importance, and the work was appreciated for its aesthetic and painterly qualities. To the museum visitor it was now simply "a Gainsborough."

A sense of exclusion—and of exclusivity—naturally focused attention on the reputation of the individual artist, who benefited from the cachet of being selected for inclusion in this artistic pantheon. At first, such cachet was enjoyed posthumously, for museums were uniquely concerned with the art of the past; only when an artist had died was his work hung in the Louvre. This changed in 1818, when the Luxembourg museum was founded specifically to display the work of living French artists. As Francis Haskell points out, this was a moment of great significance in the evolution of the art museum. He suggests that it was the prestige and financial resources of museums such as the Luxembourg that encouraged painters like Delacroix, Courbet, and Géricault to create works that because of their size alone could be hung only in museums. The museum was acting no longer as custodian but as patron—a role it maintains strongly in the present day.

The American architect Louis Kahn used to say that the way to begin to design a building was to ask the question "What does the building want to be?" Kahn believed that all buildings had intrinsic spiritual functions that transcended the circumstantial and local requirements of site, construction technology, and the commissioner's purpose. The spirit of a building was timeless; once the architect discovered this poetic inner essence, the rest was easy. For example, Kahn described a library as a place where a person could take a book to a window and sit down to read. The result was his library at Phillips Exeter Academy, where a ring of private study carrels surrounds the dark, interior book stacks.

What does a museum want to be? The difficulty, for the modern architect, is that there is more than one answer. The museum wants to be a place where people can experience art. That sounds simple enough, but the nature of this experience is different from those of the other creative arts. The play, the symphony, and the ballet are created with an audience in mind; the presence of the public is a crucial ingredient of the performance. Visual art, too, is made for a public, but unlike the other art forms, the painting speaks to an audience of one. Looking at a painting is like reading a book. Hence the first contradiction of the museum. It is a public building whose chief purpose is to provide an opportunity for an event that is not public but personal and intimate. Going to a museum, may be a social act, but looking at a painting is a private one.

The art museum, in Kahn's parlance, wants to be a room—a place of light—containing a picture, but the museum is required to accommodate many other uses; in fact, in most contemporary museums, picture galleries account for only a fraction of the total area (typically, less than a quarter of a modern museum is devoted to exhibition space). The rest is taken up by curatorial and staff offices, workshops, laboratories for restoration, auditoriums and lecture rooms, restaurants, lobbies, and the now indispensably lucrative souvenir shop and bookstore. There's also usually a large space that's intended for social occasions, galas, musical performances, banquets, and other public celebrations. As the critic Ellen Posner has pointed out, these events are often unrelated to museum life. The modern museum is just as likely to be the locale for a society wedding or a state dinner as for an exhibition. Posner maintains that the museum now stands at the center of social life, "although the art is still in there someplace." This expansion of the museum's role makes purists uncomfortable, but, given the economic pressures under which all museums labor, it is inevitable.

The architect must find a balance between art and commerce. He must provide space for all these other uses without losing sight of the soul of the museum: the rooms with the pictures. It's become a common experience in modern museums to make our way through spatially exciting lobbies and dramatic skylit atriums until, finally, our sensibilities pumped up by these overrich architectural appetizers, we arrive at the galleries, where the experience of the paintings can seem like an anticlimax.

The challenge to the architect, especially when the art museum is a large one, is to give appropriate importance to the picture galleries while organizing the building so that the visitor can find his way around. In too many museums the maze of rooms and corridors seems to have been arranged by someone enamored of Minoan labyrinths. Once embarked on this exhausting artistic quest, we soon find the pleasure of art giving way to sore feet and an aching back, and we may retreat with relief to the "non-art" spaces, the restaurant or the gift shop.

Museums contain art from many periods: Byzantine Madonnas and impressionist landscapes, modern abstractions and seventeenth-century still lifes. Some of these works were meant to be seen in intimate domestic settings; others can be appreciated only in large, loftlike spaces. The work of some painters, like Poussin and Lorrain, needs breathing space; the work of others, like Vermeer and many of the impressionists, looks small and insignificant if it is hung in a grand room. Modernist paintings are best appreciated against a neutral background, but this is not true of older paintings, which tend to benefit from richer surroundings. In old museums where eighteenth-century paintings hang in eighteenth-century rooms, there is an automatic accord between subject and setting that is not always present in newer buildings. It's not easy to hang pictures well. The recent renovations of the galleries for French paintings in the Louvre—not generally judged a success, and already slated for redesign—are evidence of the difficulty of this task. Then, too, there is no such thing as ideal lighting. Paintings from different periods need different illumination: soft or harsh, warm or cool. This is another contradictory requirement: on the one hand, a varied collection demands a variety of rooms; on the other, the architect strives to maintain a sense of continuity.

Lastly, the museum designer must consider the question of symbolism. The museum is a repository of culture, of what we consider to be the highest achievements of the visual arts. It's hardly surprising that the earliest museums often resembled temples, for the museum aspires to be a kind of shrine. But a museum, unlike a private gallery, is a *civic* monument, and hence stands as a symbol not just of art but of the importance that we as citizens place on art. The educational role of the museum requires that it be open and welcoming to the public; it must impress but also attract. This obliges the architect to tread a fine line. If the building is too grand, too palatial, it will alienate the very people it hopes to serve; if it's too ordinary, it risks trivializing its subject.

Never have museums been so popular with the public, yet paradoxically, as Mark Lilla has pointed out, never have they been so confused about their social role. This confusion is apparent in the conflicting demands for building real art appreciation and merely building attendance, or between the allocation of resources to assemble solid collections and to construct eye-catching buildings. It appears that many museums are abandoning their traditional roles as upholders of aesthetic standards in order to better reflect the changing cultural and social values of the society of which they are a part—embracing populism instead of connoisseurship. This may be a positive development, but it is also a risky one, for it puts the art museum in direct competition with television and movies for the public's favor. Under such circumstances, it's not difficult to imagine the art institution degenerating into a sort of art theme-park. Clearly, for the architect, finding the right symbolic solution for the modern museum is no easy task.

The first public museums represented a new use; one might have expected architects to invent a brand-new type of building, such as the Victorian railway station, which had no precedent in architectural history. Alternatively, it might have been possible to modify a traditional building type to suit the new function, as Thomas Jefferson did when he based the library at the University of Virginia on the Pantheon. But neither happened. The first public museums did not involve design at all, for they were housed in a variety of existing buildings, and in some cases these were buildings that already contained rooms intended for the display of art. The collection of the Medici family, for example, which Anna Maria Lodovica, the last of the line, willed to the people of Florence in 1737, was housed in the Galleria degli Uffizi, which contained picture galleries designed by Buontalenti and Vasari; the Museo Capitolino and the Palazzo dei Conservatori, both on the Capitoline Hill in Rome, had held art since the Renaissance. On the other hand, the Loggia della Signoria in Florence, an open-air museum for sculpture established at the end of the eighteenth century, was originally a fourteenth-century reviewing stand used by officials during public ceremonies; the Galleria dell'Accademia in Venice was installed in what had been a convent. Early collections were generally princely in origin and so were often housed in royal palaces, such as the Louvre in Paris and the Belvedere in Vienna. Stately city residences—the Hôtel du Luxembourg in Paris, the Mauritshuis in The Hague—were sometimes co-opted for the public display of art.

Baroque palaces were not designed as public buildings, but they were intended to accommodate large numbers of people and, with their impressive entrance halls and grand ceremonial staircases, were certainly spacious. Their lofty rooms, directly connected one to another, could be filled up with paintings in the indiscriminate manner of the earlier picture-cabinets and served the purpose of displaying art reasonably well. And displaying art was all they were required to do. These first museums did not have auditoriums, conference rooms, or staff offices, let alone bookshops, restaurants, or kitchens. The pragmatic way in which art collections were fitted into whatever large buildings happened to be handy suggests that the museum was not considered an important civic institution. It was a storehouse of the past and had not yet acquired the public role—and the public image—that we associate with the museum today.

Not all European cities had vacant royal palaces, however, and as collections grew and museums became more popular, there began to be a need for new museums. The first buildings designed especially for the purpose of exhibiting art went up between 1810 and 1840, but architects had been thinking about museums for a while. As early as 1700, the German theoretician Leonhard Christoph Sturm published a short paper that described a building for the exhibition of "rare objects"; the plan, which consisted of a sequence of squarish rooms, was essentially that of a small château. In 1783, Etienne-Louis Boullée designed a theoretical project that anticipated many elements of the nineteenth-century museum; it had a clear route through a series of long rooms (which were based on the traditional gallery), symmetrical inner courtyards, windowless walls (to increase hanging space), and a domed central space that he called the "Temple of Fame." Other French theorists of the time, like Claude-Nicolas Ledoux and Jean-Nicolas-Louis Durand, made similar proposals (never built) which became the basis for a rash of large public museums: the Altes Museum in Berlin (1824–28), the British Museum in London (1825–27), the Alte Pinakothek (1826–36) in Munich, and the New Hermitage in St. Petersburg (1840–49). It should be mentioned that the British Museum, unlike the other institutions, was based not on a royal collection but on a private one, that of John-Julius Angerstein, a Lloyd's financier. This would be the pattern followed by most North American museums.

By the nineteenth century, museumgoing had become fashionable with the middle class, and there was a growing desire among architects and their clients to give the museum an identity appropriate to its emerging role as an important civic institution. The Altes Museum, for example, was built on the most prominent site in Berlin, across from the royal palace and facing the Lustgarten. It was a splendid building that the American historian Henry-Russell Hitchcock called "the masterpiece of the period." Its architect, Karl Friedrich Schinkel, set an immense colonnade across the building, linking the museum visually to the square in front of it and emphasizing its public character. The entrance, reached by a broad set of steps in the middle of the colonnade, was through an open loggia containing a double-winged stair that led to the upper floor. (The grand stair, lifted directly from the royal palace, was a feature common to many early museums.) The plan was both elegant and logical. Long galleries were arranged on each side of the rectangular building, giving the visitor a clearly demarcated route.

The most prominent space in the Altes Museum was a large, two-story circular hall. This domed room—the heart of the museum—was a setting for Classical sculpture, but its main purpose was not display; rather, it was to convey to the visitor a sense of the transcendent place of art. With its coffered ceiling and its colonnade, the hall was a clear reference to the Pantheon; as Boullée had intended, the art palace had become an art temple.

The picture galleries of the Altes Museum, like those in the converted palaces, were illuminated by windows. (Paintings were hung on screens set at right angles to the light to reduce glare.) It is not clear why Schinkel did not use skylights; he had made a tour a few years earlier of British galleries, where skylighting was popular. As early as 1787, the British architect John Soane had designed the first skylit picture gallery, for Fonthill House in

Wiltshire. It was something of an accident: he was converting an existing corridor space without windows, and skylights were the only solution. The idea of using skylights for picture viewing caught on. Skylights have many advantages: they reduce glare, eliminate harmful direct sunlight, and free up the walls for hanging pictures. In 1811, Soane began work on a small picture gallery for Dulwich College, which is now considered a precursor of the nineteenth-century museum. This long, narrow building consisted of a series of connected rooms with octagonal vaults crowned by clerestories. There were no windows; the walls were uninterrupted. This became the standard solution for lighting galleries; Leo von Klenze used it in the Glyptothek (1816–30), which housed the royal sculpture collection in Munich. So did William Wilkins in the National Gallery in London (1832–38).

Because of the need for natural overhead light, many of the first nineteenth-century museums—like the Dulwich Art Gallery—were on one level. Eventually the typical solution became two floors: a ground floor with rooms for furniture, pottery, and textiles, and an upper floor, corresponding to the *piano nobile* (main floor) of the palace, with the skylit painting galleries.

The architecture of these first museums was usually classical, a style that both expressed their antiquarian function and provided a serene and noble setting for the experience of art. The classical style was also adopted by Richard Morris Hunt for the facade of the Metropolitan Museum of Art in New York (1894) and, on a smaller scale, by Edward and William Maxwell in the Montreal Museum of Fine Arts (completed in 1912). One of the latest examples of the classical museum is the National Gallery of Art in Washington, D.C. (1937–41), designed by John Russell Pope. A large entrance portico (a feature common to both the Metropolitan and the Montreal museums) leads to a magnificent rotunda, a hundred feet in diameter. In addition to the traditional toplit galleries, Pope designed monumental circulation spaces (this was a larger building than the Altes Museum) and glazed interior garden courts.

The next phase in the evolution of the art museum began in the 1930s, with the advent of modernism. Modernist architects generally disliked traditional solutions, so it was not surprising that their ideas for displaying art broke the patterns that had been established in a century and a half of museum design. In New York's Museum of Modern Art, for example, designed by Philip L. Goodwin and Edward Durell Stone (1937–39), the emphasis was on flexibility; there were no individual galleries at all. Instead, movable walls let the curators rearrange the spaces as needed. A straightforward entrance lobby replaced the grand rotunda. All this was a radical departure from the nineteenth-century idea of a museum; MoMA was more like a high-rise office building, which it resembled.

In 1942, Mies van der Rohe produced a design he called "A Museum for a Small City." It was a long, low building with a grid of columns supporting the roof and glass walls enclosing an open, flexible space. Twenty years later, in the Berlin National Gallery, Mies realized a similar concept on a large scale. This extraordinary building is a glass-walled hall, fifty meters square, covered by a massive roof that is supported by only eight peripheral columns. The space is entirely open and is intended for temporary exhibits; the permanent collection, offices, and other functions are housed in the podium below.

Flexible gallery planning also intrigued the French architect Le Corbusier, who built two art museums, one in Ahmedabad, India

(1954–57), the other in Tokyo (1957–59); both designs were versions of an idea he had first proposed in 1930. The plans are similar: a square doughnut with an open space in the center, surrounded by exhibition spaces with movable walls. Le Corbusier kept the tradition of a *piano nobile*, although, characteristically, he raised the main floor into the air and supported it on freestanding columns.

In the Tokyo museum, Le Corbusier experimented with unusual ways of introducing daylight into the galleries. A concern with natural light was a feature of many modernist museums. Beginning in 1936, the Finnish architect Alvar Aalto built a number of museums that incorporated ingeniously contrived skylights. In his museum in Aalborg, Denmark (designed in 1958), the skylights let in only reflected, diffused light. In an unbuilt design for an art gallery in Shiraz, Iran, the roof over the exhibition spaces was to be glazed, and a system of slats and reflectors below counteracted direct sunlight. A similar idea was implemented by Renzo Piano in his elegant design for the Menil Collection (1981–87) in Houston, where a "ceiling" of delicately curved concrete shells is suspended beneath a glass roof and reflects light into the exhibition spaces below.

Another museum in which natural light plays a central role is the Kimbell Art Museum (1967–72) in Fort Worth, Texas, generally considered to be one of Louis Kahn's masterworks. The concept is simple. The roof of the low building is a series of parallel, identical, six-meter-wide concrete vaults; light enters through a skylight at the top of the vault and is reflected onto the concave ceiling by an aluminum diffuser, producing a silvery glow. The solution recalls Klenze's vaulted galleries in the Alte Pinakothek, although the interior of the Kimbell is darker and relies on supplementary electric spotlights. As in the Alte Pinakothek, there are no external windows; instead, the vaulted area is interrupted by three interior garden courts. Unlike Klenze, Kahn left the gallery spaces open, divided only by low, movable partitions.

The Kimbell Art Museum and the Menil Collection, which represent the acme of the modernist museum, differ from the nineteenth-century models in more than architectural style: they eschew monumentalism both inside and out. Neither building has a central hall or a grand entrance lobby, for what is at the heart of these buildings is not a commemoration of culture but the visitor's experience of the art. These are neither palaces nor temples but exquisitely crafted containers—air-conditioned picture cabinets in which one is led directly to the art, without fuss and without fanfare.

Both the Kimbell and the Menil have received accolades from architectural critics and from curators. But they haven't become the model for other contemporary museums. Why not? The answer is that these museums are unusual in several respects: they are relatively small, as museums go; they house private collections; and they are privately endowed. Being small, they do not have to accommodate crowds. They don't put on blockbuster art shows, and while they do have ancillary facilities, these are relatively modest in scale. Although these museums are accessible to the public, they are not really civic buildings or civic symbols. And their financial independence allows them to be low-key in the display of their art; they don't rely on admissions for their survival.

Most large public art museums have been obliged to take a different architectural approach, one in which the building, not just the collection, must attract the public. A graphic example is the Neue Staatsgalerie (1977–83), an extension to an existing museum in Stuttgart designed by the British architects James Stirling and Michael Wilford. The architectural critic Reyner Banham once described the Menil Collection, which has a distinctly unprepossessing exterior, as "an upscale UPS depot"; in contrast, the exterior of the Neue Staatsgalerie is an eye-catching collage of unusual forms and bright colors: high-tech awnings, sloping glass walls, and hot-pink balustrades.

The most recent phase in the evolution of the art museum was anticipated by New York's Solomon R. Guggenheim Museum (1943–58). Frank Lloyd Wright took a characteristically original approach and produced a museum unlike any other. It was as if he had taken Schinkel's Altes Museum and stripped away the galleries, leaving only the great rotunda. The focus of the Guggenheim is the dramatic space in the middle, which is surrounded by a spiraling ramp that carries visitors from top to bottom and affords ever-changing views of the interior. Instead of isolating the galleries from the rotunda, Wright placed them in a series of niches directly off the main ramp.

A similar concept guided I. M. Pei in his design for the East Building of the National Gallery of Art (1976–78) in Washington, D.C. Here the central space, crowned by an impressive glass roof made up of geometric skylights, is triangular (a result of the shape of the building site), and the ramps are replaced by crisscrossing bridges and soaring escalators. The High Museum (1980–83) in Atlanta, designed by Richard Meier & Partners, is also built around a tall, dramatic space; its curved ramps and overlooking galleries consciously recall the Guggenheim.

The art critic Robert Hughes has characterized the Guggenheim as one of the most hostile environments imaginable for showing contemporary paintings. This is mainly the result of the low ceiling height, the sloping floor of the ramp, and the poor quality of the light. The High Museum and the East Building have avoided these pitfalls, but they both share a less obvious drawback. Since the galleries are relegated to the periphery, they are often uncongenial, badly lit, and awkwardly proportioned. The art, which should be at the center of the museum experience, is here pushed into leftover spaces in the background.

The glass-roofed central spaces of the East Building and the High Museum have been compared to the central rotundas of Schinkel and Pope, but what they really recall are the atriums that have become a common feature of many recent hotels, office buildings, and shopping centers. This attribute troubles some critics, who feel that a flashy, commercial atmosphere is inappropriate for a civic institution. On the other hand, these museums are undeniably popular with the public—the East Building is the most visited site in the city.

From grand palace to solemn temple to beautiful container to art emporium: the last hundred years have seen dramatic changes in the form of the museum, as the institution itself has changed, and as architects have struggled to resolve the contradictions inherent in this unusual building type. Putting art inside the walls has turned out to be a lot more complicated than anyone might have imagined.

Airports

Several months ago I was obliged to fly to East Africa on business, and my travel agent informed me that as there were no direct flights between Montreal and Nairobi, I would have to make a six-hour stopover in Amsterdam. My heart sank: six mind-numbing hours in an airport lounge. Too listless to go anywhere, too weary to read, too bored to work—under such circumstances I sink into a catatonic stupor.

Like most people, I dislike airports. I am either walking too far or sitting too long. The food is bad, the chairs are uncomfortable, and the irritating public-address system squawks unintelligibly. The tired potted plants do little to dispel the obsessively mechanical atmosphere. Above all, there is the dispiriting feeling of inactivity reflected in the weary faces of my fellow passengers, for whom ennui has replaced anticipation. They are just as torpid as I am. If Fritz Lang's *Metropolis* showed the underground city of the enslaved workers as a kind of hell, then the airport waiting room could serve as a convincing vision of purgatory.

Lang's nightmarish city was inspired by a visit he made to New York in 1924, but the German director arrived by steamship, not airplane—Lindbergh's transatlantic flight was still three years in the future. Nevertheless, the opening sequence of *Metropolis* does contain an airport; it is shaped like the top of a huge card table, and is daringly perched on one of the city's skyscrapers. The idea of the airport as a heroic aerie is still striking and has reemerged in the *Star Wars* movies, but even in the 1920s it was not original. Lang, who was trained as an architect, was certainly familiar with the Italian futurist Antonio Sant'Elia, who in 1914 had exhibited a set of drawings representing Milan in the year 2000. He situated the landing strip of his *stazione aeroplani* on a concrete platform above the Viale Vittor Pisani, a broad boulevard that leads from the railway station to the Piazza della Repubblica. Several years later, with equal abandon, Le Corbusier positioned the landing strip of his Ville Contemporaine project on the roof of a transport interchange that was set amid a cluster of sixty-story office towers.

It is easy to see the practical shortcomings of such proposals. But the exuberance of these early designs is understandable, for the airport represented a challenging opportunity to the architect: a new building type. Most buildings are variations on well-established programmatic themes. Two of Le Corbusier's best-known buildings are a chapel and a monastery; Frank Lloyd Wright is known to many as the designer of a museum and a synagogue; and both men achieved prominence because of their designs for houses. Like most architects, they were called upon to reinterpret, not to invent.

The twentieth century has seen only a few successful new building types. The drive-in restaurant and the gas station are modest but original contributions, as is the shopping mall, although it has antecedents in nineteenth-century arcades and department stores. But the paradigm for the airport has, so far, eluded us.

At the beginning, in the 1950s, it seemed easy enough. I remember as a youngster being taken to the airport just to see the planes taking off. The airport was a sort of civic institution, the pride of the city. It was also a place for sightseers—just as, I suppose, some of the more extravagant shopping malls are today. Architects responded, not surprisingly, by giving the visitor something to look at. The most prominent example of this was at New York's Idlewild (now Kennedy) Airport. The birdlike shape of the TWA Terminal, completed in 1962, suggested flight; its unusual curved concrete structure and cavelike interior hinted at science fiction and space travel. The Dulles Airport outside Washington, D.C., completed two years later by the same architect (Eero Saarinen), was just as dramatic: a vast hall resembling an aircraft hangar with glass walls. Airport terminals, unlike exhibition halls—or hangars for that matter—do not really require large open spaces, but it was visually spectacular and mirrored the excitement that the public felt about air travel. This approach was carried even further at Paris's Charles de Gaulle airport, which resembles a discotheque, and whose chromed and zigzagging escalators suggest an orbiting space station. The United Airlines Terminal at Chicago's O'Hare, which opened in 1987, is yet another version of the heroic *stazione aeroplani*, this one with an enormous glass-roofed concourse that some observers have likened to a Victorian railway terminal. The similarity is apparently intentional. The designer, Helmut Jahn, has been quoted as saying, "We wanted it to have a certain romance, a certain feeling of fantasy that you associate with travel."

The problem, of course, is that the exoticism of air travel has worn off. No one now would hazard traffic or negotiate parking lots just to visit an airport. The TWA Terminal, in particular, demonstrates that futurism is best left to the science-fiction writer or to the filmmaker; over the years its exotic appearance has paled into eccentricity. Air travel has become almost as inexpensive as bus travel, and airports, with an unfortunate logic, have begun to resemble bus stations. That is, they have slipped to an environmental lowest common denominator: molded plastic seats, harsh fluorescent lights, and acres of low, suspended metal ceilings. These buildings, which have proliferated across the continent, promise neither solace nor comfort to the weary traveler, merely utility. The message: As long as you don't lose your luggage, get shot at by terrorists, or become stranded overnight, don't complain.

I trusted that I had escaped all three perils when I landed at Schiphol airport in Amsterdam and made my way to the central lounge. Its architecture was unprepossessing: white tiled floors, a ceiling no higher than an ordinary office building's (and just as bland), a wall of plate glass overlooking the runway, and the usual collection of duty-free shops, information booths, and snack bars. It was about as exciting as my local supermarket. I took all this in, more or less—it was now 1:00 A.M., Montreal time—found an empty seat, and settled down to wait.

I must have dozed off, and when I awoke I felt rested enough to go to a nearby counter for a cup of coffee, which I took back to my seat. After I finished it, I looked more closely at my surroundings and realized that in many ways this was a different kind of airport. To begin with, the seats. They lacked armrests and resembled extremely long sofas, quite long enough to stretch out on full-length—as I had unthinkingly done—and sleep. Someone had realized that people flying in from New Delhi—or Montreal—might actually be tired. Another reason that I had been able to sleep is that Schiphol was a "quiet airport," without canned music, and whose public address system was used only to make emergency announcements.

I leaned back comfortably in my seat. Instead of hard plastic or contoured Naugahyde, these settees were upholstered in cloth and heavily padded, but flat, so that you could safely put down your belongings or a food tray without danger of its slipping off. Next to me was a low table where I had placed my cup. Cup? I realized that I had been holding a china cup and saucer and that scattered around were empty plates, glasses, and beer steins. Not a piece of Styrofoam in sight, and none of those huge and overflowing trash receptacles—a busboy with a cart came around periodically to remove the empty dishes.

If some airports evoke the lobby of a grand hotel, the homey Dutch have looked elsewhere for a model. The central lounge at Schiphol recalls nothing so much as a living room—albeit a large one, since it is about five hundred feet long, with space for more than a thousand sitters. The uncommercial ambience is reinforced by the complete absence of advertising and by the presence of large TV monitors that show not flight schedules—those are displayed elsewhere—but cartoons. On a lower level are showers and rest cabins. The relaxed atmosphere, of comfort instead of formality, encourages one to slip off one's shoes and feel at home. For the tired and disoriented air traveler, it is a welcome offer. Domesticity, instead of fantasy and romance, is an unexpected attribute for an airport. It is not what the early pioneers of modern architecture envisioned; but, then, so many things have turned out differently than they imagined.

At the Mall

I remember visiting the Museum of Modern Art in New York several years ago, following a major expansion of the building by the acclaimed Argentine architect Cesar Pelli. As I approached the familiar West Fifty-third Street entrance I looked forward to the new, expanded picture galleries. One of these rooms housed the exhibition I'd come to see—a display of models and drawings by Mies van der Rohe. The exhibit, a retrospective of the great man's lifework, was interesting; but its setting, a characterless space in the basement, was uncongenial. Without windows, and relying completely on overhead spotlights, it felt like the showroom of an old-fashioned department store.

Aboveground, things did not improve. The new picture galleries were tastefully understated, in characteristic MoMA fashion, but, also characteristically, the effect was insipid and bland. The architectural action was elsewhere. What had preoccupied Pelli and his associates was not the rooms with the pictures but the large atrium that dominated the new addition. This glazed space, which overlooks the sculpture garden, did not contain works of art (unless you counted the Bell helicopter that the curators had suspended spectacularly—and anomalously—from the ceiling) but rather was taken up by open passageways and crisscrossing escalators.

The effect was dramatic but distracting; the commotion and activity were hardly what I had expected. Like most people, I was used to the traditional idea of a museum as a place removed from the bustle of everyday life—a retreat. While I wasn't sure that I agreed with Philip Johnson, who has been quoted as saying that "museums have taken the place of churches in our culture," I thought I understood what he was getting at. Works of art have become the objects of a kind of public reverence and veneration that could be described (with some exaggeration) as religious, and the buildings that contain art have assumed something of the bearing of shrines. Indeed, during the sixties Johnson himself designed several of these art temples: imposing neoclassical buildings with grand, imperturbable interiors and even grander columned facades.

Standing on the MoMA escalator behind a troupe of noisy children, I felt that this atmosphere—of jostling crowds, commanding, glass-roofed passages, and spacious atria—was vaguely familiar, even if I didn't recognize it immediately. This space owed less to nineteenth-century art galleries than to nineteenth-century gallerias, the glass-covered streets that became popular all over Europe after the success of London's Crystal Palace. But the most famous of these arcades, Milan's Galleria Vittorio Emanuele, was really a prolongation of a public street (there were no doors) and not a building; the new art gallerias are different because they are fully enclosed.

The first museum with an interior space as the focus of attention was probably the Guggenheim. It is generally acknowledged to be Frank Lloyd Wright's masterpiece, and although its spiraling ramp proved unsympathetic to the display of most art, the building had a major impact on museum design. Its direct descendant is the East Building of Washington's National Gallery, a large addition whose centerpiece is an expansive triangular atrium. Although the atrium constitutes the bulk of the addition, this impressive space is not a display area. A Calder mobile, rather than a helicopter, is suspended from the ceiling; but as in MoMA, the majority of the art is relegated to smaller rooms on the periphery.

The architect of the East Building, I. M. Pei, completed a major expansion of the Louvre in Paris in 1989. One feature of his design, a large glass pyramid, has been the source of much debate among Parisians, who have been mystified by the presence of the Egyptian symbol in the center of the Cour Napoléon. The pyramid—which is really a huge skylight over an underground concourse—does not appear mysterious to me. It marks the new entrance to the museum in a way that reminds me of a shopping mall in upstate New York that is actually owned by an outfit called the Pyramid Companies.

Of course! These modern museums have taken their architectural cues not from Milan's Galleria but from Houston's. No wonder they feel familiar—they resemble shopping malls. And why not? The ambition of the contemporary museum is not merely to conserve works of art but to publicize and popularize the culture they represent. This is partly an intellectual decision and partly a financial necessity. Museums require the income generated by restaurants and gift shops, by films and lectures, as well as by special events (not just traveling exhibitions but also galas, dinners, fashion shows, and weddings). Given this new commercialism, it's not surprising that the art shrine should begin to acquire an entrepreneurial gloss.

I'm sure that neither Pelli nor Pei turned to the architecture of mass marketing because he lacked the imagination to produce a less derivative solution or because he intended to make an ironic social comment. Their solutions reflect the new priorities of contemporary museums: the demand for many non-gallery functions, the desire to accommodate large crowds, and the necessity of attracting them in the first place. But the setting of these cultural emporia is also a reminder of something quite different and unexpected: the growing predominance of the shopping mall as an influential architectural prototype for our time.

The extent of this influence is visible in the wide range of recent public buildings that have adopted the pedestrian mall as an organizing principle—not only museums but also airports, university buildings, and civic centers. Office buildings now incorporate an atrium as a matter of course. So do many hotels. The pedestrian shopping mall shaped the course of architecture in the 1980s in much the same way that the dome, the columned portico, and the pedimented temple front did in the more distant past.

Throughout history, specific building types have dominated architectural design. For centuries, architects adapted the Greek temple to a variety of uses—churches, houses, banks. The Renaissance dome survived its religious function and reappeared over library reading rooms and state capitols; in Montreal, a dome crowned the lobby of the city's main produce market. Throughout the nineteenth century, the aristocratic palace was the model for public buildings. But in the 1950s the image of the commercial office building became so powerful that city halls, courthouses, hospitals, even museums discarded their Classical dress and adopted the anonymous steel-and-glass gray flannel suit of the business world.

Designing buildings according to types always involves more than simply matching traditional solutions to new uses. It is a reflection of the common institutions and values that society holds dear: antiquity, the church, the monarchy, commerce. By the end of our century, with so many public sentiments made private (such as religion and, indeed, culture itself), and respect for business and authority in decline, a new prototype was required.

"The perfect fusion of the profit motive and the egalitarian ideal," Joan Didion called the shopping mall. And she's right. The mall is a democratic, convivial space; it puts the architectural emphasis squarely on the public rather than on the institution. Just as the stores in a shopping mall are accorded second place, so are the picture galleries in a museum mall. Shopping (or looking at art) is important, the message goes, but so is strolling, watching people, moving at a leisurely pace from one location to the next, and hanging out.

This architectural focus on walking has no exact historical precedent. In the past, buildings that emphasized movement, such as cathedrals and royal palaces, usually had a processional character. On the other hand, city life has always featured unstructured movement in public space, and in that regard the mall building is an unexpected resurgence of urbanity. America may yet become a nation of boulevardiers.

Curious Shrines

The Richard Nixon Library in Orange County, California, was opened to the public in July 1990. The building—a one-story structure that resembles a Spanish-style hacienda—has not received much attention in the architectural press. This may be due to its design, which, like most presidential libraries, is conservative rather than pacesetting, or it may be an indication that although Nixon has returned to public life, a pall of untouchability still hangs over the man. Or maybe the inauguration of yet another presidential library is no longer newsworthy; after all, six of these buildings have been erected in the last twenty years.

A presidential library is an unusual sort of building. All architecture is, to some extent, commemorative: a museum celebrates our respect for art; a company office symbolizes the power of the corporation; even a house can be seen as a small monument to domesticity. But in very few types of buildings—chapels, perhaps, and mausoleums—is the commemorative function predominant. The presidential library belongs to this category, for despite combining the practical purposes of archives and museum, it's chiefly a shrine. But it's a curious sort of shrine, for it's usually conceived and built by its subject.

This practice was begun by Franklin D. Roosevelt. (Technically, the first presidential library was that of Rutherford B. Hayes, but it was built twenty-three years after his death and remains in private hands.) It was Roosevelt's idea that his presidential papers should be housed in a special library that he would build himself on the grounds of the family estate at Hyde Park, New York, and then present to the nation to be operated by the National Archives.

It is fitting that it was Roosevelt who invented this new building type, because, like Jefferson, he was an architect by avocation. He designed buildings for Warm Springs, a health spa in Georgia that he bought in 1926; houses in Hyde Park and New York; two post offices in Dutchess County; and, of course, the library itself. Surprisingly, the New Dealer was not a modernist but a revivalist: the remodeling of his family home, Springwood, was Georgian; the new buildings he erected at Warm Springs were Southern Greek Revival.

But his great love was the Dutch Colonial architecture of his native Hudson River Valley, a style characterized by steep slate roofs, fieldstone walls, small windows, and simple, white-painted woodwork. This is the type of building that appears in his first, 1937 sketch of the library, and this is what was built. (The supervising architect was Louis A. Simon of the Treasury Department, but the designer was clearly the President.)

The original library, since added to (also according to Roosevelt's plans), was a U-shaped building enclosing an entrance courtyard surrounded by a deep porch. Roosevelt's design is too sophisticated to be called folksy, but it does have an appealing modesty and a domestic scale that were obviously meant to disarm critics, who were already describing it as a "Yankee pyramid."

This was not an altogether unfounded complaint, for like all the subsequent presidential "libraries," Roosevelt's was a repository of personal memorabilia as well as of state documents. Like Jefferson, he was a collector—of ship's models, books, stamps, coins, political cartoons. And the building (completed in 1940) contained these, as well as a record of the era of the New Deal, which Roosevelt, nearing the end of his second term, considered his greatest accomplishment.

The President's personal collections were not, strictly speaking, archival, but the function of the library as a museum for the public was part of Roosevelt's vision. As early as 1938 he wrote that he expected "an enormous number of sightseers . . . very easily half a million visitors a year." Well, not quite. The Roosevelt Library now receives about two hundred thousand visitors a year, but that is enough to make it the third most popular tourist attraction in New York State, trailing behind the Empire State Building and Niagara Falls.

More than forty years later, when President Nixon was planning his own library, he called at Hyde Park. He must have liked what he saw, for he specifically asked his architect, Richard Poulos of Langdon Wilson Architecture & Planning, for a design that was traditional rather than modernist. The resulting building consists of three pavilions with tiled, hipped roofs and sandstone walls; a reflecting pool forms the focus of the simple but appealing composition. The Nixon Library, slightly smaller than the Roosevelt Library, has a similar domestic scale, which sets it apart from such recent buildings as the monumental Kennedy Library in Boston and the imposing structure built by Lyndon Johnson in Austin, Texas.

There is one formal architectural gesture in the Nixon Library. In the entrance lobby, one's attention is drawn to a long axial view across the length of the reflecting pool. This vista (which might be called French Baroque if it weren't for the palm trees) terminates in an unlikely focus: a white clapboard farmhouse. This is the President's birthplace and boyhood home, which has stood on this spot since Frank and Hannah Nixon built it in 1912. The elevation of the modest homestead to such prominence is maudlin but affecting; it establishes a historical link to a real site (which also occurs in Hyde Park) and gives an additional emotional resonance to the library—an authentic *genius loci*.

Despite these conceptual similarities, the Nixon and Roosevelt libraries are very different. For one thing, Nixon's does not contain the presidential papers, which, following a 1974 congressional statute, have remained the property of the federal government. And the Nixon Library is run by a private foundation, not by the National Archives. But for the visitor, the chief difference is apparent in the displays. The Roosevelt Library (whose exhibits have been reorganized twice since it was opened) continues to display its material in a low-key and self-consciously traditional manner: artifacts in staid glass cases; no videos, films, or interactive exhibits. There is only one small theatrical gesture—the conspicuously situated presidential desk, which is arranged to appear exactly as it was on the day Roosevelt died.

The Nixon Library, by contrast, is an extreme example of the exhibition designer's art, and artifice. The real—election campaign buttons, presidential notes, televised extracts of the famous "Checkers" speech and the Nixon-Kennedy debates, even headphones on which one can hear portions of the Watergate tapes—is side by side with the re-created and the imaginary. There is a reproduction of the Lincoln Room of the White House; a Chinese pavilion symbolizes one of the Nixon presidency's greatest foreign-policy accomplishments; a scaled-down replica of St. Basil's cathedral recalls the 1972 Moscow visit. One room contains life-size plaster casts of ten world leaders who have figured in President Nixon's career: Golda Meir chatting with Anwar Sadat, a paunchy Churchill dwarfed by de Gaulle, a pugnacious Khrushchev. The final display includes a giant video screen on which the President appears to "answer" preselected questions, which the visitor can activate by pressing a button on a console.

The Nixon Library is a reminder of how much times have changed. What has not changed is the attitude of the visiting public: it exhibits the same solemn, almost reverential attitude here as in any of the earlier presidential libraries. Young and old move slowly through the museum, paying serious attention to each display.

Shrines the presidential libraries may be, but they are also educational institutions that present the record (admittedly, sometimes one-sided) of a President and his epoch. Still, the emotional, media-driven exhibits that document the political life of Congressman, Senator, Vice President, and President Richard Nixon stand as an odd memorial to a man who was so intensely private and who always seemed uncomfortable with the public aspects of the modern presidency. Unlike the Roosevelt Library, which was conceived by a master of image making, the Nixon Library tries a little too hard. Perhaps that, too, is a reflection of its driven and complex subject.

The Birthplace of Postmodernism

A small bronze plaque hangs in the lobby of Michael Graves's Portland Building. In the usual fashion, it records the names of the mayor and of the various other city officials who participated in the project. It also indicates that the building was dedicated in "this, the city of Portland, Oregon, on October 2, 1982." What it doesn't say is that the date marks a historic cultural moment, after which American architecture was never quite the same.

Graves's Portland Building was the first major building designed by a member of the so-called postmodernist school. This loose term encompassed a variety of architects who shared a dislike for the abstractions of contemporary (modernist) design and, to different degrees, looked to historical examples, especially classical buildings, for inspiration. Until the late 1970s, the proponents of postmodernism had little to show in the way of concrete realizations, except for a few private houses and a large number of pretty colored drawings. The Portland Building changed all that: it was a large urban building—a public building, in fact—and it had been chosen in an open competition over buildings designed by two widely respected firms from the architectural mainstream.

"I think the proposed Portland public office building is the funniest thing I have ever seen," a local architect wrote when the competition results were announced. The architectural establishment, which had been willing to tolerate postmodernism at the fringes of the profession, was not amused. Led by the eminent modernist Pietro Belluschi, local practitioners successfully pressured the Portland city council to hold a second competition, but the same design won again, raising the ire of its detractors. "Jukebox" and "wedding cake" were some of the milder epithets. "Billboard classicism" scoffed the *Architectural Record*, a prominent professional journal. The harshest words were contained in *Time*, whose architecture critic, Wolf Von Eckardt, called the Portland Building "dangerous and heavy-handed Pop surrealism . . . from some second-rate stage set for Mozart's *The Magic Flute*." His conclusion was the unkindest thing an architect can hear: "The Portland Building is ugly."

Almost a decade later, I went to Portland to see for myself what all the fuss had been about. Buildings, like people, should not be judged at the moment of birth. They need time to establish themselves in their surroundings, time for their inhabitants to occupy them and for the newness to wear off. Unlike books, completed buildings should be a little dog-eared before they are reviewed.

It was drizzling during the morning of my visit. This is good weather in which to see the Portland Building, for this is not "a magnificent play of masses brought together in light," as Le Corbusier once defined architecture, but a muted play of flat surfaces and soft colors—especially the latter. The base of the building is covered in green ceramic tiles; the main body is cream-colored with large areas of terra cotta; and the penthouse is blue. According to Graves, the colors were chosen for their associations: green for the garden, terra cotta for the earth, and blue for the sky.

We're not used to color in public buildings. No wonder that when it was first unveiled, the model of the project reminded people of a jukebox or of a gaily wrapped Christmas package. Even the photographs of the completed building looked garish. But glossy pictures had misrepresented the dullness of these surfaces. There's very little that's shiny on the exterior of the Portland Building, and so it has an unexpected sobriety despite its vivid coloration, making it a sympathetic neighbor to the gray stone architecture of the French Renaissance City Hall and the neoclassical Multnomah County Courthouse, which stand on either side.

I'd expected an unusual building, and the Portland Building is unusual: instead of anodized aluminum, most of its surface is ceramic and painted concrete; instead of an all-glass wall, it has even rows of discrete square windows. It is short (fifteen floors) and makes no attempt to hide its squat proportions. It has a clearly articulated base, middle, and top. It is not fronted by a plaza (like most of Portland's newer buildings) but fills the city block; its walls come down straight to the sidewalk. The ground floor is enclosed by a sheltering loggia, from which shops can be entered directly; the main entrance to the building is flanked unceremoniously by the Portland Water Bureau and Levine's Dry Cleaning.

And the surprises continue on the inside. Unlike the lobbies of most modern office buildings, that of the Portland Building lacks the air of compulsive ostentation that American business feels obliged to impose on its architecture. There's no chromed metal or polished granite here, no stainless steel trim, no smooth marble walls. Instead, the walls are made of a shoulder-high wainscot of green ceramic tiles, a blue torus molding, and, above that, ordinary plaster that has been painted fawn gray. The lobby is almost thirty feet tall and is overlooked by a mezzanine. The ceiling is a buff color; the patterned terrazzo floor is dark green; the stair railings are black painted metal. The overall effect is dark (there are no windows) and a little gloomy, but not unfriendly. It reminded me of the sort of art deco lobby that Philip Marlowe would have hung around in, waiting for a down-at-heel blonde. (The occupants of the building feel differently; Graves has been asked to prepare a new, lighter color scheme.)

I spent two hours walking around the building before I realized how comfortingly familiar it felt. The Portland Building is not a place you get lost in, either literally or aesthetically. Its relationships to its surroundings and to the people who use it are grounded in an American convention of urban building that grew up at the end of the nineteenth century. The Rookery Building, which was built in Chicago in 1886 by the famous firm of Burnham & Root, is a classic of this type. The base of the building, more elaborately decorated than the upper floors, is given architectural prominence. Following the sidewalk, it contains shops that can be entered from the street. The entrance to the office building is in the center of one facade and leads to a windowless two-story-high lobby. The Portland Building is free-standing, while the Rookery is attached to other buildings, but otherwise the resemblances are unmistakable; even the general dimensions of the two buildings are similar. So the Portland Building is radical largely in the sense that it's old-fashioned. Is that what had enraged its critics?

The clearest statement of the building's old-fashioned intentions is the sculpture above the main entrance. It is of hammered copper and huge—thirty-eight feet high—but size is not what makes the strongest impression. Tom Wolfe called this sculpture "a turning point in American public art," and so it is: no lump of granite or wall of steel, this is a human figure—a woman holding a trident. She has windblown hair and is clothed (demurely) in a swirl of cloth. The sentiment is classical (the figure was taken from the city seal), but the pose is modern: she's kneeling, with downcast eyes, and one hand outstretched in a gesture of welcome. The statue (by Raymond J. Kaskey) is called *Portlandia*.

The initial (and superficial) impact of the Portland Building on American architecture was the result of its combination of color, unexpected materials, and classical references—all of which suggested an alternative to the bland, modernist, curtain-walled box. But having seen the building in its setting, I feel that its importance is more than a question of aesthetics. The Portland Building is an important piece of architecture because it demonstrates that it's possible to create an urban building which expresses continuity with the past without becoming enslaved to it. That is Michael Graves's achievement: the building is both a surprise and a homecoming.

A National Gallery

A national gallery is not only a repository for paintings and sculpture; all museums are that. It also symbolizes the national attitude toward the visual arts. It is a sad commentary on Canadian priorities that for the last twenty-eight years, the national collection of Canada has languished in a banal commercial building on Elgin Street in Ottawa while an assortment of new and increasingly ostentatious government offices were built nearby.

After more than a century of shameful neglect and official prevarication, the National Gallery of Canada finally has a proper home—a building suitable for this important public institution. Although it was formally established in 1880, for the next two and a half decades the gallery existed largely on paper—the young Dominion was building railways, not museums. Later, it was housed in five different premises, all makeshift, none intended for displaying art. There were attempts to remedy the situation. As early as 1936, the gallery itself commissioned plans for a new building, but the government of Mackenzie King, although it was embarking on an ambitious program of public works, had different priorities; it built the Bank of Canada instead. In 1952, a national architectural competition for a new National Gallery was announced. It took some time for the jury to reach a decision—not because there were one hundred and four entries, but because, partway through the selection process, the government changed the site from Cartier Square to a less central location near Rideau Falls. It was a beautiful setting for a lackluster design: the winning scheme resembled a suburban office building. No construction was undertaken, however, since shortly after the jury made its choice, the government decided to revert to Cartier Square. Unfortunately, this site was occupied by wartime buildings belonging to the Ministry of Defence and was unavailable for the next decade. To pacify the agitated curators, the Department of Public Works proposed a compromise. A new building would be built near the future site, on Elgin Street; it would be a temporary home for the Gallery until Cartier Square was available. The new Lorne Building, named after the celebrated governor general who founded the National Gallery, also looked like an office building—not surprising, as it was designed for conversion to office use once the museum moved out.

Fifteen years later, a major renovation of the Lorne Building was undertaken—not because the museum finally had a permanent home, but because the exterior walls were falling apart owing to the high humidity required in the picture galleries. In 1976 the then director, Jean Sutherland Boggs, managed to revive interest in a new building sufficiently for the government to announce another architectural competition. Several hundred architects were invited to submit applications, and ten were chosen to submit complete plans. There was a flurry of excitement, and a year later a winner was announced. But that project, too, was shelved. Down the street, the Bank of Canada, which had flexed its muscles again, now occupied a new, expensive addition.

In 1982, the government formed a Crown corporation whose mandate was to select a site, designate an architect, and oversee construction of a new National Gallery, as well as of a National Museum of Man. Given the history of false starts, it was an unremarkable decision. One could now expect a decade of public hearings, design-review committees, and feasibility studies, culminating in a traditional political compromise, satisfying everyone, exciting no one.

But the Trudeau government had taken three unusual steps in establishing the Canada Museums Construction Corporation. Instead of putting a bureaucrat in charge, it recalled Jean Boggs, who had been teaching at Harvard, to be chairman and chief executive officer; it made her a firm budgetary commitment of Cdn$185 million for both buildings; and it set a firm deadline—five years.

Boggs had requested—and was given—a great deal of autonomy to recommend a site and an architect. The former decision was relatively straightforward: the National Capital Commission had provided five alternatives. Picking an architect was more difficult. With her staff, Boggs visited and interviewed seventy-nine architectural firms, finally recommending a dozen to the government. The winner of this unorthodox contest was Moshe Safdie. With the exception of Arthur Erickson, Safdie was the only Canadian architect whose work had earned him an international reputation. Still, the choice caused a furor. "The one thing I did not anticipate," says Boggs, "was the hostility that would be expressed towards the architect." It was true that Safdie had built almost nothing in Canada after Habitat, and the bulk of his completed work was not even in North America but in his native Israel. And there was the undeniable fact that Safdie had not even been short-listed in the 1976 competition, which had been won by the Parkin Partnership, a corporate firm known more for its technical competence than for architectural brilliance. (Safdie was asked to associate with Parkin on the final project but retained control over the design.) Boggs's Museum Corporation stood firm, and the furor died down. In November 1983, a schematic design was presented to the public, and almost immediately, groundbreaking commenced for the building. In all, it had taken Boggs only eighteen months to get the ball rolling.

The new National Gallery opened to the public on May 21, 1988, and I think it is a notable piece of architecture, though this view has been debated. Safdie has been a vociferous opponent of postmodernism, which places him firmly, and unfashionably, to the right (or is it to on the left?) of many of his colleagues, and of many of the architectural critics. Some criticisms are valid—the design has flaws, and not only minor ones—but they cannot detract from the building's major achievement. For where it counts, the National Gallery has delivered the goods.

Where it counts, in an art gallery, is not in the lobbies and the public spaces, not in the gardens, not in the views of and from the building; it is in the rooms with the pictures. And in the National Gallery, art *is* displayed in familiar and comfortably sized rooms, not in amorphous "spaces" of the kind that characterize so many modern museums. The display areas are organized in what amounts to three discrete galleries: one for historic works, one for contemporary art, and a third area for special exhibitions. This division not only provides the visitor to this large building (almost half a million square feet) with a sense of orientation; it also creates different settings for different types of art.

The Canadian, European, and American collections are hung in a series of rooms arranged in the classical manner—the visitor passes directly from one room to another through clearly defined doorways. The oak floors and trim, the sometimes strongly colored walls, and the vaulted ceilings suggest the intimacy of a grand house rather than the antiseptic anonymity of a public building. Since the art displayed here was originally intended for homes and palaces, this domestic atmosphere is particularly suitable.

Unlike the Musée d'Orsay in Paris, whose revamped interiors have a tendency to overwhelm the art, the rooms of the National Gallery are decorous and restrained. This restraint is even more evident in the cool, white spaces that contain the contemporary art, and that accordingly dispense with a domestic imagery; they remind me of a SoHo loft. The third gallery *is* a loft—a great barn of a room the size of a hockey arena—and is intended to be dressed for special exhibitions and traveling shows, such as the large 1988 Degas retrospective.

What is surprising, in the light of Safdie's firebrand reputation, is the traditional solution that he has adopted, particularly for the galleries containing the historical collections. Like all nineteenth-century museums, these are divided into a series of rectangular rooms, each provided with skylights. No one would accuse Safdie of being a classicist like John Russell Pope, but he has included two glass-roofed inner courts reminiscent of Pope's National Gallery of Art in Washington, D.C., which provide a pleasant refuge for the tired visitor.

Safdie's one major innovation signals a landmark in museum

design. It has long been recognized that the best conditions for viewing paintings are achieved with diffused natural light through skylights. The disadvantage, of course, is that galleries with skylights restrict museums to a single story, which results in large, sprawling buildings. The National Gallery of Canada is the first museum that has attempted to combine overhead natural lighting with two levels of galleries. The upper galleries have straightforward skylights. The lower rooms resemble the upper, but the daylight is transmitted through mirror-lined shafts that extend forty feet down from the roof above. It sounds gimmicky, but it works. The result is that almost all the galleries are bathed in serene, natural light that complements the architecture and creates a congenial environment for viewing the gallery's collection, which literally sparkles in its new setting.

Despite the unorthodox light shafts, this is a building that happily acknowledges the nineteenth-century museum. For resisting the temptations of modernism, much credit must go to the architects, to the curators, and to Jean Boggs. "Whatever form the building has taken has her major imprint," Safdie generously concedes. The National Gallery does break with its Victorian antecedents in the treatment of the public spaces. Whereas the traditional museum was a tranquil place, where scholars and connoisseurs were only occasionally interrupted by small groups of visiting schoolchildren, the average contemporary art gallery plays host to thousands of people who have come to see the widely advertised shows that now tour the continent like rock groups or circuses. And like the fairground, the gallery must provide space for the crowds—space for getting in and out, for lining up, for loitering, for eating, and for buying souvenirs.

The problem is that the festive nature of these crowded spaces is in sharp contrast to the private enjoyment of art. Faced with this dilemma, the architect can respond in several ways. He can choose to turn the entire museum into a single public room. Whether this is a spatial tour de force, like Wright's Guggenheim, or a neoclassical hangar, like Mies van der Rohe's Berlin National Gallery, the result is a distinctly inhospitable home for art. Or he can, like Richard Meier in the High Museum in Atlanta, create a great public atrium as the focus of the building and leave the curators to fend for themselves in the leftover spaces.

A more satisfactory solution is to separate the two functions, but to give them equal architectural presences. In James Stirling and Michael Wilford's Neue Staatsgalerie in Stuttgart, it is the public spaces that are colorful and exuberant; the galleries are a series of sedate rooms, arranged in the traditional manner. Safdie opted for a similar approach. Unlike the galleries, the public spaces are contained in transparent steel-and-glass structures, including a polygonal entrance pavilion, a soaring great hall, and, between them, a long, glass-roofed colonnade. The scale of the colonnade, and of the pavilions, is appropriately monumental, as is the ramp leading to the great hall. If there is a valid grievance, it concerns the execution of the public spaces. Early sketches of the great hall showed a delicate skein of steel and faceted glass, and a crystalline appearance reminiscent of the *Glasarchitektur* of the German visionary Paul Scheerbart. Unfortunately, the structure of the completed building is far from lacy; it is heavy, and the details are clumsy and inelegant, which severely compromises what could have been a wonderful, phantasmagoric space.

The decision to make the public spaces transparent was the right one. The National Gallery is built on Nepean Point, a promontory projecting into the Ottawa River, and the glass walls provide a marvelous vista of the Gothic Revival spires of the Parliament Buildings, the river, and beyond—the (fortunately distant) ugly government complexes in Hull and the Gatineau Hills. The view is particularly welcome in the ramped colonnade that greets the museum visitor—in such circumstances, waiting for Degas can actually be a pleasure.

This site is, after Parliament Hill itself, the most prominent location in the Canadian capital, and an inspired choice for the National Gallery. It is also a site surrounded by several notable buildings, not only Parliament but the Château Laurier, the Notre-Dame Basilica, and the War Museum. Although the new building responds effectively to each of them, the exterior of the Gallery is not an unqualified success. Safdie once published a criticism of postmodernism titled "Private Jokes in Public Spaces." Predictably, his design has none of those arcane historical references that delight architects and mystify the public. On the other hand, although jokes would have been unbecoming in a national monument such as this, one wishes that a lighter touch had been brought to bear on the facades, which take themselves altogether too seriously. The pink granite cladding, the most attractive feature of the exterior, is used with a grim solemnity that becomes wearying. A little playfulness would not have been out of place.

But, as I said, where it counts, in the rooms for displaying art, the National Gallery is a remarkable accomplishment. Its many visitors will come for the sizzle, to see the blockbuster art shows and the great glass hall, and to experience the breathtaking vistas. But they will return for the greater delights of the galleries, of the calm, still rooms with the pictures.

A National Billboard

An embassy is unique among building types. It is culturally and legally foreign, even though it may be a familiar part of the city. It is usually forbidding—not altogether private, nor yet really public; indeed, most people never go inside an embassy, and when they do, it is likely to be that of another country, not their own. The first Canadian embassy that I visited was in New Delhi. I was not sure what to expect. Once through the front door, I felt immediately at home. Not only the familiar accents of the embassy staff but the furnishings—the desks and chairs, the pictures on the wall, even the staplers—were recognizably Canadian. The building itself made little impression; it was merely one more official edifice along embassy row, distinguished only by its maple-leaf flag and its Canadian diffidence.

On the other hand, visitors to the Canadian embassy in Washington, D.C., cannot help noticing the architecture. Officially opened in 1989, this is an unusual design, an unusual embassy, an unusual location, and, not the least, unusual for a building representing Canada.

The design first. The critical reaction has been mixed. Defenders of modernism, such as Wolf Von Eckardt, castigated the architect for incorporating "useless" neoclassical elements, such as a giant colonnade and a decorative rotunda, into what was otherwise an unequivocally sleek and abstract composition. So did Adele Freedman, whose sarcastic piece in the *Toronto Globe and Mail* made it clear that the building did not meet with her approval. Proponents of postmodernism, on the other hand, found fault with the building's lack of traditional detail and considered it a shallow pastiche—"classicoid," rather than classical. To Benjamin Forgey of the *Washington Post* the building was a masterpiece; another Washington critic described it as "the thing on Main Street." Paul Goldberger of the *New York Times*, steering a middle course, found it to be "an odd mix of the grandiose and the graceful, the pompous and the inviting, the awkward and the appropriate."

So—too modern, or not modern enough? The partisan bickering that passes for architectural criticism today is unlikely to inform the public on this matter. The buildings of Arthur Erickson, the architect of the embassy, generally have been more popular with the public than with the professional critic. This is partly because Erickson has always been a builder rather than a theoretician. His architecture is meant to be enjoyed, not analyzed; to be an object of pleasure for the user, not the subject of discourse for the critic. Erickson is also detached from the mainstream in his unique blend of unfashionable modernism and an equally unfashionable concern for a traditional, but currently neglected, attribute of architecture—beauty.

The new Canadian embassy is, indeed, a very beautiful building. The walls, of cream-and-gray-streaked stone, are lovely; so are the hanging roses, azaleas, and hawthorn blossoms that cover the stepped-back facade inside the courtyard. The materials are assembled with great attention to detail. There are satisfactions for the ear as well as for the eye: a sheet of water spills over to sheathe the base of the rotunda and gurgles mysteriously into a gap beside the sidewalk. There is also the pleasure of movement—up a wide stair, between columns, and under the building—and of shifting views.

The twelve pillars of the rotunda are intended to symbolize the ten provinces and the two territories of Canada. As if anticipating Canadian expansion or subdivision, the circle is not quite closed—space is left for one or two more pillars. Oddly, the provincial pillars don't stand on solid ground but emerge from water, like islands. Is this a sly comment on the state of Canadian federalism? The rotunda is dwarfed by a row of six mammoth fluted columns inside the court. Here the symbolism is less clear. Do these represent the federal government? If so, why are these columns headless? And why do they support nothing more substantial than a giant planter?

The difficulty with the game that Erickson is playing is that it raises precisely such questions. The results demonstrate not so much the limits of his talent as the limits of the modernist approach, at which he is usually so adept. As a beautiful abstract sculpture, the building is a success; as a postmodern symbolic architectural statement, it sends ambiguous messages.

The interiors, by contrast, are strictly in the modernist idiom, which is to say cool, metallic, and, to my mind, uncongenial. There is a handsome semicircular staircase, but the lobby is rather too splendid. It makes the casually attired staff and Bermuda-shorted visitors look out of place. The offices—and an embassy is really an office building—are unremarkable, except for the ambassador's suite, which is a concoction of puffy decor and cream-colored leather furniture. I cannot imagine that it will be too long before they are replaced by dark wood paneling and sensible Georgian wing chairs.

As one approaches from the street and climbs the stair leading to the court and the main entrance, which is marked by an unprepossessing, pyramid-roofed pavilion, the sequence is so smooth, so skillfully orchestrated, that one never notices the absence of a fence or gate, or of a barrier of any kind. When I visited, people were strolling around the court, children were throwing coins into the fountain, and two tourists were testing the acoustics of the rotunda dome. There were no members of the Protective Service (a uniformed division of the U.S. Secret Service) accosting loitering photographers, no security guards in view. As everyone knows, the land on which an embassy is built is extraterritorial, in this case a piece of Canada; here is a piece of Canada that is open even to the most casual passerby.

This unrestricted access is partially continued inside; there are a public art gallery and a library, also open to the public. The decision to make a large part of the embassy in effect a public place is a truly unusual one and required a range of security devices: strategically located checkpoints, zoned access, much bulletproof glass, and, I assume, a battery of hidden electronics. Whatever the cost of such gadgetry—and a spokesman for the Department of External Affairs would provide no figures, although he assured me that it was "not expensive"—it was well worth it. Such openness makes this embassy, as far as I know, unique, and both the client and the architect deserve much credit for the achievement, largely ignored amidst all the talk of modernism and classicism.

The open character of the embassy is a direct result of the very public nature of its site, on Pennsylvania Avenue overlooking the ceremonial route from the Capitol to the White House, adjacent to Capitol Hill and directly across from the National Gallery of Art. If you are going to have a national billboard—and that is an important function of an embassy—the location is important, and this is certainly a prime one. An American friend told me that the building site had been given to Canada in return for services rendered during the Iranian hostage crisis. He was wrong on both counts; the land was purchased (for $4.5 million U.S.), and in 1978, almost two years before the seizure of the American embassy in Tehran. Still, there is no doubt that making this prominent site available was a special gesture of friendship. Or maybe Americans were simply returning a favor; after all, the site of their own embassy in Canada—the very first to be built in Ottawa, in 1932—is on Wellington Street, opposite the Parliament Buildings, directly on the axis of the Peace Tower.

According to Arthur Erickson, "Our instructions [from the Canadian government] were that they wanted something that was open and friendly, and which demonstrated that we are a good neighbour." The openness and friendliness obviously have been realized in this magnanimous building. The neighborliness is evident in the attempt to make the embassy respond to its particular surroundings—the modernist East Building of the National Gallery and the gallery itself, as well as the many older neoclassical buildings that line the avenue and the adjacent park. The response has created the architectural problems and awkward juxtapositions of the design, but on the whole it has accomplished its purpose. John Sansing, executive editor of the *Washingtonian*, told me, "I like it; it tries to fit in with our Federal look. It's not a glaring personal statement of a country—not like the Japanese embassy, for example."

Sansing recently prepared the *Washingtonian*'s annual "Best and Worst" feature, which involved sending ballots to about a thousand readers, who were asked to name the best and worst examples in categories like Most and Least Admired Senator, Best Light Beer, and Worst Scandal. There were two Canadian winners: Wayne Gretzky, as Best you-know-what, and the Canadian embassy, which took first place for Best New Architecture. Does everyone agree, then, that the Canadian embassy is number one? Well, not quite. The building was also voted second place as Worst New Architecture, just behind "Any Tysons Corner building."

According to Sansing, such double billing is not uncommon—Ronald Reagan, for example, was often found on both lists. It might not be unusual for Ronald Reagan, but it is certainly un-Canadian to be in the public, American eye, let alone the center of controversy. Nevertheless, in a period of free trade, and closer ties with a brash southern neighbor, Canadians will have to abandon their characteristic reticence and stand up and be noticed. This the new Canadian embassy achieves admirably.

A Homemade House

My feelings about houses designed by famous architects are mixed. I cannot help admiring the mind that contrived such a marvelous variety of spaces, or orchestrated such an exciting experience of interior and exterior views. I can appreciate the imagination of the designer and his ability to will into existence the complex, interlocking arrangement of materials, textures, shapes, light, and space. The beauty of this kind of house is not only that it is a work of art but that the art contains, reflects, and celebrates familiar, everyday activities: cooking a meal, sitting around the hearth, looking out a window.

At the same time, such buildings make me sad, for the architect's brilliance masks many of the qualities that make homes so precious. There is no sense of time in these perfect houses, sprung fully formed from the minds of their creators. There is no room for the peculiar but endearing idiosyncrasies that are revealed when houses are lived in and lovingly molded to fit the lives of their owners. Everything is part of an architectural ideal. As a result, while these houses display the attitudes and personality of their designers, they communicate almost nothing about their occupants.

That is why I find the Swedish artist Carl Larsson's house so appealing. It is both beautiful and eloquent. It is carefully fashioned yet has an unaffected air. It is full of odd spaces and quirky details that few architects would attempt, partly because its designer was a painter, and partly because the house came together over a long period of time, not as an exercise on paper but as the result of constant tinkering and adjustment. Now over one hundred years old, it continues to speak, both of artistic intentions—which have worn surprisingly well—and of the lives and preoccupations of its owners. It is that rare example (Jefferson's Monticello is another) of a famous house that is also a famous home.

In 1889, Carl Larsson, then aged thirty-six, and his wife, Karin, also a painter, received as a gift from Karin's father a log cabin in the small village of Sundborn in central Sweden, over a hundred miles from Stockholm. The traditional four-room, sixteen-foot-wide house stood on a slag heap beside a river. "But I called it my own," wrote Larsson, and it was an excuse to return to Sweden from France, where the couple had lived for several years. They named it Lilla Hyttnäs—the little house on the point. As time went on and the Larssons' family grew, it became their permanent home. Then, in 1899, the Stockholm publisher Albert Bonnier, who was also an art collector, brought out a slim book of Larsson's paintings titled *Ett Hem*—"A Home."

Ett Hem consisted of an introductory text followed by twenty-four full-page color illustrations. The paintings, all done in ink and watercolor in a realistic style, portrayed a characteristic Swedish inland settlement: a shingled church, a curving wooden flume carrying logs downriver to the sawmill, and rough-hewn houses shrouded in snow under the pale light of a winter sun. There were also summer scenes of rural family life—the swimming hole, lunch in the garden, children crayfishing in the river and dressing up for a party. In addition to these vignettes, there were several paintings of domestic interiors, all from Lilla Hyttnäs—the "home" of the title. Unlike the domestic genre work of artists such as Vermeer and De Hooch, where the center of attention was the human figure, in *Ett Hem,* the primary focus was the room itself.

The Swedish public would have recognized *Ett Hem* as a painterly version of the contemporary fashion for creating souvenir albums that documented (in photographs) not the family but the house. What was unusual about Larsson's book was the unorthodox appearance of the rooms. One of the pictures, "Papa's Room," shows a small room almost entirely filled by a large bed. The bed is a fourposter, with embroidered curtains, and a cotton tester fixed to the ceiling. It is more like a ship's bunk than a bed, for it incorporates not only a place for sleeping but also a bench, apparently used for removing boots, a pair of which stand beside it, and a low locker that doubles as a step up to the high mattress. There is also a built-in night table, just visible on the far side. The effect might have been monumental were it not for the ordinary construction, the plump straw mattress, and the plain color—white. The posts are attached to the low ceiling, making the bed appear solid and immovable, like a little house in the center of the floor. This novel piece of furniture stands in a room whose decor is equally original, a combination of sophistication and contrivance. Around the walls, just below the ceiling, is a bookshelf supported by little columns. A scoured wood floor and whitewashed plaster walls set off the vivid red and blue of the shelves, which contrast with the green washstand under an opaque window of leaded glass.

This watercolor is distinguished from the stiff renderings of architects and interior decorators both by its painterly qualities—the pair of black boots in the foreground firmly anchors the composition—and by the lifelike way in which the odds and ends of everyday existence are scattered around the room. This is not just a beautiful room, but the beautiful room of a particular person. The particular person, Carl Larsson, is visible behind the bed, adjusting his cravat in the mirror.

Then forty-six years old, Larsson was already well known in his own country. The year before, he'd turned down a prestigious professorship at Stockholm's Fine Arts Academy to devote himself to painting. He was a rare figure in the history of art; of his hundreds of works, as many as two-thirds were of his own family, usually set in and around his home.

Ett Hem was a success (over the years it went through half a dozen editions, the last in 1969) and was followed by *Larssons* ("At the Larssons") and *At Solsiden* ("On the Sunny Side"), which appeared in 1910. That same year, the Larssons' home was revealed to a wider European audience thanks to a popular German book entitled *Das Haus in der Sonne* ("The House in the Sun"), which sold ten thousand copies in two years and which was succeeded by *Lasst Licht Hinein* ("Let in More Light"). These books used the same format as *Ett Hem*, and although they were not translated into English, their illustrations made them accessible to a large public.

Carl Larsson understood the potential of inexpensive three-color printing, and he used the new technology to promote his ideas about interior design. In the introduction to *Ett Hem* he wrote: "The results of this remodeling of my shack are what I want to show you—you, some of whom may own bigger country places than I do, maybe even only castles in the air. I'm doing it, not only out of vanity in showing off how I have things, but because I think I have gone about all this with so much common sense that I feel—dare I say it?—it might serve as an example (there, I've said it!) for a lot of people who feel the urge to furnish their homes nicely."

"Nicely," to Larsson, meant a departure from the current fashion. The typical turn-of-the-century Swedish bourgeois home was influenced by Victorian tastes. It was the sort of dark, comfortable, crowded, and richly embellished interior that cossets the Ekdahl household in Ingmar Bergman's period film *Fanny and Alexander*. Larsson had a low opinion of such "gaudy rubbish," as he called it, and encouraged his readers to adopt a style that drew its inspiration from Swedish peasant traditions and combined old-fashioned and even homemade furniture with bright colors and natural materials. The sunlit rooms of Lilla Hyttnäs, although cheerful, were sparsely furnished and simply decorated: instead of velour, handwoven cotton; instead of gleaming mahogany, plain pine; instead of exotic palms, native plants and flowers; and instead of fussy wallpapers, walls painted in stylized colors and decorated with folk motifs.

As early as 1904, the progressive British art journal *The Studio* published an article on Larsson's work that included reproductions of six of his domestic paintings, including "Papa's Room." The text referred to the painter's "artistic bungalow" and admiringly described its decorations and bright colors, and the combination of traditional craft with artistic motifs. *The Studio* frequently featured illustrations of houses, interiors, and furniture by avant-garde architects and earlier that year had presented a residence by the

Viennese designer Josef Hoffmann, an interior (the famous Peacock Room) by J. McNeill Whistler, and a country cottage by the British Arts and Crafts architect M. H. Baillie Scott.

Larsson's approach to design is often compared to that of his contemporaries in the Arts and Crafts movement. But despite their informal appearance, the country houses of Baillie Scott and C. F. A. Voysey were large, modern villas built for wealthy clients. Professionally conceived, constructed, decorated, and furnished, their picturesqueness was a romantic conceit. By contrast, the patched-together quality of Lilla Hyttnäs was authentic; its creation took over two decades. Between 1889, when the Larssons acquired the original log cabin, and 1912 (seven years before Carl's death), the house was modified on eight separate occasions. First a small studio was built against one side. This became a family room when the Larssons moved in permanently in 1901; Carl, by now more prosperous, built a "big box of a studio" (at that time the largest in Sweden) at a right angle to the house, eventually linking the two structures to form an L-shaped cottage. These expansions and additions produced an exterior that was a haphazard, carefree collage of materials: logs, whitewashed stucco, painted siding, clay tiles, tin roofing. Windows were placed according to interior convenience rather than exterior composition; chimneys popped out as needed, creating a whimsical roof silhouette.

The interiors, too, reflected the passage of time. Rooms were altered as the family grew—there were seven children eventually—and as Larsson acquired his eclectic collection of antique furniture. He used many props for his historical murals and illustrations, and often mercilessly repainted his purchases in bright colors. The decor also included a wall of Frisian wood paneling in the "Old Room" and traditional porcelain-tile stoves, whose floral ornament spilled over onto the walls. This slow accretion, more like *bricolage* than design, is what makes the house so charming, so human, and, to my mind, so much more appealing than the beautiful but stillborn artifacts of the Arts and Crafts practitioners. If buildings were clothes, this house would be like a worn and carefully mended patchwork jacket that has taken on the shape of its wearer over time.

Lilla Hyttnäs has another attribute that is rarely encountered in Arts and Crafts interiors: it is fun, not to be taken altogether seriously. The bright colors, the nooks and crannies, and the interconnecting maze of little rooms recall the play world of children. In the workshop, the newel post is crowned by a caricatured carving of Larsson and contains pigeonholes where he kept his oil paints; a painted window above the sofa shows a medieval castle with Karin and Carl in period costume.

There are surprises around every corner: peepholes from one room to another, beds in closets, and painted surfaces everywhere. There are orange doors and yellow window frames, green ceilings and ocher walls, cupboards and panels nonchalantly decorated with paintings of the children. Many of the walls are adorned with aphorisms, but instead of the pompous mottoes that Baillie Scott sometimes included in his interiors ("We Two Will Stand Before That Shrine, Occult, Withheld, Untrod"), Larsson inscribed such doggerel as "I tell you what: be glad and good," "Love one another, children, for love is all," and—in English, curiously enough—"There was a little woman, lived with C.L., and if she is not gone, she lives there still—very well." Karin—the "little woman" and Larsson's lifelong partner and collaborator—is depicted on the lower panel.

Despite his lighthearted approach to interior design, Larsson was a complex man who developed into a stern reactionary in later life. This side of him is not apparent in books like *Ett Hem*, which cajole rather than hector. Still, there is no doubt that he and Karin were quite consciously advancing a particular set of artistic attitudes. "The Larssons were in effect promoting not just a decorative style but a way of life," writes Stephen Calloway in his book *Twentieth-Century Decoration*. He goes on to suggest that their books were intended to be what today would be called "lifestyle manuals." I am sure that the Larssons would have hated this description, but it is not inappropriate. The house's natural and relaxed appearance—and remember, this was a century ago—cannot be separated from the natural and relaxed life that it contained. This integration is recognizably modern, although compared with, say, the domestic advertisements of Ralph Lauren, which also present decor as a setting for a particular way of life, Larsson's watercolors, like his home, are infinitely less contrived, less artificial, less self-consciously sentimental.

It is rare that artists of the Larssons' sensibilities turn their talents to interior decoration, and rarer still that they do so not for self-aggrandizement but to celebrate their common pleasure in ordinary family life. Lilla Hyttnäs was an original contribution to the Arts and Crafts movement, yet it has been largely ignored by historians, perhaps because the Larssons, unlike Baillie Scott and Voysey, were amateurs who built for the pleasure of building, and for themselves. The rest of us are fortunate that they have also left behind a glorious record of their creation.

III. The Art of Building

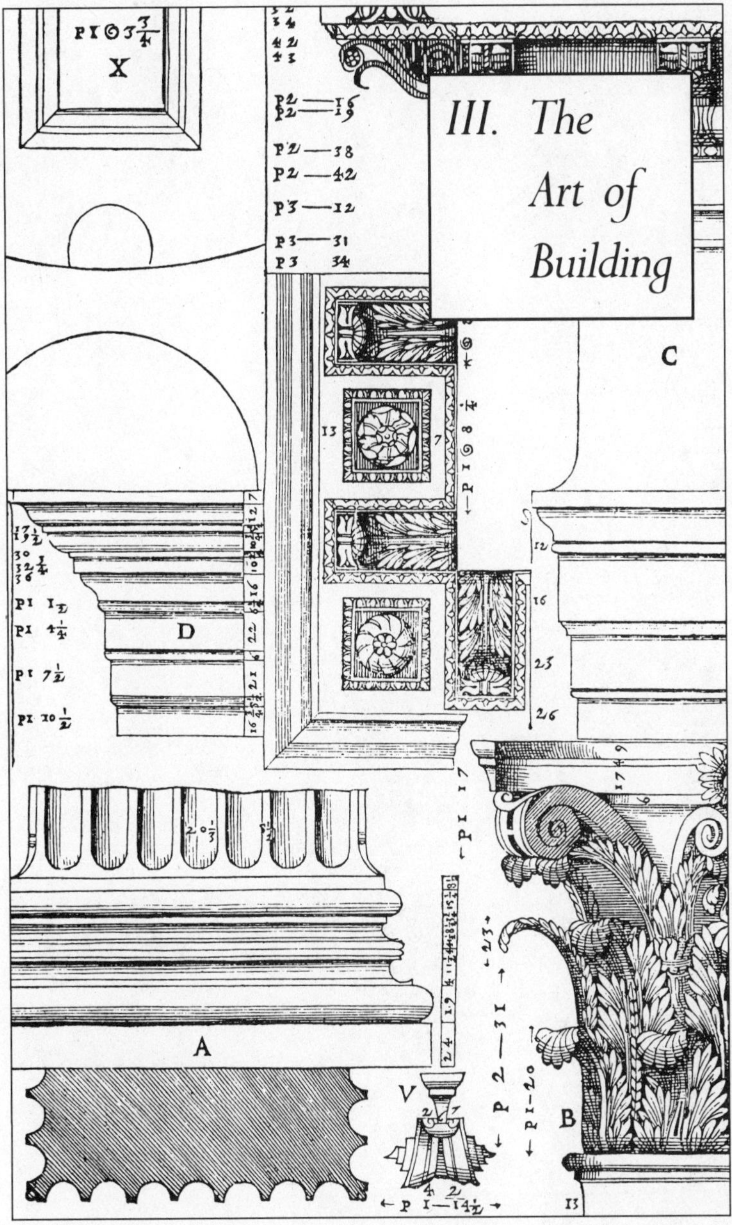

Little Architects, Little Architecture

I played with architectural toys as a child; but, then, who didn't? Wooden blocks, tiny buildings, and construction games are so common that it's easy to forget that they, too, have a history. The oldest surviving toy catalog dates from 1793; it is from Nuremberg and includes a "Box of Building Bricks." The earliest mention I have found of building blocks for children in English is in Maria and R. L. Edgeworth's *Practical Education*, which was published in 1798. It is no coincidence that this is a pedagogical text, as building toys were, from the beginning, conceived for more than fun. Building blocks were called "rational" toys, and they were intended to teach children about assembling many small different parts into a whole; about gravity and physics; and about how buildings were made. John Ruskin, referring to the Edgeworths, wrote that thanks to his wooden toy blocks—"my constant companions"—he had mastered "the laws of practical stability in towers and arches" by the time he was seven or eight years old. Ruskin was eight in 1825. Twenty years later, Henry Cole's famous series of Victorian children's books, *The Home Treasury*, included a box of terra-cotta toy blocks and a set of actual building plans.

Toy manufacturers stressed the link between architecture and building toys throughout the nineteenth and early twentieth centuries. The Anchor Stone Blocks, manufactured by Richter in Germany from 1879 to 1963, came in a box adorned with a female figure representing Architecture. Made of compressed and dyed sand and chalk and covered in linseed-oil varnish, the Richter blocks were invented by the Lilienthal brothers, the pioneers of manned flight. But several other building toys had architectural pedigrees: the German educator Friedrich Froebel, whose building blocks were the fourth of his Nine Gifts (a series of play materials of increasing complexity), began his career as an architect's assistant; the collection of tiny stone bricks manufactured by A. E. Lott in Britain was designed by Arnold Mitchell, an architect; Lincoln Logs was patented in 1920 by John Lloyd Wright, son of the celebrated architect.

I played with a version of Lincoln Logs as a child. They were not very versatile—whatever I built, it always looked like a log cabin—but they smelled good. Later I was given a set of Meccano, which included a box of brass-plated nuts and bolts, a little metal wrench, and a set of instructions illustrating extraordinary contraptions that I never quite managed to complete. I favored a mismatched collection of worn wooden blocks of assorted shapes and sizes. Their ordinariness was an advantage, for they could be used to build a variety of structures: forts for my toy soldiers, bridges for my electric train, or garages for my Dinky toy cars.

When I was eight or nine I received a more refined architectural toy, called Bayko, which consisted of a green plastic base perforated with a grid of holes into which could be inserted short metal rods. Little grooved pieces of colored Bakelite representing walls, doors, and windows slipped down between the rods. I remember Bayko particularly well, since it bore a resemblance to the toolshed that I watched my father and uncle build one summer at the foot of the garden. The walls of the shed consisted of heavy, two-foot-square, grooved concrete panels, and instead of rods there were lengths of thick reinforcing bar, as thick as my finger. This distinction between scales—between my father's big shed and my own little Bayko model—is fundamentally mysterious and is, I believe, the chief fascination of architectural toys, not only for children but for adults.

Toy buildings make us feel like interlopers in a small world, but they also make the real world look bigger. When I placed one wooden block on top of another, my arm became a crane, and forever after, cranes lifting steel beams to the tops of tall buildings have assumed a human shape. When I built my first house as an architect, at the age of twenty-five, with notched and grooved cedar logs, I couldn't shake the feeling that I was Gulliver in the land of the giants, struggling with the plaything of a huge child.

Miniaturization has an ancient ancestry. The oldest use of doll-like figures was probably funerary; the little people and animals that were buried with their owners were intended as company on the journey to the world of the dead. Architectural toys are company of a different sort. The child playing with building blocks, absorbed and solitary, is also accompanied on a magical journey to another world—an imaginary one of his own making. No doubt, the scale of architectural toys, like that of dolls and toy soldiers, has a particular appeal for children, because it reverses the order of the world around them and gives them an opportunity to control and dominate their surroundings.

We know that architectural toys influence certain children in their later choice of a vocation, but playing at being an architect may have a wider significance. Surely our understanding and appreciation of architecture and of how buildings are made is conditioned by this early exposure. Whenever we see a building, some part of us remembers a process of construction, of testing the limits of height or balance. That buildings gain our affection, as they often do, may be a function not only of adult sensibilities but also of childhood memories—memories, in Robert Browning's words, of "That far land we dream about, / Where every man is his own architect."

"But Is It Art?"

In November 1989, Paul Goldberger, the architecture critic for the *New York Times*, reviewed the Wexner Center for the Visual Arts in Columbus, Ohio, designed by Peter Eisenman and Richard Trott. This was the first large public building in the United States in the so-called deconstructivist style, a highly abstracted and geometrical type of architecture. The director of the museum had decided not to hang any pictures in the galleries until several months after the building opened, so that the space would be better appreciated by the public. Goldberger praised this "masterly" decision on the grounds that it guaranteed that the museum, rather than the art, would be the focus of attention. "The building," Goldberger wrote, "is exhibition enough." Three weeks later, a letter to the editor of the *Times* took issue with this judgment. How, the puzzled correspondent wondered, was it possible to appreciate a building in the absence of its primary focus? Or, as the mischievous headline to the letter put it, what was an art museum without the art?

The obvious answer is that architecture, like painting, is an art, and hence can be appreciated on its own merits. In the sense that "art" refers to any skill applied to a creative activity, architecture certainly qualifies. The design of buildings clearly involves artistry, and architecture traditionally has been described as "the mother of the arts." But calling architecture an art puts it, in the minds of most people, in the same category as painting and sculpture, whereas designing buildings actually has little in common with the other plastic arts.

The major difference is, of course, that a building exists not solely as a vehicle for the skill or expression of the architect but as an object with a function. Although there are a few types of buildings in which practicality takes second place to architectural effect—garden pavilions and funerary structures, for example—the fulfillment of mundane uses occupies the architect to an extent unknown to sculptors or painters.

Function demands propriety. A cottage does not, and should not, resemble a town hall. The function of each requires a different intensity and mode of architectural expression—the one private and domestic, the other public and monumental. This prevents the architect from developing what is usually the hallmark of an artist: a consistent personal style. Or, at least, it should. The juxtaposition of traditional domestic elements and exaggerated classical details has recently become the trademark of the office of Robert Venturi and Denise Scott Brown, which has produced such anomalous designs as the Izenour residence on Long Island Sound. With its caricatured temple facade and its flat clapboarded Doric columns, this house sits uneasily among its less pompous neighbors and lacks the discreet and modest presence of Venturi's earlier domestic designs, such as the Trubek and Wislocki houses on Nantucket. The buildings of Michael Graves, another architect who has pursued a personal style, sometimes exhibit the same tendency toward overblown architectural language. Graves's monumental treatment of the Portland Building, in Oregon, is appropriate to a civic building; charged symbolism is less convincing when applied to an ordinary commercial office building, such as the Humana Building in Louisville, Kentucky.

Unlike paintings and sculptures, which are created in the studio, exhibited in a gallery, and end up in a museum, architecture is always attached to a particular place: the Portland Building backs onto a city park, the Humana Building sits by the bank of the Ohio River. Given suitable natural light and no distractions, paintings and sculptures can be appreciated anywhere. Buildings are designed to be experienced from specific vantage points. Andrea Palladio's symmetrical Villa Rotonda, for example, which sits on top of a hill in Vicenza, has four identical facades, which it presents to the four points of the compass; this is very different from the flat and one-dimensional Villa Barbaro in Maser, which is seen against the backdrop of a wooded mountain as one approaches down a long drive.

Buildings respond to geography and climate, and take their place in specific architectural settings. Frequently it is these settings, and not only the imagination of the architect, that suggest the materials, form, and arrangement of a design. The aggressive shapes and tough materials that Frank Gehry used in the Loyola Law School, and which appear idiosyncratic and "artistic," are really a response to, and a product of, the urban disarray of Los Angeles's Olympic Boulevard. I am less convinced by his subsequent Yale Psychiatric Center, in which the exuberance of Southern California has been transported to a corner of New Haven. Gehry's signature elements—chain-link fencing, industrial materials—appear uncongenial both to the city and to the building's curative function.

There is one concern, however, that the architect shares with the artist, and that is beauty: even Gehry, who often uses commonplace materials in his buildings, assembles them with uncommon care, and his originality is always buttressed by a concern for proportion, order, and detail. And like all architects, he is obliged to work with conventional parts—doors, windows, stairs. All buildings are, to some extent, assemblies of standard, traditional elements. This use of convention is an intrinsic characteristic of all architectural design, traditionalist or not.

The modern artist is supported by the sale of his work, or he may enjoy the backing of a patron—a gallery or a foundation. The architect works for a particular client. Patrons offer support but leave the artist to his own devices; clients make demands. According to John Burgee, who together with Philip Johnson designed the AT&T Building in midtown Manhattan, the chairman of AT&T explicitly insisted on a trend-setting design. The result was the first skyscraper to depart from the modernist glass-box aesthetic.

The artist generally initiates his own work. Since the architect is always employed by a client, the decision to build is not his. Dominique de Menil is said to have rejected some of the world's leading architects before engaging Renzo Piano to design a museum to house her art collection. The production of an outstanding building is as much the result of her demand for intimate public rooms with controlled natural light, and for a building that would be sympathetic to its suburban Houston setting, as it is of Piano's considerable talent. On the other hand, the sheer size of the Pan Am Building—the requirement of an inflexible and callous client—overwhelms Park Avenue just as it seems to have overwhelmed its designer, Walter Gropius.

The architect must share the credit—and the blame—with others as well as the client. The architectural press refers to a "Renzo Piano building," as if it were an individual creation, like a Rauschenberg or a de Kooning painting. But architecture has more in common with movies than with painting or sculpture, as it has always been the result of a collaborative effort on the part of the designers, the engineers, and the builders. Yet whereas movie directors make one film at a time, a successful architect carries out many projects simultaneously. In April 1990, for example, the office of Robert A. M. Stern had about forty buildings under way; even a dynamo like Stern, who was also a teacher and an author, needed help—in his case, sixty architectural assistants, on whose creative and technical input he relied.

In the sense that design and construction involve many people, architecture is a collective pursuit. But buildings are also the product of society as a whole—of legislation, of wealth, of technology, of custom, and, above all, of cultural traditions. That is why buildings are so precious: they tell us who and what we are—or wish to be—not only as individuals but as a community.

This quality is visible in a building such as the New York Public Library, designed by Carrère and Hastings in 1897. The building was patterned on Henri Labrouste's Bibliothèque Sainte-Geneviève in Paris, and it admirably resolved the complex technical problems inherent in creating a massive container for books. But it was more than an extravagant monument to nineteenth-century patrician philanthropy. Built for the ages, with public funds (only the contents were privately donated), the building spoke of civic responsibility and civic pride, and continues to do so. It serves—the word is apt—both the city and its inhabitants.

Is architecture an art? It is both less and more. The making of architecture has always been a compromise—between the beautiful and the practical, between the ideal and the possible, between innovation and tradition. This compromise is itself a kind of achievement, but of a different order from the lonely quest of the artist. Works of art stand apart from time; buildings, like people, have a life, perhaps even a soul. They age and weather and show the marks of human habitation and prolonged use. In the process, they acquire character, a quality that embellishes and amplifies the architect's original intention. My office at McGill University, for example, is in a stately Montreal greystone building designed ninety-six years ago and originally intended to house the chemistry department. The massive walls, which once enclosed laboratories where white-coated scientists balanced retorts over Bunsen burners, now contain architecture students hunched over drawing tables. The interior has undergone some modifications, but the building's character is unmistakable: a crusty Victorian gent, willing to change with the times (up to a point) but holding fast to prescribed conventions; a little stuffy, a little formal; built for comfort, not for speed.

If they last long enough, buildings, like all good tools, gain our affection and fondness, and to the Vitruvian trilogy of commodity, firmness, and delight must be added benevolence—a quality not normally associated with works of art. For good buildings faithfully shelter and protect us, and as time passes they become old friends.

How to Pick an Architect

In 1983, Peter Rose was given the opportunity to do something that all architects dream of but few experience: he was selected to design a prominent building for an enlightened client in his native city. The building was to house the newly founded Canadian Centre for Architecture (CCA), and the client was Phyllis Lambert, herself an architect, and one of the heirs to the Bronfman fortune. The city was Montreal.

Whether a building is big or small, the client is a decisive part of the creative process. Pairing the right architect with the right job is a crucial responsibility. In the case of an urban building, it's a responsibility owed not only to oneself but to one's fellow citizens, for in the city, one person's architecture is another person's environment. How does a client choose an architect? It is a question not simply of deciding who is the most impressive architect, but rather which architect will best respond to the opportunities and limitations of a particular place.

This would not be the first time that Phyllis Lambert had selected an architect for a major project. In 1954, Samuel Bronfman, her father, decided to build an office tower on Park Avenue in Manhattan to house the headquarters of the family whiskey business, Joseph E. Seagram and Sons. Lambert, who was twenty-seven, had left New York two years earlier; since then, she had been living in Paris, estranged from her father. When she heard that the commission was being awarded to a competent but lackluster Los Angeles firm, Pereira & Luckman, she returned to New York and remonstrated with her father. She argued that a major company such as Seagram had an obligation to the city, and to the public, to erect a building of distinction. Seagram claimed that its whiskey was made with "integrity, craftsmanship, tradition"—shouldn't it apply the same standards to its architecture? Bronfman conceded the point but added an unexpected condition: that his daughter choose the architect. "And now I must say my prayers every day to be able to do the job as it should be done," Lambert wrote to a classmate. "What a unique chance I have!"

Although Lambert had taken courses in art history, her major at Vassar had been American studies, and she had no architectural training. Nevertheless, with professional help—she consulted both Lewis Mumford and Philip Johnson—she compiled a list of the leading practitioners of international modernism. It naturally included Le Corbusier and Ludwig Mies van der Rohe, the pioneers of the movement, as well as America's master builder, Frank Lloyd Wright. Lambert also considered younger designers: I. M. Pei, who was building a large office tower in Denver; Marcel Breuer, the Bauhaus prodigy (Mumford's choice); and the rising star, Eero Saarinen, who had just completed a large research complex for General Motors.

Lambert's dilemma was one that most architectural clients face: whether to side with age, experience, and proven abilities or to take a chance on a younger designer of untested but perhaps greater talent. Opting for the first course, Lambert narrowed the list down to Le Corbusier and Mies (Wright, whom she considered a "nineteenth-century architect," was rejected almost immediately). The work of Le Corbusier, who had never built anything in America, seemed to her "too sculptural," and not likely to fit well in an urban setting. Mies, an émigré from Nazi Germany, had lived in Chicago since 1938 and had produced an impressive body of work there, most notably the campus of the Illinois Institute of Technology, whose architectural school he headed. Although he had never built an office building, his severe, formal, and abstract designs appealed to Lambert and were perfectly suited to the 1950s gray-flannel business world.

Lambert made her recommendation, and the commission went to Mies. Her involvement with the project continued; as director of planning she was, in effect, the client. With an architect of Mies's stature, her role was obvious. "I had one clear goal," she recalls. "To build the building that Mies wanted." The outcome, four years later, was a 516-foot rectangular shaft covered in glass and bronze, one of the first towers in New York in the International Style (the nearby Lever House is slightly earlier), and what Mies's biographer Franz Schulze has called "the most important tall building of the post–World War II period." As for Lambert, after graduating with a master's in architecture from the Illinois Institute of Technology in 1963, she established her own practice in Chicago.

While she worked on the Seagram project, Lambert became interested in architectural drawings, photographs, and books, and in 1979 she founded the Canadian Centre for Architecture to house her collection, which then numbered 2,000 drawings. The following year she began to think about finding a permanent home for the Centre. She decided on her native Montreal, where, after an absence of more than twenty-five years, she was now spending much of her time.

When a renovated downtown warehouse proved too small, Lambert resolved to build a new building for the CCA, an unusual combination of archive, museum, and study center. Not only would it store a large collection of books, drawings, and photographs—currently 150,000 volumes, more than 20,000 drawings and prints, and 45,000 photographs (the collection is second only to those of the Royal Institute of British Architects in London and the Avery Library at Columbia University)—but it would provide office space for the curatorial staff (then six, now one hundred twenty), researchers, and visiting scholars, as well as space for photo and conservatorial labs and for exhibitions and associated public lectures—a substantial building that would eventually require an area of 150,000 square feet.

Lambert began to design the new building herself. She owned a full city block in downtown Montreal, at the center of which stood the Shaughnessy House, a French Second Empire–style mansion she had saved from demolition. She had intended to use it as the basis for the Centre, but she was having a hard time combining this greystone survivor of Montreal's Victorian heyday with a classical Miesian box. Dissatisfied with several alternative designs—the final one was an underground building—and increasingly absorbed by her administrative responsibilities at the Centre, Lambert decided to engage another architect.

The last time Lambert had organized a search for an architect, she had felt that "the question to be asked was not who should be the architect, but who was going to make the greatest contribution to architecture." In 1954 the answer was Mies; twenty-nine years later, the great masters—Mies, Le Corbusier, Louis Kahn—were all dead, and none of their successors stood head and shoulders above the rest. Architecture had changed: modernism was no longer a *cause célèbre* but a *bête noire.* What would replace modernism? Lambert admired the work of James Stirling, Frank Gehry, and Robert Venturi, but she approached none of them. This time she opted for someone from a younger generation. She herself had changed. No longer a novice, she now had ideas of her own. Although she had given up the central role, she still wanted to be involved in the architectural process. This was evident in the question she put to Peter Rose when she offered him the commission: "Will you do this building with me?"

Rose's architectural background was very different from Lambert's. Since graduating from Yale in 1970, he had designed several homes that attracted the attention of architectural critics, as well as a popular ski pavilion at Saint-Sauveur in the Laurentian Mountains, one of the first Canadian buildings in the postmodern style. He was one of six architects invited to submit designs for the new National Gallery of Canada (the commission that was accorded to Moshe Safdie), but he had not, in 1983, realized any major buildings. (This is not unusual for a young architect; it takes a long time to build up the knowledge, reputation, and staff to implement large buildings, and practitioners generally hit their stride in late middle age.) Rose's practice employed fewer than ten people. He was best known locally as the organizer of a well-attended annual lecture series that brought dozens of celebrated architects to speak in Montreal.

Although Rose lacked experience and professional maturity—Mies had been sixty-eight when he was chosen by Lambert; Rose was thirty-nine—he had one qualification that Phyllis Lambert considered essential: a feeling for the city. "I wanted the building to grow out of Montreal's architectural history, not out of an implanted idea," she recalls. Rose, like Lambert, was a Montrealer who had lived in the United States but had chosen to return home. As a postmodernist, he was at ease blending traditional and modernist elements—a fluency that would come in handy in dealing with the architectural problem posed by the Shaughnessy House. The fact that he had not yet designed any large projects did not worry his client. "Peter didn't have the experience of large buildings," she says, "but I did, and I felt I could intervene where necessary."

Intervention suggests a bossy client, but that's not the way Rose sees it. "Architecture is collaborative," he says. "A strong, intelligent client is what you want. In the case of Phyllis—a terrific client—it was her understanding of the architectural process, and of the time it sometimes takes to work things out, her commitment to making a great building, which involved not only materials but also engineering and such ephemeral things as the quality of light, and her ability to make constructive and timely criticisms."

Rose's view is at odds with the common notion that a "good client" is one who is on call with a checkbook and otherwise recedes into the background. There are very few designers—Mies was an exception—who have the self-control, and the integrity, to produce their best work under such circumstances. The work of most architects is enriched by the demands of their clients, as long as these are reasonable, consistent, and clearly expressed. The worst client is not one who interferes but one who cannot make up his mind. The most notorious historical example is that of the Dutch industrialist A. G. Kröller and his wife, Helene Müller, who between 1910 and 1922 engaged and fired four of the leading avant-garde architects of the day—Peter Behrens, Mies van der Rohe, Hendrik Berlage, and Henri van de Velde—to design their country villa. (Van de Velde finally built Kröller a "temporary" building in 1938.)

For Lambert, being a good client meant "having a deep but informed conviction about architecture, and the ability to see the building as something larger than oneself—in terms of history and of the city"—an attitude that is, alas, rare. Today's developers seem intent on building five-day wonders, buildings whose impact—and physical fabric—is calculated to last only as long as the first lease, and whose designs neglect to observe even the most elementary urban proprieties by obstructing sunlight, blocking views, and visually assaulting the passerby. Even public buildings, which should rise above such mundane considerations as marketing, fare little better when niggardliness and shortsightedness rule the day.

Lambert's experience with the Seagram Building taught her that buildings must respond to the needs of the people who will occupy the space. In the case of the CCA, that meant chiefly the needs of the curatorial staff. Instead of presenting Rose with a complex, predigested list of functional requirements—what architects call a "program"—she asked him to talk with the staff. This kind of direct communication sounds commonsensical, but in the design of large public buildings, bureaucratic committees generally represent the people who will be using the building, and individuals are rarely consulted.

While it's far from being a steel-and-glass box, the CCA does embody a typically Miesian concern with quality. Quality, in a building, means resistance to wear. "When someone presents a detail of design," says Rose, "Phyllis asks, 'Will this last a hundred years?' " As a result of this outlook, the CCA's exterior wall is covered in four to six inches of limestone rather than the more usual cardboard-thin veneer; the interior window frames are solid maple; and the exterior fence is constructed of heavy aluminum rather than painted steel.

Lambert's emphasis on the longevity of the structure had also been a factor with the Seagram Building, whose enduring bronze facade pushed its construction cost up to $45 million. There is no question that a good client is one with deep pockets. "If you want a building that is well built out of good materials, you must pay for it," Lambert concedes. "Money does play a role." The CCA, like all museums, is an expensive and technologically complicated building, but it gives the impression of solidity rather than luxury. Although Peter Rose describes the budget of $38 million as "generous but not lavish," it is clear that his client's wealth was an important asset.

The design and construction of the CCA took six years. The resulting building combines traditional and modernist elements. The large new wing wraps around the Victorian mansion on three sides but manages to preserve the integrity of the older structure while asserting its own individual character. Robert Stern has described the CCA as a reinterpreted classical civic building, and its plain, almost uninterrupted north facade is a model of classical restraint. Despite the general critical acclaim, it is too early to say what the building's place in architectural history will be. The CCA might not be a milestone in the way the Seagram Building was, since ours is a period of architectural consolidation rather than revolution. But its place among the buildings of Montreal is clear: a calm and urbane neighbor that both adapts to and enhances its surroundings—and this, in the final analysis, is more important than a place in the history books. The collaboration between an unusual client and a gifted architect has resulted in an original building—a Miesian postmodernism, one might say, classical in its conception, modernist in its detail, and resolutely old-fashioned in its craftsmanly execution. The building raises my spirits each time I pass it.

Fame

It is a well-known and widely deplored fact that the United States is inundated with lawyers. Yet of the major professions, the one whose membership has grown fastest in the last three decades is not law but architecture. Between 1960 and 1989, the number of lawyers increased by a factor of 2.7, while the number of architects quadrupled. Of course, lawyers still far outnumber architects; but the increase is dramatic.

The reason there are more architects is not that there is more architecture. Unless you live in a public housing project or a luxury high-rise, it is likely that your home was built without the benefit of an architect; it is estimated that fewer than 15 percent of new houses in the United States are designed by architects. What has changed is not the amount of building in which architects are involved but the nature of what's being built and why. Commercial architecture has become bigger and more complicated; large buildings such as office towers, hotel complexes, and shopping malls can be financed and built—and designed—only by large organizations. The result is that architectural offices, while smaller than corporate law firms, are larger than they ever were in the past.

Before the 1960s, only a handful of architectural offices contained fifty or more employees; by the end of the 1980s there were over two hundred fifty firms of that size and another half dozen employing several hundred architects each. Not only are these offices in a position to provide a broad range of services, including interior design, landscaping, project management, and engineering, but they can support the marketing and public-relations staff required to attract clients, particularly in the commercial and institutional fields, which is where architects are most active and where the competition is most intense. A relatively small number of architects manage what are really architectural corporations, with branch offices in several cities (or countries), sophisticated technical resources including mainframe computers, and organizational structures that mirror those of their corporate clients. Like IBM or AT&T, they prefer to be known by their initials—HOK of St. Louis, CRS of Houston, RTKL of Baltimore, and SOM of Chicago.

At the other end of the business, in basement offices, renovated lofts, and suburban storefronts, are tens of thousands of individual practitioners designing small houses, boutique interiors, and kitchen extensions. These architects combine many roles: they meet with clients, talk to salespeople, argue with contractors, and prepare the drawings required for construction. This is how architecture was practiced a hundred years ago. Now, as in the past, personal independence and freedom make up for scant monetary rewards: an architect's starting salary in 1989 was $35,000, about two-thirds that of a law school graduate. According to Robert Gutman, a sociologist at Rutgers, three-quarters of the twenty-five thousand or so architectural practices in the country have fewer than five employees; the majority consist of an architect working alone or with a single secretary—Sam Spade with a T square.

Nevertheless, architecture (along with law) is considered a glamorous profession among college freshmen, who have been seduced by the buildings featured in the architecture columns of newspapers and magazines. These buildings are usually the product of a third kind of practice, organized around a single well-known individual, a Frank Gehry or a Richard Meier. These practices are large enough to undertake significant commissions—they usually employ between twenty and sixty people, more than half of whom are architects—but unlike the architectural corporations, their chief assets are neither organizational resources nor technical competence. What they offer is the ability to create innovative and original designs. They don't necessarily build the largest projects, but they do tend to win the choice commissions: public monuments, corporate headquarters, museums.

In the past, a prominent commission did not automatically make the architect a public figure. The tourists who admire the Lincoln Memorial are unlikely ever to have heard of its architect, Henry Bacon. The designer of William Randolph Hearst's fabulous estate at San Simeon was Julia Morgan, the first woman to study architecture at the Ecole des Beaux-Arts. Morgan disliked publicity and was devoted to her work (she designed more than seven hundred buildings). There were architects who were better known, of course: Richard Morris Hunt, for example, who designed the Administration Building at Chicago's 1893 World's Columbian Exhibition, as well as the Vanderbilts' extraordinary Biltmore house. Hunt was a prominent member of New York's Four Hundred and is generally considered to have been the first society architect—the social equal of his wealthy clients rather than a mere employee. He was followed by Stanford White, whose notoriety owed more to his scandalous romantic life than to his rather discreet buildings.

Forty years ago, most people, if asked to name an American architect, would probably have answered "Frank Lloyd Wright"; if pressed, they might have added "Howard Roark," the hero of Ayn Rand's *Fountainhead*, allegedly based on Wright. Wright carefully cultivated his image as an eccentric maverick, but his celebrity was unusual for an architect. More typical was the taciturn and withdrawn Mies van der Rohe, who was idolized by his colleagues but barely known to the public.

The rising profile of individual architects in the last two decades has a lot to do with changes in architectural ideology and with the role that buildings now play in public life. The International Style (a term coined by Henry-Russell Hitchcock and Philip Johnson in 1932) dominated architecture in the 1920s and thirties and emphasized function above all. This no-frills aesthetic resulted in forms that made little distinction between a public building (for example, C. F. Murphy's 1964–65 Civic Center in Chicago) and an office building. Today, no one would ever mistake the monumental Harold Washington Library Center in Chicago, designed by Thomas Beeby of Hammond, Beeby & Babka, for an office building.

Not only public buildings are different, however. Property developers have discovered that flamboyant design can be used to attract a public weary of restraint and good taste. Higher rents can be charged in a building whose architecture suggests luxury and indulgence. This is not exactly a new discovery—think of New

York City's 1913 Woolworth Building, with its cathedral-like lobby—but it does represent a change in direction, from cool modernism to flashy postmodernism.

The architect and developer John Portman realized in the late 1960s that architecture could be lucrative. His extravagant hotels, with towering interior atriums, were anticipated by the 1950s Miami Beach hotels designed by Morris Lapidus. But neither Portman nor Lapidus was taken seriously by architectural critics, and neither had a significant influence on the profession. The first large building by an established architect to break with the past was the AT&T Building, designed in 1978. Fittingly—for its chief impact was made not by its construction or materials but by its image—the building stands on Madison Avenue. In contrast to the chaste asceticism of earlier modernist office towers, the AT&T Building incorporated traditional symbols of imperial power (Roman vaults and arches), prestige (a Chippendale-inspired silhouette), and old money (a huge golden statue which once stood in the lobby of the original AT&T building on lower Broadway). It was—to paraphrase the title of a Norman Mailer book—an advertisement for itself. That its powerful public image masked the reality of a corporation in the process of losing its power is a curious characteristic of monumental architecture, which is often used to bolster, or even camouflage, reality.

Buildings have always provided images of status and accomplishment for the clients who commissioned them, but the public perceiving these images has changed. Now people are entertained by an endless variety of consumer goods and services, and if buildings are to catch the public's attention, they, too, must present something new. Mies van der Rohe, who deliberately eschewed novelty, was once quoted as saying that he was not trying to invent a new architecture every Monday morning. Now architects are being asked to do just that.

Naturally, the people who produce these dazzling and startling works find themselves cast in a new role. In 1974, when Louis Kahn, whom many consider the greatest American architect since Frank Lloyd Wright, died of a heart attack in New York City's Penn Station, his body went unclaimed for more than a day. Nobody knew who Louis Kahn was. Now the architect is not merely a builder but an image maker, a conjurer, who is expected continually to pull new tricks out of his hat. When Richard Meier, known for his reinterpretations of the International Style, was named architect of the new J. Paul Getty Center in California—probably the most prestigious commission in the country—the chief question was "What will Meier do next?" The same anticipation accompanied Michael Graves's appointment as architect for an extension to the Whitney Museum. Where once architects were merely celebrated, now they have become celebrities. Frank Gehry, who first came to attention for his use of chain-link fencing, has only recently started to receive large commissions, but he has already been the subject of a retrospective, at Minneapolis's Walker Art Center. Robert A. M. Stern, who has been called the Stanford White of the eighties, hosted a television series on American architecture that was broadcast over PBS in 1986. And Graves, the most talented proponent of postmodernism, has achieved enough notoriety to appear in magazine ads for Dexter shoes.

Another indication of the new celebrity status of the profession is the sudden popularity of household objects—rugs, dishes, chairs—designed by well-known architects. Earlier in the century, Marcel Breuer and Eero Saarinen designed chairs that became famous and enhanced their architectural reputations. Today, it's the other way around. The unremarkable (and downright uncomfortable) chairs of Robert Venturi and Richard Meier are really signature pieces, a marketing device that is the architectural equivalent of the Eddie Bauer Bronco or the Bill Blass Continental.

The growth in the size of the architectural profession is probably not a bad thing; after all, there's no architectural equivalent of the ambulance chaser. I'm not so sure about the influence of architectural celebrity. Our perception of stardom, which has been fashioned by the mass media, is fickle. Reputations rise like meteors, and when fashions change, they can as quickly fall. This is what happened to Paul Rudolph, who fell out of favor during the seventies, and to Moshe Safdie (although he appears to have made a comeback). Meanwhile, new names are added as fast as the old ones fade. The shelves of architectural bookstores, more heavily stocked than ever before, are already overflowing with monographs on living architects; the lecture circuits are jammed with speakers who present their modest achievements as evidence of new theories of design; and galleries exhibit drawings by architects barely out of school. Never have there been so many celebrated architects; rarely, so few great ones.

Low-Cost Classicism

He has been described by architectural historian James Ackerman as the most imitated architect in history. Alberti? Wren? Many would argue that the honor should be laid at the feet of Mies van der Rohe, copies of whose buildings proliferate throughout the world, from Chicago's Loop to Lagos. But if Mies was the most imitated architect, it was an imitation that, at least for the moment, has not proved to be particularly long-lived. The old man was barely in the grave and Skidmore, Owings & Merrill, surely his most ardent imitators, were already dropping the characteristic steel-and-glass box in favor of more stylish postmodern designs. Nor will there be any public appeal for a revival of the Mies style, judging from the Mansion House Square imbroglio in London, where a 1967 design by Mies for an office building became the focus of public opposition so intense that the building permit was revoked. The Miesian decorative I-beam may yet stage a comeback—given the vagaries of architectural fashion it is by no means impossible—but not even the most ardent disciple would dare to hope that the Mies van der Rohe style could survive four hundred years after its creator's death.

Four hundred years after *his* death, "the most imitated architect in history" is still going strong, more admired than ever. Andrea di Pietro della Gondola, better known as Palladio, a sixteenth-century Veneto architect, has not merely survived. His is the rare case of an individual architect giving his name to a popular architectural style—Palladianism. That he did so was the result of a recognizably modern phenomenon: Palladio was the first architect whose international reputation was based not on firsthand experience of his buildings, most of which were in remote locations, but on written and pictorial descriptions of them. Palladio's fame was the result of a book. Resurrected by Inigo Jones, Palladio's *Four Books of Architecture* was published in England at the beginning of the eighteenth century and formed the basis for the durable Georgian neoclassical style. Except for an introduction to basic principles and a historical section, the *Four Books* is largely a self-promotional catalogue of the author's work, the kind of presentation you might see from a large architectural firm today.

Palladianism has never been completely out of fashion. It influenced William Kent at Chiswick, Thomas Jefferson in Virginia, and Claude-Nicholas Ledoux in Paris. From Leningrad to Montreal, any building with a pedimented, columnar central porch owes something to Palladio. A 1984 book on contemporary English country houses lists more than two hundred stately homes that have been built in the last thirty years. What is surprising—apart from the large number—is not that few are in the modernist style but that the majority are neo-Georgian, and to a great extent, Palladian. Hence, the current popular interest in his work is not really a Palladian revival but part of a continuing fascination.

In 1985, the Italian magazine *Domus* published a kit that consisted of a punch-out cardboard model, at 1:100 scale, of a Palladian villa; a Milanese publishing house has recently produced a facsimile edition of the *Four Books;* Edizioni Cartoleria Zamperetti has produced a handsome poster that illustrates over thirty of the great architect's buildings; and several illustrated books of Palladio's buildings have recently been published. Nor is interest in Palladio confined to the architectural profession: the Baker Furniture Company of Grand Rapids, Michigan, in 1984 introduced a Palladian Collection. This is a quirky idea, since, as far as is known, Palladio designed no furniture. But if the AT&T office building can emulate a Chippendale tallboy, why not a drop-leaf commode that resembles a building?

Architects have been featured in glossy magazines far more frequently of late, but in terms of mass appeal, they are still small beer. At most, a famous architect may have a street named after him. There is a Boulevard Le Corbusier in Montreal—a drab street of warehouses and industrial sheds in the suburbs—although Corbusier never built anything in Montreal, never honored it with one of his quickie master plans (as he did Buenos Aires and Stockholm), never even visited the place. There is not, as far as I know, an Avenue Boullée in Paris, a Lutyens Mews in London, or a Richardson Drive in Boston. But in Vicenza, Palladio's adopted home, the main street is named Corso Andrea Palladio. There is also a Palladio Real Estate Company, a Palladio trucking firm, and a Palladio Hair Salon. In a small square—named the Piazzetta Palladio, of course—stands a statue of the architect himself. A sturdy, no-nonsense type (just the man to entrust with your florins), he is shown in robust middle age. But this is speculation, as no one knows what he really looked like.

There are more than two dozen buildings by Mies van der Rohe in Chicago, but in that huge metropolis even such a large body of work makes only a small impact. In Vicenza, a provincial capital with a population of slightly over one hundred thousand, the visitor encounters a Palladian building around every corner in the old city center. At one end of the Corso Palladio are two bays of the unfinished Palazzo Porto-Breganze; at the other end, scarcely half a mile away, the large Palazzo Chiericati (now a civic museum), dominates a tree-filled square. Across the street a large gate leads to the Teatro Olimpico, which is still used for performances. Elsewhere in the city there are five more palazzos, as well as a chapel, not to mention the so-called Casa del Palladio, whose contested authenticity (James Ackerman doubts it is by Palladio), like that of Juliet's house in nearby Verona, is more disturbing to the historian than to the tourist. The main square, the Piazza dei Signori, is dominated by the Palladio's great copper-roofed Basilica (a public meeting-hall, not a religious building, recalling the proper, pre-Christian meaning of the word), and facing it is his Loggia del Capitaniato, a civic pavilion. Altogether there are thirteen Palladio buildings in Vicenza, the first built when he was thirty-two, the last—the Teatro—completed forty years later, just before his death.

The most famous of Palladio's buildings in Vicenza is on a hill in the outskirts, overlooking the city. It is best approached not by the modern highway that runs past it to the busy *autostrada* but by foot along a narrow, steeply climbing lane. The rocky track, hemmed in by tall stone walls, is much as it was four hundred years ago, when Palladio and his patron visited the building site on donkeys. From this approach, the first view of the building is at once modest and dramatic. Without warning, a pair of large iron gates opens onto a long ascending ramp cut into the hill—what appeared to be a garden wall is really a retaining wall—and squarely at the top of the ramp is the porticoed villa. When Goethe made the ascent in 1786, he was moved to write, "Never, perhaps, has art accomplished such a pitch of magnificence."

The suburban Villa Rotonda that Goethe described is a reminder that Palladio was above all a domestic architect—the first architect whose career and reputation were founded not on religious buildings but on residences. Of course, he did build churches, one of them, the Redentore in Venice, a masterpiece; and every visitor to the Piazzetta of San Marco has admired the magnificent white facade of San Giorgio Maggiore, shimmering across the water of the Canale di San Marco. But Palladio was fifty-seven when he designed the monastic complex of San Giorgio, and another decade passed before he was commissioned to build the Redentore. In the meantime, he had built dozens of palaces and villas in and around Vicenza, in the part of Italy that is known today as the Veneto, and which was then a part of the Venetian Republic.

The sixteenth century is called the golden age of the Venetian republic, and, indeed, it was a golden age of art. But politically and economically, the republic was no longer the power it had been in the fourteenth century. A series of exhausting wars with the Turks, a decline in commercial prosperity thanks to the discovery of the Cape route to the Indies and the resultant reduction in Mediterranean trade, and the ganging up of her European enemies, who formed the Anyone-But-Venice League of Cambria in 1508 (the year of Palladio's birth), signaled the beginning of the republic's economic decline. This decline was slow and did not affect the visual arts—Veronese, Tintoretto and Titian were all contemporaries of Palladio—but it did affect architecture, not so much in its design, which was as splendid as ever, but in its execution.

While strict in their political life, the Venetians were unrestrained in their enjoyment of beautiful buildings—a fondness that their material prosperity allowed them to indulge. The Basilica of San Marco is assembled from assorted plunder taken during holy wars waged against the infidel. Its exterior resembles, in Mary McCarthy's words, an Oriental pavilion, half pleasure house, half war tent. Although San Marco is built out of brick (lightweight brick is the predominant Venetian building material, as it is in that other city built on piles over the water, Amsterdam), the facade is an astonishing patchwork veneer of marble, alabaster, porphyry, and mosaic encrustations. The famous checkerboard facade of the adjacent Palazzo Ducale—the Doge's Palace—was clothed in white Istrian stone and pink Verona marble. The old palazzos that line the Grand Canal were also clad in stone—marble above and water-resistant Istrian limestone below—and all the important details were carved in stone. The delicately gothic Ca' d'Oro was so named because its stone tracery was originally gilded.

Only one of Palladio's buildings, the Basilica in Vicenza, his first large commission, was built entirely out of stone. Dressed masonry was—and is—an expensive technology, and if not enough funds were available, construction tended to drag on. Work on the Basilica proceeded for sixty-eight years, continuing long after its architect's death. The lesson was not lost on Palladio, who never again designed a building made entirely of stone; the structure of all his later buildings was brick. A building of importance, such as San Giorgio, was provided with a marble facade, although the structural brick of the side walls, the adjoining monastery buildings, and the campanile was left exposed. Lesser buildings incorporated stone only in selected areas—at the base of columns or around windows. An even cheaper solution that Palladio and his contemporaries found to duplicate the style that they admired most—that of ancient Rome—was to imitate stone with stucco plaster. Columns, pilasters, rustications, friezes, metopes, and quoins—the classical vocabulary of stone masonry—were all built out of brick and rendered in plaster. Even the statues and decorations that adorned the cornices and pediments of the palazzos were stucco.

Nevertheless, construction remained expensive, and large buildings often took years to build, or were left unfinished. Not one of Palladio's urban palaces in Vicenza was completed according to his plans; usually, as in the case of the Palazzo Valmarana, only the front block was built, and money ran out before the large Roman-style courtyards could be enclosed on all sides. The Palazzo Thiene, the most complete, has only two wings out of a projected four. Construction of the Porto-Breganze was halted during the financial crisis of the 1570s, leaving only two bays out of a planned seven, and producing a queer, one-room-wide building. Even publicly financed buildings such as the Loggia del Capitaniato were affected by the economic recession; only three bays out of five were built.

Unlike the urban palaces, most of Palladio's country villas, of which some twenty examples survive, were finished as planned. Credit goes to the gentlemen farmers who engaged Palladio. Today they would be called agro-businessmen. Not traditional landowners, they were Venetian noblemen who had settled on the mainland, participating in a large-scale attempt to develop progressive agricultural estates that would diversify the sagging economy of the republic. They had been awarded unused public lands, in return for which they invested in land reclamation, irrigation, new crops, and new methods of cultivation. Like the plantation owners in the Old South, whom they resembled, these sixteenth-century capitalist families wanted homes that would provide a measure of grandeur to their provincial lives. But these businessmen were hardheaded enough to insist on architecture that was affordable and could be easily and quickly built. Palladio's success as a country-house architect derived in large part from his ability to satisfy these aspirations.

The rural villas of the Veneto were not country homes in the English tradition. A summer pavilion like the Villa Rotonda was exceptional; most of the villas were intended as permanent residences and the centers of large agricultural estates. The Villa Emo, still inhabited by descendants of the original clients, continues to function according to its original plan. Its great flanking wings contain barns for livestock, equipment, and grain storage. The broad "terrace" in front is really a threshing floor. The wonderful curved gables at each end of the Villa Barbaro at Maser contain dovecotes. The landscape that stretches out on either side of the great poplar-lined, axial *allées* leading away from both of these houses consists not of parks or gardens but of cultivated fields. Where England created rural palaces, the Veneto agricultural barons built larger, more sophisticated, and elegant farmhouses.

Palladio was forced to adapt his designs to the economic reality faced by his clients, but because these were rural buildings in remote locations he was free to innovate. He developed a stripped-down architecture, which relied for its effect not on fine materials or careful detailing but on proportion and composition. This style was not only cheaper to build but cheaper to design; then, as now, reduced budgets meant reduced architectural fees. The roofs were simple—undisguised village tiles. The construction was in plastered brick, but there was no attempt to imitate stone. Instead, the plastered wall was rendered flat and given a coat of paint. The results are curiously modernist (and markedly unpostmodern) in their almost complete lack of exterior ornament. There are no frames around the doors and windows, which appear punched out of the wall in a Corbusian manner. The white walls of the Rotonda are unrelieved by pattern or ornament. The arcades of the colonnaded wings of Emo have a simplified capital—just a block—and no moldings. Those of the Villa Barbaro are similar, although a nominal keystone is added at the top of the arch. The sole exception is the entrance porch, which is invariably columnar, pedimented, and surmounted by a triangular frontispiece. This not only gave prominence to the front door—always an architectural requirement—but according to the *Four Books*, it was a convenient location for the owner's family coat of arms. Like the grille of a Rolls-Royce, every Palladio villa had this distinctive feature, inexpensive but prestigious.

Palladio's international reputation did not rest on his economic innovations. An eighteenth-century reader of the *Four Books of Architecture* would have assumed that he was looking at buildings of stone, and my 1929 edition of the *Encyclopaedia Britannica* still maintains that although they were executed in brick, the buildings of Palladio were intended to be built out of stone. This erroneous view neglects one of Palladio's greatest architectural achievements.

The *Four Books* does not discuss the interiors of Palladio's villas, which, because they are difficult to photograph, still have not received the attention they deserve. Unlike the exterior, the rooms are elaborately decorated with classical architectural motifs. Tall Corinthian columns support the roof beams, stone dadoes with carved panels surround the rooms, and the familiar broken pediment, a Palladian trademark, crowns doors and windows. Niches contain allegorical statues, and busts are placed on carved stone brackets; garlands hang between the pilasters. An octagonal room in the Villa Barbaro has a decorated vaulted ceiling that springs from a balustraded gallery high above the floor. There are figures visible leaning over the gallery railing. The room is entered through a door on one side, and directly across the room is an identical door, this one half open, with a boy mischieviously looking out. He does not move; he has been peeking out of that door for more than four hundred years, ever since Paulo Veronese painted him on the wall. Everything here—the columns, the dadoes, the broken pediments, the statues, the lifelike figures, even some of the doors and windows (those required by symmetry, not function)—is only fingernail thick: a coat of paint.

Like his collaborator and friend Palladio, Veronese was responding to the limited resources of his clients. If they couldn't afford a gallery, they could enjoy the sense of space afforded by the trompe l'oeil simulation. Removed from the sophisticated charms of Venice, their homes at least could offer their eyes the sensual delight to which they were accustomed. These paintings, whose first stimulus was economic, are much more than large-scale *faux marbre.* They are also a mirror of their owners' lives, for the figures that look down from the gallery or stand in the doorway are portraits of real people: the lady of the house, her husband, and their children. Their motionless presence simultaneously reinforces and undermines the illusory effect of the painted interior, for Veronese has transformed what might have been simple decor into a disquieting and moving work of art. This house within a house, peopled by magical ghosts, makes the modern visitor feel like an interloper.

An air of poignancy is present also in the buildings themselves. It is less literal than the melancholy of the frescoes, although the sculptured human figures that have been placed on and around some of the villas seem likewise to inhabit, or at least to guard, these houses. Palladio, because he was an architect, not a painter, could not resort to trickery, his brick-and-plaster capitals notwithstanding. Obliged to observe a restraint in his design—by economic necessity, not by choice—Palladio mourned his loss, but he did not conceal it, and herein lay his greatness. His respect for the past was too great to permit tinkering, and in his classical farmhouses, he skillfully retrieved what he could from the buildings he admired and unwillingly discarded the rest. We, of all people, should be able to understand his achievement.

A Decade of Disorientation: 1910–19

Unlike the twenties, the sixties, or the eighties, the decade between 1910 and 1919 has no popular designation. The twenties were the age of jazz; the sixties were characterized by youthful (hence temporary) rebellion; and the eighties were exemplified by a widely deplored, but hardly novel, acquisitiveness, which appears to be on the wane. But it is evident that what changed most during these decades was fashion. In contrast, during the period between 1910 and 1919, the world was altered in fundamental and lasting ways. Before 1910, one could view life from the comfortable perspective of the nineteenth century; after 1919 that was no longer possible. The modern era had begun.

The chief event that symbolized modernity was World War I, whose effect was not only political—two vast empires, Turkey and Austro-Hungary, disappeared, and a third was transformed by the Russian Revolution into the Soviet Union—but also psychological. It was a question not merely of casualties, which were enormous, but of a change in the nature of warfare, which escalated to include such barbarisms as poison gas, attacks on merchant ships, the indiscriminate aerial bombing of towns and cities, and reprisals against civilian populations. "When all was over," wrote Churchill, "torture and cannibalism were the only two expedients that the civilized, scientific, Christian states had been able to deny themselves."

It was not only World War I, however, that marked this period of change; the ideas of two intellectual giants were also transforming human perception. Albert Einstein, who began publishing his work on relativity in 1905, proposed the General Theory of Relativity in 1915, and it was conclusively proved correct four years later. Time and space, which had seemed to be of absolute duration and extent, turned out to be elastic, and Newtonian physics, which had stood the test of the previous two hundred years, was fundamentally altered. Sigmund Freud, too, called into question traditional beliefs and introduced new concepts of guilt, personal responsibility, hidden meaning—the famous "Freudian slip"—and sexual gnosticism.

The world was no longer what it seemed. The effect of this apparent disorder was felt throughout society, but earliest among the so-called avant-garde, a term coined slightly earlier to describe new and unconventional movements in the arts. Many of these were centered in Paris: Stravinsky's first big success, *The Firebird*, was performed in 1910; the word "cubism," referring to the work of Cézanne, Braque, and Picasso, was already in common use by 1911; Diaghilev staged *The Rite of Spring* in 1913. In 1918, Oswald Spengler published the first volume of *Decline of the West*, which reflected the new, brittle sensibility; by 1919, Proust had produced the first volume of A *la recherche du temps perdu*, Thomas Mann had published *Death in Venice*, and James Joyce was writing *Ulysses*. The modern movement in the arts was well under way.

What about architecture? Architects were slower to respond to the new intellectual reality, for buildings, unlike paintings and books, were ill suited to serve as vehicles for avant-garde experimentation. For one thing, they cost a lot of money. Proust published at his own expense; an architect, if he wanted to build, had to find a wealthy client. And the audience for the demanding and difficult avant-garde literature, music, and art was tiny; while architecture, a social art, had to appeal to a broader public. Urban buildings, especially, tended to reflect a societal consensus, which was firmly conservative. That is why many of the protomodernist Parisian buildings of the period, by architects such as Tony Garnier and Auguste Perret, while sometimes technically adventurous, exhibited what Reyner Banham called a "stripped classicism" that fell well within the academic tradition.

In Vienna, the originators of the ultraprogressive, turn-of-the-century Secession style, Josef Hoffmann and Otto Wagner, though elderly, were still active. Wagner's buildings incorporated inventive details and ornamentation, but they were increasingly grounded in classicism, and his 1911 book on city planning proposed a recognizably traditional metropolis. The younger generation was more adventurous. As early as 1910, Adolf Loos built what was arguably the first European example of a cubical, undecorated (at least on the exterior), white-walled villa—the Steiner house, in a Viennese suburb. But his downtown office building on Michaelerplatz, completed two years later, incorporated Doric columns and marble cladding, and its reinforced-concrete frame was hidden behind a traditionally composed facade.

The only architectural movement of the time that could be called avant-garde was to be found in Germany, where in 1907, Hermann Muthesius founded the Deutscher Werkbund. The most influential

German buildings, in terms of the later evolution of modernism, were Peter Behren's AEG turbine factory (1909) in Berlin, Hans Poelzig's chemical factory (1911–12) at Luban, and, above all, Walter Gropius and Adolf Meyer's Fagus factory (1911) and their model factory at the 1914 Werkbund Exhibition; it is no wonder that modernism would later incorporate a "factory aesthetic." Industrial buildings were intended to be functional, and as long as the requirements of use were met, factory owners allowed their architects a latitude for experimentation not found in public buildings, whose formal language was circumscribed by convention. Architects understood this, and when Behrens designed the new German embassy in St. Petersburg (1912), or when his assistant, Ludwig Mies (the van der Rohe came later), entered the competition for the Bismarck monument (1910), they both adopted a neoclassical style.

Nikolaus Pevsner called Behrens, Gropius, and the Werkbund architects the "pioneers of the modern movement," but it is misleading to characterize the laying of the foundation for modernism as the sole accomplishment of this decade. After all, the same period that saw the construction of Josef Hoffmann's masterful Palais Stoclet in Brussels encompassed both Edwin Lutyens's striking Viceroy's House in New Delhi and Frank Lloyd Wright's rural retreat at Taliesin. Eliel Saarinen's Helsinki railroad station (completed in 1914) was contemporaneous with Charles McKim's masterpiece, Pennsylvania Station; the year after Bruno Taut's Glass Pavilion was shown at the 1914 Werkbund exhibition in Cologne, Bertram Goodhue built his influential California Building at the Panama-Pacific Exposition in San Diego. Before the war, when Le Corbusier was still Charles-Edouard Jeanneret, an unknown domestic architect in the Swiss town of La Chaux-de-Fonds, the Greene brothers, Charles and Henry, had already perfected their individualistic residential style in Pasadena.

Nothing marks the period as strongly as the achievements of the many domestic architects. The English master was undoubtedly Lutyens, although Robert Lorimer also produced some beautiful, grave country houses in his native Scotland. But it was in America, already the richest country in the world, where the design of large houses flourished. On the East Coast, society architects such as Thomas Hastings, John Russell Pope, and Charles Adams Platt were building dozens of wonderful country villas, and in southern California, a Mediterranean domestic style was being developed by skilled designers such as Bertram Goodhue and Myron Hunt, who completed the stately Huntington house in San Marino in 1911.

American architecture of the period was anything but the "aesthetic wasteland" that James Marston Fitch described in *American Building*. Like most architectural historians of the 1940s, Fitch simply would not tolerate the eclectic movement that characterized this period. But many contemporary architects were equally uncomfortable with the variety of styles and approaches. In an essay published in the September 1913 issue of *Architectural Record*, the architect Ralph Adams Cram enumerated at least seven major tendencies. To begin with, there was classicism, of which he described three types: pure classicism, advanced by the venerable firm of McKim, Mead & White, and still the style of choice for public monuments like Henry Bacon's moving Lincoln Memorial (1912–17); Beaux-Arts, typified by Carrère and Hastings's design for the New York Public Library, which had opened its doors in 1910; and neo-Colonial, chiefly visible in the country-house movement. Then there were two variations of Gothic: one, more or less canonic, which was exemplified by Cram's own work at Princeton and by his many fine religious buildings; the other, a freer interpretation of the medieval style, such as his partner Bertram Goodhue's robust designs for West Point. Next, Cram included steel-frame construction among the influences of the moment. It had liberated architects from the constraints of traditional masonry building twenty years before and was still, as he put it, "having its fling." Lastly, Cram cited what he called "Post-Impressionism." Though he mentioned no names, he presumably was referring to the work of architects who did not take their cue from historical styles: Louis Sullivan, then in the final productive phase of his career; his disciple, Frank Lloyd Wright; and southern California innovators such as Irving Gill.

"What lies before us?" Cram asked. "More pigeon-holes, more personal followings, more individualism, with anarchy at the end?" His description of architectural chaos could serve just as well to characterize the 1980s, a heady decade of architectural pluralism during which critics were barely able to keep up with the apparently inexhaustible invention of new theories and new—and old—styles. Indeed, 1910–19 was, at least architecturally, a period resembling our own. Like the orthodoxy of modernism in the 1980s, the orthodoxy of classicism, which had held sway for more than two decades, had been questioned and found wanting, and with the opening of Pandora's box, individual architects were free to go off in a multitude of directions, combining, and recombining, old forms with new materials.

Regardless of their stylistic preferences, all architects of the early 1900s shared the use of up-to-date technology; in that sense, at least, the modern revolution in architecture had already occurred. The year 1913 saw the completion of what *Architectural Record* admiringly called "the latest and greatest of our skyscrapers," the Woolworth Building. At fifty-five stories, it was the tallest building in the world, and it was by far the tallest Gothic tower ever built. Cass Gilbert's tour de force was a curious blend of canonic design and modern construction. It had exquisitely carved ornament, flying buttresses, and grinning gargoyles, but it also incorporated a host of technologies that even fifty years before were either unknown or uncommon: a steel-frame structure, elevators, hot and cold running water, central heating, telephones, and electrical lighting. The only device that was needed to make this a fully modern twentieth-century office building was air conditioning; the first air-conditioned office building was not built until 1928.

The Woolworth Building is a reminder that although the aesthetic pioneers of the modern movement may have been in Europe, the technical innovations in architecture were taking place in North America. In 1914, Charles-Edouard Jeanneret produced the Domino house, an idea for a reinforced-concrete structural system that he proposed for low-cost housing reconstruction after the war. It was never realized, but through his own promotion, and the support of critics, his famous sketch became a seminal symbol for a new architecture. Four years earlier, however, the New York architect Grosvenor Atterbury had already begun work on a concrete building system for housing that used precast, hollow-core panels for walls, floors, and roofs, and which combined these with precast concrete porches, chimney tops, and other components. All the elements were cast in a factory and transported to the site for erection. This was not a theoretical proposal; between 1910 and 1918, Atterbury built several hundred inexpensive houses at Forest Hills Gardens, a new railway suburb in Queens. Atterbury was a curious blend of reformer and society architect, and his remarkable building system produced housing that was comfortingly traditional. His houses had pitched roofs, dormers, gables, mullioned windows, and an overall appearance that has been described as German-Tudor. This conservatism satisfied the occupants, although it also undoubtedly explains the neglect of this inventive architect by the proselytizing historians of modernist architecture.

The first two decades of our century saw the consolidation of housing as a key concern and as a fit subject for architectural study. The British Garden City movement, begun by Ebenezer Howard at the turn of the century, produced housing developments such as Letchworth and Hampstead Garden Suburb, where Barry Parker and Raymond Unwin pioneered mass housing design; on the Continent, the chief housing architects were Muthesius and Heinrich Tessenow. In the United States, most new housing was suburban, spurred by the phenomenal growth in automobile ownership. Ford introduced his inexpensive Model T in 1908, and by 1913 one million passenger cars were registered; two years later, the number had more than doubled. Many middle-class suburban houses were designed by architects, and as early as 1912, *Architectural Record* ran a seven-part series titled "Building a House of Moderate Cost." One architect who had long been interested in low-cost housing was Irving Gill, whose Lewis Courts (1910), in Sierra Madre, California, and several later bungalow courts, are exemplary projects that provided inexpensive and attractive housing in a communal setting. But Gill, like Atterbury, was before his time, and it was not until the postwar housing shortage of 1918 that attention was focused squarely on mass housing. Although *Architectural Record* continued to publish its annual country-house issue, articles began to appear regularly on "industrial" housing, featuring the work of Atterbury, Clarence Stein, and Henry Wright.

The new interest in housing was symptomatic of a change that had taken place in the architectural profession. The war and its aftermath had shifted architects into new roles, designing war installations (such as Cass Gilbert's extraordinary Brooklyn Army Supply Base), factories, factory housing, hospitals, and veterans' homes. These contingencies suggested that architects had a social role to play in the new unsettled postwar world—a world in which the debate between the classicists and the Gothicists ("between Tweedledum and Tweedledee," as one observer put it) seemed to many to be increasingly irrelevant.

The year 1919 closed a chapter on American architecture that had begun thirty years before. Beaux-Arts classicism was out, but no one style had yet moved in to replace it. Would it be an outgrowth of Gothic, as Ralph Adams Cram hoped, or some form of indigenous style of the type that Sullivan had explored? The answer, we now know, lay across the Atlantic, for 1919 saw the establishment of two European institutions that would change the face of architecture around the world. That year, Gropius founded the Bauhaus, and Jeanneret and two friends decided to start a new magazine called *L'Esprit Nouveau*. Cram closed his essay on style in American architecture on an optimistic note, suggesting that the future held "the promise of a new day." Little did he know just how new it would be.

High Tech

Go into a jewelry store, ask for a high-tech watch, and the salesclerk will know what you mean immediately. You will be shown an assortment of wristwatches that not only give you the hour—in several time zones—but will also store your broker's phone number and your parents' anniversary date, wake you up in the morning, remind you to call home, and calculate your grocery bill. The point is not that you will ever use all these capabilities, but that by wearing this Dick Tracy device, you can demonstrate that you are a forward-thinking person, a Fourth Waver, a technology booster.

High tech doesn't just mean watches or computers. It's also a look, like retro or traditional, and a mass-market fashion. Its influence is apparent in skiing equipment, running shoes, bicycles, desk lamps, and microwave ovens. High tech has connotations of Florida moonshots and Silicon Valley, of synthetics and computer chips, of efficiency and technical competence—in other words, of modernity.

Perhaps because it's so pervasive, high tech sometimes appears to be an ad man's creation—a creature of the 1980s, more style than substance. In that sense it resembles the streamlining fad of the 1940s, when the curvy and sinuous shapes of airplanes were applied indiscriminately to vacuum cleaners, radios, and automobiles, regardless of how fast these devices moved, or if they moved at all. Even buildings were rounded off, with long strips of stainless steel attached to their facades to simulate motion. High tech has also affected architecture, for example, in the headquarters of Lloyd's of London, completed in 1986. Assertively technological, the building's futuristic image announces that this corporation is no fusty Victorian relic. Is it better than a billboard, or is it a billboard? Like streamlining, high tech projects a message of technological optimism; it represents an enthusiastic embrace of the Modern Age, chips and all.

It comes as a surprise, then, to discover that the high-tech style is now more than half a century old, and that it originated not in electronics or aerospace engineering but in something as earthbound as a house. Moreover, this house was neither in Florida nor in California, but in a courtyard behind the rue St.-Guillaume in Paris.

The most striking feature of the so-called Maison de Verre, built for a doctor and his wife, is its exterior, which is constructed entirely of glass blocks; but its use of industrial materials does not stop at the outside walls. The structure is steel, and the riveted beams and girders are everywhere exposed. Stair railings are steel pipes; treads are open metal grilles. The floor of the living area is covered in white, studded rubber tiles; elsewhere, floors are white or black ceramic. Books are stacked on banks of perforated metal shelving that seem to have been transported from a warehouse; but like most things in the house they are custom-made. Instead of wall switches, all electrical controls are clustered in freestanding pods. The mechanical atmosphere is heightened by prominent metal ventilating louvers that can be cranked open, as in a greenhouse. Revolving closets in the bedroom, as well as pivoting glass screens, sliding walls, folding partitions, a retractable stair linking two rooms, and, a final novelty, adjustable track lighting all demonstrate remarkable ingenuity. The self-assuredness of this design is arresting—all the more so since the house was completed in 1932.

The Maison de Verre stands in a dark courtyard behind an eighteenth-century town house, which explains the need to preserve as much light as possible. The architect, Pierre Chareau, had to insert the house under existing upper floors, whose owner refused to move. These floors are supported by the exposed steel structure. But it would be a mistake to describe the Maison de Verre as merely a "functional" solution to a difficult building site. It's much more than that. Here, technology and industrial materials (glass block, rubber tile, steel, aluminum) are not only used but displayed—not out of necessity, but out of delight.

Chareau was interested in using new materials, and he was unusually inventive. At the 1925 Exposition Internationale des Arts Décoratifs et Industriels Modernes, which launched the so-called art deco style, Chareau devised a study-library with an overhead dome of palm-tree wood that could be opened at night to disclose an illuminated ceiling consisting of several layers of thick white glass. Mechanical innovation pervades the Maison de Verre, whether it is the heated aluminum towel-drying cabinet in the bathroom or the overhead gantry track for a horizontal dumbwaiter that leads from the kitchen to the neighboring dining room. This exuberant attention to detail prompted the architectural historian Kenneth Frampton to describe the Maison de Verre as an enlarged piece of furniture.

It is true that Chareau was trained as a furniture maker, and his career was primarily in the field of interior decoration. In that sense, the Maison de Verre was an exercise in decor—albeit industrial decor. This is not to say that Chareau's design was purely aesthetic. Many of the mechanical elements of the house were functional, and all performed as intended. But what distinguished Chareau is that he used industrial elements in a visually decorative way. Technology could be fun. This was a novel discovery, and it has remained one of the touchstones of the high-tech style.

The Maison de Verre was the high point of Chareau's career; he never equaled it, and perhaps for that reason this "machine for living"—which was far more technically sophisticated than anything that other modernist architects were building at the time—remained unknown, exerting little influence on other designers. It may also have been ignored because Chareau, like Eileen Gray and Jacques Dunand (who also produced strikingly original interiors), was not an architect but a *décorateur*.

Nineteen years later, another furniture designer, Charles Eames, built a house that, while very different from the Maison de Verre, also demonstrated the possibilities for an aesthetic based on industrial materials. Designed with his wife, Ray, in Santa Monica, California, the Eames house uses ordinary, mass-produced construction elements—open-webbed steel joists, prefabricated steel decking, factory windows. As in the Maison de Verre, there is no applied decoration (although some of the panels are painted in primary colors), nor any traditional domestic imagery. What is striking about the Eames house is that the common industrial components are assembled in an uncommonly careful—one might almost say handcrafted—way. This precision became a unifying feature of all future high-tech buildings.

The Eames house achieved great renown during the 1950s, as did the buildings of other Los Angeles architects, such as Craig Ellwood, Raphael Soriano, and Pierre Koenig, whose work on the so-called Case Study Houses was characterized by both the extreme lightness and the large spans of their delicate structural steel frames, and by a pragmatic use of industrial details.

Houses often have served as vehicles for architectural experiments, but it is large buildings that catch the public's eye. High tech's first opportunity for a major architectural project came in 1971, when two young architects—Renzo Piano, an Italian, and Richard Rogers, an Englishman—won an international competition to build a national cultural center in the heart of Paris. The extraordinary-looking Centre Pompidou opened its doors in 1977. Described by some as an oil refinery, by others as an Erector set, the building is a giant glass box draped in a crisscrossed scaffolding of structural elements, escalators, elevators, air ducts, and conduits, all painted in vivid colors.

The point of exposing the structure and the mechanical elements was to give the building a dynamic appearance that would attract the public, since the French government specifically wanted this to be an untraditional museum. But the industrial imagery of the Centre Pompidou was reminiscent of such nineteenth-century engineering works as the Crystal Palace and the Eiffel Tower. This, and the fact that Piano and Rogers had drawn heavily on the industrial imagery of the Maison de Verre and the Eames house, led some architectural critics to characterize the design as "Late Modern." This was not a flattering epithet, for the implicit suggestion was that the industrial aesthetic had run its course.

The critics were wrong. Less than a decade after the Centre Pompidou opened, Norman Foster, another Englishman, designed a new headquarters for the Hongkong and Shanghai Bank in Hong Kong. The result was not only the most expensive office tower in the world at the time, but one in which technological imagery was conspicuously present in every detail, from the transparent escalator housings at the base to the helipad on the roof. At forty-seven stories, this was high technology indeed.

The Hongkong Bank suggested that the technological sophistication of the industrial aesthetic had a broader appeal; no longer avant-garde, high tech had moved into the corporate mainstream. If there was any doubt about this, the head office of Lloyd's, in the City of London, made it clear that high tech was the style of the moment.

Designed by the office of Richard Rogers (he and Piano parted ways in 1977), Lloyd's is a monochrome, stainless-steel echo of the Centre Pompidou. The fourteen-story building contains a large, glass-roofed atrium, below which is the famous Room, where the insurance traders work. Unlike the Hongkong Bank, which, despite its technological appearance, looks sober, Lloyd's is an unrestrained exercise in what the architectural historian Reyner Banham called "functional gizmology." Its exterior is stacked with a startling array of fire stairs, snaking mechanical shafts, protruding service rooms, and glass-walled elevators. At the top of the stack projects a miniature gantry from which dangles the window washers' platform; it resembles a lifeboat, or the gondola of a hot-air balloon.

The designs of Richard Rogers are technologically accomplished (Lloyd's required planning flexibility that would accommodate changes for at least fifty years). They also include a great deal of technological imagery; indeed, looking technical is as important as functioning well. But this concern for appearance is one of the pitfalls of high tech, because it results in a desire to redesign every part of a building, no matter how minor, in a technological-looking idiom. At its best, it produces new solutions to old problems; at its worst, it is superficial and results in irritating and awkward details: uncomfortable furniture, disagreeable hardware, uncongenial decor.

The imagery of the Lloyd's building is sometimes futuristic, as in the android computer consoles that stand in the Room, and sometimes suggests a nostalgia for the past, as in the old-fashioned gantries. The atrium roof mimics the barrel vault of the Crystal Palace. As in the Centre Pompidou, the obsession with displaying machinery recalls the heroic period of modernist architecture, when pipes and ducts were exposed and painted in bright colors. This combination of new and old makes me think of the celebrated Swiss custom-car builder Franco Sbarro, who produces curious, not-quite replicas of classic automobiles, such as a seven-eighths-scale Bugatti Royale or a fiberglass prewar BMW 328 with modern (BMW) mechanicals. It is hard to know if these are new cars with old styling or old cars with new engines. In that regard, at least, the buildings of Norman Foster, the architect of the Hongkong Bank, are unequivocal: the architectural equivalents of a 500-series Mercedes-Benz—technology in the service of luxury.

The association of industrial products with luxury would have surprised Chareau or Eames, whose interiors have a frugal, almost ascetic quality. But in its latest reincarnation, high tech has emerged as a costly and extravagant style whose primary message is not only up-to-dateness but status. Buildings such as the Hongkong Bank and Lloyd's are probably among the best crafted (and, paradoxically, the most handcrafted) in the world. This makes them expensive, and hence exclusive. Architecture itself becomes a luxurious consumer product.

The future of high tech—and its persistent survival over the last fifty years suggests that, in one form or another, it has a future—may lie beyond the aggressive, industrial allusions of Foster and Rogers. In 1980, Renzo Piano was asked to design a museum in Houston to house the Menil Collection. The building opened in 1987. One block long, the predominantly single-story building resembles at first glance a nondescript suburban shopping center. The characterization is not unfair, for the museum is situated in an unprepossessing neighborhood of small bungalows; and despite its size, it does its best to fit in. The delicate white-painted steel frame is filled in not with glass or metal or plastic, but with cypress clapboard siding. The architecture is decidedly low-key.

On closer inspection, however, the building reveals itself to be an unusual structure, almost entirely roofed in glass. This glazing is supported on cast-iron trusses. Suspended beneath the trusses is a protective "ceiling" of specially designed delicately curved concrete shells, whose function is to deflect and diffuse the natural light into the galleries.

"I am not primarily an environmental architect," Piano has said. "I come from making things." As in all high-tech designs, the engineering and the assembly of the structural elements give life to the architecture. But in the Menil, the jumble of pipes, ducts, and air-conditioning equipment is discretely hidden from view, not exposed. The attention of the visitor is drawn to inner courts filled with tropical plants, not to the machinery. The chief impression is one of a gentle, ethereal light—and, of course, of the art itself. Architecture takes second place.

Piano's is the latest reincarnation of high tech, but with different aims from the high tech of Rogers and Foster. Although technology is visible in the Menil, it almost never dominates. Piano's preoccupation with machinery is put at the service of the user; it is not there merely to be admired. This is not a consumer product; nor is it an ingeniously packaged corporate image. High tech has finally come down to earth.

Will the Real California Architecture Please Stand Up?

I'm anything but an expert on California architecture. Although I have visited the state half a dozen times, the experience has not managed to shake my Easterner's clichéd view of California as a landscape consisting chiefly of tract houses interspersed with shopping malls, drive-in churches, and theme parks. If pressed, I suppose I'd describe the real California architecture as a low, freestanding building, in bright sunlight, on a highway strip not far from the ocean. Several convertibles would be parked in front, and inside, people would be wearing sunglasses and colorful clothing.

The California I know best is not real at all. It is the southern California of Raymond Chandler and Ross Macdonald, a sinister Los Angeles of seedy private-eye offices and decadent hillside villas—the sort of city that Polanski captured so well in *Chinatown*. It's also the gritty San Francisco of Jack London and Jack Kerouac, the rowdy Monterey of John Steinbeck, the Big Sur of Henry Miller. Like Dickens's London and Flaubert's Paris, this literary California is a moment in time frozen in my imagination, which only makes it more tenacious. All readers know the experience of seeing a place that we have never visited. The first time I visited Shanghai, it seemed only a pale reflection of the prewar city that J. G. Ballard described in *Empire of the Sun*. Having first experienced Shanghai through that author's eyes, I could not shake his image of it.

For me, as for so many people, California is also a cinematic fantasy. One of the earliest television programs I remember seeing as a boy is "Dragnet." Thanks to movies like *Bullitt* and *Dirty Harry*, I feel that I could almost find my way among the gingerbread-lined streets of San Francisco. Hollywood brought California to the world's moviegoers and television watchers. The first time I visited L.A. it all seemed so familiar: the high-rise tower where Mackenzie, Brackman have their offices; the beach bungalows; the impossibly wide freeways. I didn't see Jim Rockford's oceanside trailer, or the office building where Philip Marlowe hung out his shingle in *The Maltese Falcon*, but I knew that they were there somewhere.

There's also another California in my imagination. I came of age during the 1960s. For us, San Francisco was the capital city of the counterculture; northern California, its nascent republic. It was the home of the Grateful Dead; it was where Ken Kesey played his pranks, and where the Free Speech movement began. During the 1970s, we learned about northern California from the *Whole Earth Catalog*: people lived in communes in geodesic domes, houseboats, and handmade houses. They used composting toilets and solar heating; they went hang gliding, rode mountain bikes, and kept in touch with each other on their personal-computer bulletin boards.

My sense of mainstream California architecture was much less well defined. I knew that there were important modernist buildings in California, but they seemed to be largely the work of Europeans like Richard Neutra and Rudolf Schindler, or of outsiders like Frank Lloyd Wright and, later, Louis Kahn. Of course, there were some very good California architects, but I only learned of these later, through Esther McCoy's excellent book *Five California Architects*. I was only vaguely aware of the Case Study Houses, steel-and-glass exercises in West Coast high tech. They seemed to me then—as now—to be a sterile exercise in reductivism: Mies, but without the substantial and somber solidity of the German master.

The first indigenous Californian work of architecture that caught my attention—as it did that of so many architects around the world—was Moore, Lyndon, Turnbull, & Whitaker's condominium at Sea Ranch, one hundred miles north of San Francisco. This striking complex exhibited all the hallmarks of modernist design: it had exposed structure; it was built out of the same material inside and out; it was composed of repetitive modules. Although the roof was sloped, it was an acceptably low slope, clearly inspired by the Finnish architect Alvar Aalto's masterful Säynätsalo Town Center, built in 1950, and his Villa Carré, a large house built outside Paris in 1956.

But Sea Ranch was not merely another example of international modernism. Charles Moore and his co-designers were up to something new. The shapes of the buildings at Sea Ranch were influenced by local constraints such as topography and climate. Their post-and-beam construction and redwood siding made them look more like barns than ranches, an intentional and explicit reference to northern Californian building traditions. Sea Ranch, then, was an accomplished example of architectural regionalism.

Regionalism has been a part of the architectural debate since the end of the nineteenth century, when the Arts and Crafts movement produced different, local adaptations in England, in Scotland, and on the European continent. The Arts and Crafts movement was subsumed by the International Style, but calls for a more regional approach to design crept back into architecture again during the 1950s. Regionalism was a concern of the second generation of modernists, such as the Swedish architect Ralph Erskine and the Italian Giancarlo de Carlo, both members of that international architectural forum and kaffeeklatsch, Team Ten.

Attention to regionalism reflected a growing dissatisfaction with the absolutism of orthodox modernism and with its adherence to the concept of universal and absolute needs—an idea that did not adapt to local traditions or local constraints, such as climate and culture. This universality initially seemed to be one of its strengths: modernists could build anywhere and everywhere, and modernist design could be absorbed by anyone who was willing to learn its few dictums. It accounted for the rapid spread of modernist architecture, fueled by the rapid and total spread of modernist architectural education, an extraordinary phenomenon that bears more study than it has received.

The problem for young architects in the 1950s was that the modernist style was *too* successful, with the result that around the world, not only buildings but entire neighborhoods began to resemble each other. Unwilling to be bored or boxed in, architects began to look for design rationales beyond only function and construction.

By the early 1960s, there began to be an interest in the work of architects who while not overtly regional in a sentimental way nevertheless exhibited traces of a local aesthetic in their buildings. I am thinking of architects such as James Stirling in Britain, Ernesto Rogers in Italy, Kenzo Tange in Japan, and the young Paul Rudolph in the southern United States. Their work seemed to offer a way out of the anonymity of the International Style while not questioning the principles, aesthetic and functional, of the modernist approach.

With Sea Ranch, the regionalist tendency was acknowledged explicitly, and the stage seemed set for a new style of locally influenced architecture. We now know that this flirting with regionalism was only the beginning of a successful departure from orthodox modernism. But while the postmodernism that followed did have some regionalist tendencies, on the whole it looked farther afield. Postmodernism might have promoted regionalism—after all, contextualism was one of its watchwords—but in practice, it, too, was international in flavor. It was part of a global architectural phenomenon, driven by the media, international marketing, and globetrotting practitioners. The same gable roofs, square windows, Palladian motifs, pastel colors, and skewed axes were just as likely to show up on the West Coast as on the East, or even in the Far East.

Postmodernism also opened the door to a reconsideration of a variety of early avant-garde, modernist tendencies. Postmodern architects are interested in history and tradition, but in a highly selective and sometimes curious way. A design by the firm of Perkins & Will for a government center in a Chicago suburb is based on Dutch architecture of the 1920s; Kohn Pedersen Fox's award-winning World Bank headquarters in downtown Washington, D.C., consciously recalls Italian modernism of the 1940s. Obviously, this bizarre kind of historical borrowing has little to do with regionalism.

At the same time, the idea of regionalism—or at least a recognition of stylistic regional influences—has by no means altogether vanished. It continues to be a factor in many of Charles Moore's designs, as one might expect, and it has also re-emerged as a concern in the work of Antoine Predock in New Mexico and Taft Architects in Texas, and in the South Florida houses of Andres Duany and Elizabeth Plater-Zyberk. Regionalism has also affected the design of buildings by B.V. Doshi and Charles Correa in India and Manuel Manzano-Monís in Spain. In Canada one sees regionalist influences in projects as disparate as Moshe Safdie's Museum of Civilization in Quebec City and the Canadian Centre for Architecture by Peter Rose, who studied under Charles Moore.

The quest for a regional style is always an attempt to identify authenticity, as well as a determination to deny inauthenticity. In most cases, regionalism is a reaction against what might be called cultural colonialism—that is, the imposition of an architecture from without. This imported architecture is perceived as foreign, inappropriate, and artificial. That is to say, it is definitely not the real thing.

Regionalism in architecture often has been tied to nationalist movements. National Socialism in Germany in the 1930s promoted "Germanic" art, which in architectural terms meant a firm rejection of internationalist, modernist architecture. Instead, the Nazis adopted a folksy *Heimatstil* ("homeland style") in rural buildings and, like the fascists in Italy, neoclassicism for public buildings. *Heimatstil*, with its reliance on folk motifs, is obviously a type of regionalism. The studio that Albert Speer built for himself in upper Salzburg in 1936 recalls a medieval barn or a large rustic bungalow by Gustave Stickley.

The Third Reich lasted only a dozen years, so we will never know what the outcome of this large-scale experiment in architecture regionalism would have been had it not been halted with Germany's defeat in World War II. But it probably would have run into trouble, for regionalism has several built-in contradictions. To begin with, there is something static about the idea of a regional building style. It's an idea derived from anthropologists, who have always preferred studying remote and isolated societies. It's no coincidence that the most distinctive regional styles of building were produced by cultures in which the pace of change was extremely slow: early medieval Europe, for example, or Polynesia, or imperial China. Most of the places that were the focus of Bernard Rudofsky's influential 1965 exhibition and book *Architecture without Architects* were far removed from urban centers. It's hard to disagree with Rudofsky's observation that the picturesque domestic architecture of places like Mykonos, rural Morocco, and Apulia, is unblemished and virtuous compared with the jumble of any modern town. But is that really a sign of greater understanding and native ingenuity on the part of the untutored builders, or is it merely the result of isolation and cultural stagnation?

Traditional buildings such as pueblos, African dogons, and Yemeni earth houses are all hallmarks of impoverished societies. Without wealth and freedom of movement, choices are limited and change is extremely slow, in architecture as well as in dress and customs. Building techniques are handed down from generation to generation, little altered. Houses are built and rebuilt with traditional methods and materials, and according to traditional patterns. In these cultures, architecture changes slowly because civilization changes slowly.

By contrast, dynamic societies are characterized by rapid and frequent change that affects all cultural activities, including building. Part of this change is evidenced by fashion, which most architects consider trivial and frivolous. But the French historian Fernand Braudel has suggested that fashion may be more important than we like to think. For one thing, fashion has always been a way for the privileged to distinguish themselves from the masses; for another, it literally makes material progress visible.

In addition, as Braudel writes, fashion is "a search for a new language to discredit the old, a way in which each generation can repudiate its immediate predecessor and distinguish itself from it." The most extreme examples of this repudiation occur during revolutions, which typically pioneer new fashions in clothing. Think of the dress changes that accompanied political change in Maoist China, communist Cuba, postindependence Israel, or postcolonial East Africa. In all these cases, dressing right (blue caps, army fatigues, open-necked shirts, safari suits) symbolized thinking right. But any social change can be manifested in a change of dress. The fashions of the Roaring Twenties, for example, were a way to celebrate, and emphasize, the new postwar world. In the 1960s, fashion in the guise of long hair, blue jeans, and tie-dyed T-shirts also played an important role in repudiating the values of an older generation.

There is an interesting example of such architectural repudiation in postindependence India. The first buildings erected by the British during the Raj were classical, as in England. During the late Victorian era, Gothic migrated to India where it eventually developed a curious, exotic variation called Hindu-Gothic. Starting in the early 1900s, when the new capital city was being planned in Delhi, a concerted effort was made to develop a more authentic style of building adapted to India's cultural heritage—what we would call a regional style. This movement was spearheaded by Edwin Lutyens and Herbert Baker, the architects of the chief buildings of New Delhi, and by Claude Betley, who was head of the Bombay School of Architecture, then the only school on the subcontinent. The result was the Indo-Saracenic style, an amalgam of traditional classical composition and planning with indigenous architectural elements gleaned from a study of historic Hindu and Moghul monuments.

After India's independence in 1947, the Indo-Saracenic style quickly lost favor. Whatever its local characteristics, it was seen as a remnant of British rule, and hence its authenticity was called into question. Most Indians (with the exception of Gandhi and his followers) were interested in looking forward, not backward. During the early 1950s, many young Indians chose to study architecture abroad, chiefly in the United States—at Harvard, where Walter Gropius was an influence, or at other, similarly modernist schools. Not surprisingly, when these architects returned home, they brought the new dogma with them. There was also the considerable influence of Le Corbusier, who in 1951 was invited to design the major buildings of the new city of Chandigarh. Nehru, the prime minister, was explicit about the fact that Chandigarh—and, by extension, modernist architecture—was to be a symbol of the new, progressive India. Whatever its merits—and any visitor to New Delhi knows that they are considerable—the Indo-Saracenic style had to go. By the early 1950s, it had been supplanted by international modernism.

Almost by definition, regionalism is ill-equipped to deal with changing fashions. That is why anthropologists are often so critical of the influence of modernity on so-called traditional societies. With modernity comes change: sandals give way to Nikes, ponchos are replaced by nylon anoraks, and adobe is displaced by concrete blocks. All of these changes, accompanied by new developments in culture, politics, and economics, represent Braudel's "new language." It is no coincidence that religious fundamentalism resists new fashions in clothing. It recognizes that modern dress announces a rejection of old habits—and, of course, old beliefs.

The problem with defining a regional architecture is doing so in a way that accepts that it, too, will change. How can one guarantee that it will retain its authenticity? Even if it were possible to develop different styles of building to suit different regions—a very big if—how do you prevent contamination? Without the barriers of isolation, fashions migrate from one place to another. How many societies will be prepared to elevate cultural mullahs to protect their regional purity?

There are two other forces that work against regionalism today. The practice of architecture has become increasingly international, because information about architecture travels. Go into any design school in America, Europe, or Asia, and you will find the same books in the libraries and the same magazines lying around in the studios. I once asked a group of students in Chongqing, a relatively remote city in the heart of China, which architects they most admired. The answer was Michael Graves, James Stirling, and I. M. Pei.

The other tendency that works against regionalism today is the universality of building technology. I've spent several years studying housing in Third World countries, and one of the striking features of urban slums in Africa, Asia, and Latin America is the similarity of building materials and techniques. The small-scale reinforced-concrete frame, for example, has turned out to be extremely adaptable to the needs of poor owner-builders. It is simple to construct, durable, resistant to hurricanes, flooding, and earthquakes, and flexible enough to meet any contingency. Just leave a few bars protruding, and construction can be resumed any time in the future. As a result, reinforced-concrete construction has swept the world in only a few decades, repeating the performance of an earlier technology, the corrugated tin roof.

Universal technology does not necessarily mean universal architecture—Bombay slums are very different from Mexico City slums—but it does tend to alter radically local building traditions, since it obviously introduces a distinctly foreign ingredient. To that extent, the idea of regional styles is becoming increasingly difficult to imagine, whether for small urban houses or large buildings.

If regionalism cannot survive changing fashions and social aspirations, dynamic economies, and standardized building practices, what is the alternative? How can we combine the aesthetic ideals and technological innovations of universal modernism with a response to local needs and local problems?

I am always struck by the contrast between contemporary buildings in, say, Montreal, or Los Angeles, and the earlier architecture of those cities. Whether it is the Edwardian greystone public monuments of my own city or the buildings of Irving Gill, Bertram Goodhue, and Myron Hunt in southern California, the older examples always seem to me more at home in their surroundings.

It's easy to forget that modernism is not the first universal style. For the previous several hundred years, classicism, or some variation of it, was the foundation of the art of building. The greystones of Montreal, like the Spanish Colonial buildings of southern California, were the work of men, and sometimes women, whose architectural skills were grounded in the classical tradition.

What is interesting is that in hindsight, it is obvious that this universal tradition was extremely adaptable to local needs. Myron Hunt's beautiful library in Pasadena, with its welcoming patio and cool, protective interior, is both classical and Californian; so is Irving Gill's simplified (reinforced concrete) classicism of the Women's Club in La Jolla.

An investigation of classical architecture around the world demonstrates that universal solutions and local needs can be compatible. As Robert A. M. Stern has pointed out, classicism offers architects a canon, but it is a liberal and tolerant one. It has provided its practitioners with an architectural language that is rooted in the past but adaptable to the present. It is amenable to modification and crossbreeding, and in talented hands can respond successfully to new building programs. Like modernism, it is a universal style, but it lacks the absolutism and rigidity that characterize the modernist approach to building.

I am not arguing here for a historical style as much as for a historical attitude—déjà vu, as opposed to avant-garde (in Derek Walcott's phrase). An awareness of history—of the successes and failures of the past—should inform architectural design to a greater degree than it now does. If a "real" California architecture is possible, it's likely that it will find its chief impetus in precisely such an awareness.

Shaping Chicago's Future

Some cities are memorable for their settings—Vancouver and Seattle come to mind, or Rio de Janeiro and Hong Kong. Others are impressive for the character of their public spaces—the boulevards of Paris, the parks of London, the streets and avenues of New York. But of the great American cities, only Chicago derives its physical impact almost solely from the quality of its buildings, and this despite its dramatic lakeside location. For more than a hundred years, it has been the site of unparalleled architectural creativity and innovation, and the home of such architectural giants as Daniel Burnham, Louis Sullivan, Frank Lloyd Wright, and Mies van der Rohe.

"New Chicago Architecture," a show exhibited at Union Station in Washington, D.C., and then at the Chicago Athenaeum in 1991, was more than a preview of new buildings; it was a look at the future face of the city. What will the new Chicago be? Currently the site of the world's highest building—the 1,454-foot Sears Tower—Chicago will soon outdo itself in the 125-story Miglin-Beitler Tower, a 2,000-foot stalagmite designed by Cesar Pelli. Several other new skyscrapers have been designed by the Chicago architects Helmut Jahn and Perkins & Will, and by that local powerhouse Skidmore, Owings & Merrill, including their recently completed AT&T Corporate Center, the NBC Tower, and the projected 80-story Dearborn Tower. Tall buildings will continue to dominate the new Chicago, with one notable exception: Hammond, Beeby & Babka's impressive Harold Washington Library Center, which was nearing completion in the spring of 1991 and which promises to be an outstanding piece of architecture.

Despite the patronage of local architects, many of the new Chicago skyscrapers have been designed by architects foreign to the city. In addition to the Miglin-Beitler Tower (and 181 West Madison, also by Pelli), there are several office towers designed by the New York firm of Kohn Pedersen Fox, as well as work by John Burgee and Philip Johnson, Kevin Roche, a rather lackluster office building by the Japanese master Kenzo Tange, and a decidedly silly neoclassical tower (under construction) by the Spanish architect Ricardo Bofill.

"There was a time when only Chicago architects built in Chicago," writes the exhibition's curator, Christian K. Laine, in an introductory essay. Well, not quite. The famous Boston architect H. H. Richardson built four buildings in Chicago between 1872 and 1887, including the huge Marshall Field Wholesale Store, now demolished; his successors, Shepley, Rutan & Coolidge, designed the city's chief museum, the Art Institute, in 1892. Another Bostonian, Ralph Adams Cram, built the Fourth Presbyterian Church in 1912, a gem of the Gothic Revival on North Michigan Avenue. And one of Chicago's most familiar urban landmarks, the Tribune Tower, was designed by Raymond Hood, a New Yorker, in 1925.

Yet Laine is right in suggesting that after World War II, the city became something of an architectural enclave, owing chiefly to the arrival of Mies van der Rohe. His work, and that of his followers and students at the Illinois Institute of Technology, dominated the city. The rectangular steel-and-glass buildings by Mies, as well as by the offices of Skidmore, Owings & Merrill and C. F. Murphy & Associates, give the Loop an architectural homogeneity unique among American cities.

There is a marked difference between the buildings of the Miesian period (Mies died in 1969) and the new Chicago architecture, which is either adventurous or lacking in conviction, depending upon your point of view. The flat-topped boxes of the fifties and sixties have been replaced by a variety of highly articulated and imaginatively conceived shapes, and the monochrome vocabulary of steel and glass has given way to a diversity of forms, materials, and colors.

Freed from the constraints of Miesian rationalism, designers have explored a variety of new solutions. But the freedom has produced a curious result: most of the new buildings reinterpret older ones. The silhouette of Pelli's soaring stalagmite recalls Wright's visionary mile-high skyscraper the Illinois, and Pelli's other tower is a conscious re-creation of Eliel Saarinen's entry in the 1922 *Chicago Tribune* competition (won by Raymond Hood). John Burgee and Philip Johnson have said that the design of their handsome office building on South LaSalle Street is based on an 1892 tower by Burnham & Root. Lucien Lagrange's proposal for a 55-story tower is capped by a Greek temple in the manner of the Second Chicago School of the 1930s; the crown of Kohn Pedersen Fox's tower at 225 West Wacker Drive is inspired by the nearby Navy Pier. One of Perkins & Will's skyscrapers is a vertical version of De Stijl modernism; another recalls Italian futurism. And buildings such as the Dearborn Tower and the NBC Tower both evoke the art deco style of the 1920s and thirties.

Perhaps, as Laine suggests, this revival of past styles represents a "renewed romance with the skytowering form." Or is this haphazard eclecticism born of a kind of resignation? The chief determinants of tall office buildings are commercial rather than architectural and appear to offer the designer little scope for real innovation beyond the patterning of the exterior walls or the addition of extraneous spires and rooftop paraphernalia. Inside, architects replicate the traditional arrangement of a grandiose lobby surmounted by identical, anonymous office floors.

That real innovation is still possible in skyscraper design is apparent in Norman Foster's celebrated bank in Hong Kong. Foster breaks with the stereotype of the office tower and introduces new forms of movement (a combination of elevators and escalators), unconventional construction, and innovative organization of the upper floors (intermittent two-story sky lobbies). The result is not just an alteration in appearance but a reflection of concern for the quality of the public areas of the bank and for the environment of the workplace.

Paradoxically, the forerunner to the Hongkong Bank is a Chicago building now more than twenty years old, the John Hancock Center. This skyscraper, known locally as "Big John," was the tallest building in the world until the Sears Tower usurped its position. Designed by Bruce Graham of Skidmore, Owings & Merrill, the Hancock building is an unusual combination of functions that includes a department store on the first three levels, seven floors of parking, twenty-nine floors of offices, and above that forty-seven floors of apartments. It is a vertical city enclosed in an attenuated tower whose chief architectural impact is derived from the exposed crisscrossed structural bracing (a Miesian motif, adapted from that architect's 1953 design for a convention center) on the exterior wall and from its tapering form. Twenty years have done nothing to diminish the Hancock's compelling image of structural robustness and functional clarity; beside it, the conceits of the new Chicago architecture appear flimsy and unconvincing.

God Isn't in the Details, After All

The work of celebrated architects has one thing in common. Their buildings are not necessarily more beautiful than those of their less acclaimed colleagues, nor are they imbued with loftier aspirations. Yet they do stand apart; they embody an air of detachment from the world around them. Often this isolation is due to the form of the building. There is nothing else in New York—or in any other city—like the spiral of the Guggenheim Museum. Sometimes the difference is the result of structural legerdemain, like the odd, reverse-stepping facade of the Whitney Museum, or Edward Larrabee Barnes's IBM Building on Madison Avenue, which looks ordinary enough until one notices the gravity-defying corner, floating unsupported over the sidewalk. Frequently, famous architects simply have the opportunity to do things on a bigger scale than anybody else. Arthur Erickson's Law Courts in Vancouver are located under a glass roof, a greenhouse 350 feet long.

Some buildings startle us with unorthodox materials, such as Frank Gehry's chain-link fencing, lead-coated copper, and raw plywood. James Stirling is particularly skillful at the shock effect. No one who has ever seen his extension to the Fogg Art Museum at Harvard will forget the alternating stripes of colored brick or the anomalous pair of colored posts (actually cooling towers) at the entrance. The crazy-quilt facade of the Clore Gallery in London is equally memorable. Antoine Predock's designs have often used color to effect; the exterior of the United Blood Services building, a blood-donor clinic in Albuquerque, New Mexico, is startlingly, but appropriately, red, and a pueblolike apartment complex, also in Albuquerque, achieves its major impact from its unusual polychromy.

A striking difference between works of architecture and, say, your local Kmart is that the architecture usually costs a lot more to build. There is nothing like expensive materials, exacting workmanship, custom-made fittings, and elegant appointments to create an atmosphere of exclusiveness. It is the architectural equivalent of the "thunk" that you hear when you close the door of a luxury sedan.

Mies van der Rohe is reputed to have said, "God is in the details." The origin of this statement, like that of his other well-known aphorism, "Less is more," is obscure; no one is sure exactly when he said it or, indeed, if he said it first (it has also been attributed to the art historian Aby Warburg, to Gustave Flaubert, and to Saint Teresa of Avila). Was the famous architect answering a question? Had someone asked him about his design for the Illinois Institute of Technology chapel, the one that resembles a boiler house? "Professor Mies, where is God in this building?" Or did the question address his consuming, almost obsessive concern for precision and exactitude in building construction?

What characterized all of Mies's buildings was the careful and studied way in which they were built. Every corner, every meeting of materials, every joint, inside and out, was a part of an aesthetic whole. No detail was too small to be designed. When the British property developer John Palumbo engaged Mies to design an office building on London's Mansion House Square (it was to be Mies's last commission), the first communication Palumbo received from his architect was not a preliminary sketch but a parcel containing brass door handles and travertine ashtrays. "Is this what you had in mind?" Mies queried in his accompanying note.

The architectural consequences of such fastidiousness are impressive, but they can also be disconcerting. Whenever I go into a Mies van der Rohe building I am slightly intimidated. I feel like an interloper in a flawless, unequivocal, and absolute world—a perfect world for perfect people.

Mies's influence has waned since his death in 1969; but in one sense, at least, all contemporary architects are Miesians, for all share his overriding preoccupation with perfection. Whether they are modernists, postmodernists, or deconstructivists, their buildings exhibit the same desire to bring every facet of the building under their aesthetic control and the same tendency to replace conventional details with designs that carry their personal stamp.

Mies der Rohe designed his window frames, using standard steel profiles, to make them appear an integral part of the building. Le Corbusier, seeking a different effect, often set the window glass directly into a groove in the concrete wall, thus doing away with the window frame altogether, and producing an unexpectedly rustic impression. The work of Louis Kahn derives its impact from a careful articulation of the joints. The location of every brick was predetermined; some of his buildings look more like the work of a cabinetmaker than an architect. An interior by Richard Meier achieves its minimalist impression because the designer has ingeniously done away with most of the moldings and joints found in ordinary rooms. All the surfaces—walls, ceilings, soffits—blend seamlessly into a sculptural whole. The simplicity is deceptive; such subterfuge is both difficult and expensive to achieve.

This emphasis on the minutiae of construction is modern. In the past, architects relied on craftsmen and builders to carry out their work and did not concern themselves with inventing new construction details, which followed strict conventions. Ornament, not construction, was the way architects dealt with joints and junctions. When the modernists banished ornament from architecture, they were obliged to replace it with something, and so construction details became a new type of decoration. In time, this technical adornment became more imaginative and personal, but also more precious and fussier. Beauty had been reinterpreted as mechanical perfection.

Some architects are returning to an interest in figurative ornament. The recent work of Hammond, Beeby & Babka, for example, achieves its chief architectural impact through figurative decoration and the ornamental treatment of surfaces rather than from finicky joints. The result is buildings like the Harold Washington Library Center in Chicago, which lose nothing in originality but also feel more familiar.

The Seven Implants of Postmodern Architecture

In 1954, Philip Johnson gave a famous talk at Harvard University that was later published as an essay titled "The Seven Crutches of Modern Architecture." Lampooning John Ruskin's "Seven Lamps of Architecture," Johnson listed what he considered to be the current beliefs impeding the art of building and, in the process, took several potshots at some of the sacred cows of the same modernism that, only two decades before, he had been so instrumental in promoting.

While some of Johnson's crutches—the Crutch of History, for example, or the Crutch of Pretty Drawing—are even more apposite today than they were thirty-eight years ago, others—like the Crutch of Cheapness and the Crutch of Utility, which represented a heretical dig at Walter Gropius's teaching legacy of function taking precedence over artistic invention—have lost their edge; the designs of our best architects have long since ceased to be governed by usefulness or by economy. No; Johnson's prosthetics need updating, so here goes: the Seven Implants of Postmodern Architecture.

Surely no architectural device today is more overused than the square window. Facades composed entirely of uniform rows of individual square windows were originally a trademark of Aldo Rossi, and later Michael Graves. Square windows, usually divided into four by crossed mullions, are now ubiquitous. They are so common, in fact, that it's easy to ignore their novelty. Square windows are totally absent in traditional building styles, such as Georgian and Colonial (where windows are always vertical), and they appear only rarely in classical architecture, usually in the attic story. The advantage of using square windows is, of course, that the designer needs no skill in the art of proportioning. Ditto for circular windows, another favorite.

A close second is the symbolic gable. This shape pops up just about anywhere: on top of skyscrapers, in front of shopping malls, at the entrance to motels. Occasionally, it even includes a piece of gable roof behind it; but more often it's a false front, perhaps intended to remind us of traditional domestic architecture or, to stretch a point, of Greek temples. These references are meant seriously, although I think they often strike the public as humorous; the funniest symbolic gable can be seen in the postmodern rehab of the haunted house in the movie *Beetlejuice*.

In the 1970s it was atriums; in the eighties, no office building was complete if it didn't have a triumphal arch marking the entrance, and the bigger, the better. In some buildings the arch was stretched into a barrel vault, evoking imperial Rome. The most conspicuous contemporary model is certainly Johnson & Burgee's AT&T Building, completed in 1984. By no means the first office tower to incorporate an arched entrance, it nonetheless provides the grandest example, rising one hundred feet from the sidewalk, as if to welcome home some Cyclopean victor. Masters of the Universe, indeed.

The fourth implant is the pinnacle. The origin of this architectural feature is obscure (San Simeon? Disneyland?), but recently more and more buildings have been sprouting turrets and spires —to identify entrances, to articulate corners, sometimes merely to hide air-conditioning equipment on the roof. Romantic pinnacles were a feature of H. H. Richardson's robust neo-Romanesque and of Gothic Revival, but postmodern turrets are stripped of decoration, which gives them an insubstantial, toylike air.

The traditional chair rail was a strip of wood on the wall at waist level to protect the plaster from being damaged by the backs of furniture. Robert Venturi reintroduced the chair rail in 1961 in a house designed for his mother, but he went one better and applied it to the exterior as well. Since then, bits and pieces of moldings have appeared on the facades of buildings, often in the unlikeliest places—on the twentieth floor, interrupted by windows, seemingly glued to the surface. Unlike traditional architectural moldings, which have an integrating role in the facade, these discontinuous fragments, devoid of visual function, produce a curiously incomplete effect.

The bowstring truss was a common feature of nineteenth-century industrial architecture and produced a characteristic roof shape: a very low, flat vault. Now, for reasons that have little to do with structure or function, airplane-hangar roofs are added to schools, museums, and theaters. Four of the winners of the 1991 Progressive Architecture Awards incorporated bowed roofs.

Lastly, colors. More and more buildings that are unremarkable in other respects catch our attention because of their unusual coloration: acid-green floors, gaudy turquoise window frames, garish crimson columns. The first generation of postmodern architects broke with their monochromatic predecessors and (tentatively) introduced colors into their designs; inevitably, these gave way to brighter and more violent hues as the public got used to, and tired of, pastel pink and gray. James Stirling deserves a lot of the credit (if that is the word) for this trend.

The props that Philip Johnson was kicking out from under modern architecture were intellectual concepts (he also singled out Comfort, Structure, and Serving the Client). It says a lot about the current state of architecture that the Seven Implants are largely cosmetic, with little intellectual content. It is true that previous periods have included architectural stereotypes: pedimented porches, domes, grand staircases, and, in the modernist era, flat roofs and white walls. But these were part and parcel of an ideology. It would be difficult to situate the Seven Implants within any coherent architectural doctrine.

What is the explanation for the spread of visual platitudes in contemporary building? Since the reign of modernism, the art of building has been increasingly transformed into an art of packaging; architecture has become influenced by fashion. And fashion implies rapid change. From the same offices come a series of styles in quick succession—art deco one week, updated classicism the next. There is no time to develop a well-grounded knowledge of the craft; one might say that there is no learning curve. Little surprise that the harried designer resorts to cosmetic surgery. Square windows, symbolic gables, and arched entrances have been turned into clichés.

The superficiality of the Seven Implants also underlines an increasing powerlessness on the part of most of the architectural profession. As marketing and economics increasingly govern architectural decisions, the average designer, who lacks the authority of the celebrity architect, exerts less influence on the overall form and organization of buildings, and is cast in the role of stylist. Like a stylist, he must content himself with adding "little touches" to predetermined solutions. The problem is not only that so many architects are using artificial implants but that they are allowed nothing else.

Listen to the Melody

Goethe once described architecture as frozen music; if he was right, could cities be described as congealed concertos? The metaphor is flimsy, but music, architecture, and cities do share one striking characteristic. Just as rich music requires both solo and ensemble playing, and expanses of serenity provide the setting for moments of soaring drama in great architecture, so, too, successful cities carry an underlying melody. The pleasures of Venice or Florence are both the wonderful churches and civic buildings and the rich fabric of the more numerous commonplace structures in which people live and work. It is the street architecture that provides character in a city—the Georgian terraces and squares of London, the nineteenth-century brownstones of New York. Great cities celebrate not only their master architects but also the dozens of smaller talents who provide the less dramatic but equally precious background buildings.

One of the greatest architectural shortcomings of most of our modern cities is the apparent inability of builders to produce large numbers of unassuming but satisfying buildings that can form the backdrop for the occasional important landmark. Instead, what we have are cities composed increasingly of aspiring landmarks, which is to say cities without any landmarks at all.

There is a difference between background buildings and buildings that are merely undistinguished or indistinguishable. The criticism leveled against modernist design is that the buildings produced under this aesthetic were anonymous, faceless, identical. A post office looked the same as a schoolhouse; both resembled nondescript factories. The return to a more traditional language in architecture—loosely referred to as postmodernism—has given designers a great deal more freedom to make richly expressive buildings with individual character. In the hands of a talented and knowledgeable practitioner like Michael Graves or Robert Venturi, this has produced evocative and eloquent public buildings.

At the same time, the newfound freedom has provided less gifted architects with an assortment of architectural tricks (the Seven Implants), yielding some of the least satisfying buildings of recent times. Forms are resuscitated from the past, but for the purpose of novelty, not clarity. Style layers style; a facade is transposed from medieval Italy, miniaturized or elongated, and mated to a Victorian gazebo or Georgian urns on the roof.

Traditional decoration is used—or abused—to evoke a vague connotation of the past, or merely to suggest luxury. An apartment building is made to look like a multistory palazzo; the variegated-stone-decorated storefronts put the Doge's Palace to shame; entrances of ordinary office towers imitate those of a cathedral, and their lobbies might have been designed by Albert Speer at the height of German National Socialism. Run-of-the-mill commercial buildings have sprouted floating keystones, split pediments, and a grab bag of ornamentation.

Is this the result of architectural hubris? Only partly. It is true that the emphasis on personal creativity in our individualistic society encourages mediocre talents to overreach themselves. Nor has the celebrity status awarded to prominent architects fostered any modesty in an egoistic profession. But a building is not only a reflection of its creator. Though writers, composers, painters, even filmmakers may choose to undertake commissions, their art allows them to initiate their own creations. Architects work for clients, who are not to be confused with patrons. Patrons say, "Do what you want"; clients demand, "Do what I want."

What do building clients want? Today, commercial buildings are required to stand apart from their neighbors—to provide status, prominence, an image, and corporate recognition for their owners. Today's architecture has become colorful packaging, intended to catch the eye like a detergent box on the supermarket shelf. Monarchs, popes, civic leaders, and, yes, architects from ancient Egypt to ancient Rome have used architecture as advertising; but in the past, classical architecture reserved its most charged vocabulary for important public buildings, such as libraries and cathedrals. A pedimented temple front could announce the entrance to a market; its architect would use rustic Tuscan columns, and through appropriate proportions and a judicious use of ornament he would modulate the intensity of its appearance. An analogous front on a university building could utilize refined Ionic columns, finer materials, and more ample moldings. Decorations, too, communicated a building's function: bas-reliefs of books and scientific implements (or of vegetables), sculptures of famous people, Latin mottoes incised into the frieze.

The communication of meaning, more than beauty, distinguishes architecture from engineering. A bridge must be solid, functional, and attractive; a good public library must be all of these, but it also carries cultural baggage. Its architecture defines our attitude toward reading and celebrates a sense of civic pride. A library is more than a warehouse for books; it is a built evocation of an intellectual ideal.

Classical architecture managed to convey meaning in a fashion that was not only rich enough to be used in a variety of public buildings but also widely understood and cherished. Its potency and its longevity were enhanced by its widespread application in the modest architecture of homes and places of work. The selective use of classical details produces buildings that are less architecturally charged than, but not unrelated to, their more impressive neighbors. As the architect Allan Greenberg has pointed out, the front door of a Colonial Revival cottage is a simplified version of the entrance to the White House. This concern for a fitting expression of a building's importance—whether a President's house or a private citizen's dwelling—produced cities of a wide range of intelligible architecture: mundane and monumental, familiar and commandingly grand.

The best-known examples of this sensitive balance between public and private buildings are the eighteenth-century Georgian extensions to Dublin and Bath, and Bloomsbury in London. The residential streets of the New Town of Edinburgh, planned in 1767 by James Craig, exhibit an admirable uniformity of materials (brick, stone, stucco), a constant roofline, and common repeating elements like columns, windows, and doors. The anonymity of the streets is relieved by public gardens and open spaces (squares, crescents, ovals) and by the monumental public buildings of Princes Street. The planned expansion of Barcelona by Ildefonso Cerdá in 1858 was based on a grid of octagonal blocks that were to be built on only two sides, with the remainder to be landscaped.

In seventeenth-century Amsterdam, Daniel Stolpaert, a surveyor-architect, established an explicit framework for the city—sites for large, important buildings beside the three main canals, and those for smaller homes along smaller canals. The houses themselves were variations on three simple canons: narrow decorated gable-fronts, large multipaned windows, and a consistent face along the sidewalk, interrupted by a multitude of stoops and shallow projections. In Boston's Back Bay, planned in 1857 on a filled-in tidal marsh, the precepts were different and governed the height of the house, its setback from the street, and the distribution and proportions of the characteristic bay windows. The result was an environment of rich and varied urbanity, the architecture of the narrow side streets contrasting with the stateliness of Commonwealth Avenue.

Such architectural propriety is absent today, owing to the attitudes of architects and their clients. Our cities lack a satisfying background. There is no melody, no ensemble; only solo players, many of whom are commonplace. To fashion the modern equivalent of the classical city, it is not enough to incorporate classical forms into individual buildings. They must be used in a classical fashion—with intelligence, restraint, and decorum.

No simple formula guarantees this goal. But achievements like Edinburgh's New Town and Boston's Back Bay were not accidents; they were the result of a unified control of land and buildings, an intelligent plan, and knowledgeable individuals—developers, architects, and builders—to execute them. These conditions were buttressed by a consensus—often explicit—about what constituted architectural good manners.

Rules, not inspiration, guided the growth of the town of Seaside, a Florida resort community. The enlightened developer, Robert

S. Davis, engaged Andres Duany and Elizabeth Plater-Zyberk as planners and architects, and they made an unusual decision. To avoid the sterility of a "project," they resolved that the buildings be designed by a variety of architects. Rather than a master plan, they compiled an urban code—an architectural etiquette—that would guide all future construction. The rules dictated the presence of porches, vertical window proportions, painted wood siding, and consistent roof slopes. The result, while not a historical re-creation, suggests the comfortable sociability of small Southern towns, in which the majority of buildings fit in rather than stand out.

One of the consultants to Seaside was the London-based Luxembourgian architect Leon Krier, who has made several urban proposals based on distinctly traditional rules. His designs demonstrate a special concern for identifying architectural elements that produce satisfying and familiar background buildings. Although he is best known as a theorist and critic of modern town planning, it may well be Krier who will realize the first modern classical city. In 1988, he was engaged to devise a plan for Poundbury, a new town for ten thousand people in southwestern England. Preliminary descriptions, as well as Krier's previous work, suggest that the planning will be compact and scaled to the pedestrian, while the modest buildings will be low in height and will incorporate recognizable classically inspired forms. This will undoubtedly please the client, himself a vocal critic of modern architecture—H.R.H. the Prince of Wales, Prince Charles. One looks forward to seeing the result of this unusual collaboration.

Reprise: The Art of Building, or the Building of Art?

On the corner of La Huerta Road was a miniature Rhine castle with tarpaper turrets pierced for archers. Next to it was a highly colored shack with domes and minarets out of the *Arabian Nights*. Again he was charitable. Both houses were comic, but he didn't laugh. Their desire to startle was so eager and guileless.

It is hard to laugh at the need for beauty and romance, no matter how tasteless, even horrible, the results of that are. But it is easy to sigh. Few things are sadder than the truly monstrous.

NATHANAEL WEST
The Day of the Locust

The title of this essay is a question that would have been unthinkable ninety years ago—or even, for different reasons, thirty years ago. At both of those moments in our century, architects and their patrons agreed about what constituted good architecture. This is no longer the case.

Perhaps I feel this lack of agreement more acutely because I teach in a school of architecture; and at McGill University, as at all schools on the North American continent, there is no longer an accepted canon of architectural principles. Instead, a multitude of contradictory intellectual positions jostle for primacy. This disarray is evidenced, first of all, in the content of the courses. Until 1941, architectural teaching at McGill was influenced by ideas from Britain, chiefly Scotland. The school was founded in 1896 by Stewart Capper, who, although an Englishman, was educated and trained in Edinburgh, where he lived and worked before immigrating to Montreal. The next two directors, Percy Nobbs and Ramsay Traquair, were both Scots and brought with them an approach based largely on the Scottish Arts and Crafts movement. They also inculcated the school with a curiously Scottish mixture of romanticism and pragmatism. Architecture was taught as a discipline founded on historical examples, responding to local conditions (such as a rigorous climate, which Montreal shares with Edinburgh) and requiring the learning of particular skills, especially sketching, drawing, and modeling.

After 1941, under the leadership of John Bland, a Canadian, the course was modified to stress functional requirements, modern construction techniques, and a modernist aesthetic. The new curriculum loosely followed the lines of Mies van der Rohe's 1937 program at the Illinois Institute of Technology. Regarding his teaching goals, Mies wrote: "It is the business of education to implant insight and responsibility. It must turn irresponsible opinion into responsible judgement and lead from chance and arbitrariness to the rational lucidity of an intellectual order." The emphasis at Mies's school was on understanding construction and building materials, studying functions, and learning how to integrate these to produce complete architectural forms. Courses were organized sequentially to bring the student slowly to the realization, first, of what was possible; second, of what was necessary; and finally, of what was significant.

Both the Arts and Crafts and the Miesian approaches represented an integrated, comprehensive method of teaching architecture that was shared by the staff. The widely varying content of courses in architecture schools today is a function of how different professors interpret the subject. In rapid, bewildering succession, a student is taught that buildings should represent their function; that they are really personal essays in which function plays a secondary role; that the responsibility of the architect is to respond to the needs of the client; that the duty of the architect is to challenge societal values; and that commercial concerns or user preferences must be ignored if the purity of the architectural ideal is to be maintained. One teacher sets a problem in which students are required to explore a specific historical style; another denounces any historical references as mere pastiche. It's difficult to teach students about housing, as I've tried to do, when they have been told in another class that housing is not the proper concern of an architect—indeed, that housing is not really architecture at all.

This confusion is reflected in the work that students do for their final projects. The final project represents a long tradition in architectural education. At the end of the program, the student is asked to design a building of his or her own choosing. It is an opportunity for students to demonstrate the skills that they've acquired in the previous three and a half years and the architectural equivalent of the free program in figure skating: after many imposed exercises, students are let loose to strut their stuff.

Students' choices tend to mirror the concerns of the moment. During the early 1960s, when social issues were paramount, the final project was usually an ambitious housing development; in the late sixties, there were a lot of idealistic projects for low-income housing, community centers, and small-scale neighborhood infill. Revolutionary rhetoric replaced traditional architectural discourse, and discussion concerned sociology rather than construction. The seventies, in reaction to this radicalism, saw a revival of interest in architectural history and in the design of traditional types of buildings, such as city halls, libraries, and museums. Beautifully rendered drawings, up to Beaux-Arts standards, made a comeback.

The hallmark of the last ten years has been an intense individualism, in keeping with the Me Decade. What was striking was the way in which this individualism asserted itself architecturally. Buildings with strict functional requirements, such as housing, office buildings, factories, schools, and hospitals, were rarely undertaken as final projects. Even at McGill's conservative School of Architecture, students were encouraged to explore problems that incorporated a large emotive component. This produced a rash of exhibition pavilions, opera houses, and churches, and such esoteric buildings as monasteries, cemeteries, and commemorative monuments. Some ventured even farther afield: a hospice, a meditation center, a museum of ecology, and a floating theater. Not only were projects imaginative, but they were often imaginary: "A Church for a New Religion" or "An Airship Terminal." I think that students were attracted to such unusual buildings because their functional requirements were marginal—sometimes nonexistent. This allowed the tyro to deal with what was increasingly seen as purely architectural concerns.

And what were these concerns? Above all, self-expression. During the Me Decade, architecture was seen as an opportunity to express the individuality of the designer. The users of the building and the client were scarcely mentioned. Such personal expression in a building manifested itself chiefly in the creation of unusual forms. One student produced an odd-looking office building that turned out to be based on television components—tubes, circuitry, speakers—that had been copied from a manufacturer's repair manual. The bits and pieces were then greatly enlarged and assigned building functions. The student's rationale for this appropriation was that the project would house the Canadian Broadcasting Corporation. Another memorable project involved a center for political retreats—a sort of grandiose Meech Lake—whose form was derived from an interpretation of Pliny the Younger's description of his seaside villa at Laurentum.

The nineties promise a continuation of this self-indulgence. There is no longer any consensus among students or teachers about what the societal role of architecture is—or indeed that it has one. There is no general agreement about whether the responsibility of the architect is to the community, to the users of the building, to the client, or merely to himself. There are no more universally accepted rules for the making of buildings, which is why I would say that, at least in the traditional sense, there is no more teaching.

Am I perhaps exaggerating? Is this a simple case of a middle-aged professor's burnout? Or maybe this architectural ferment is a temporary outbreak of youthful exuberance and delayed adolescent rebellion, students sowing architectural wild oats before getting down to the serious business of a professional career. In any case, the general public need not concern itself about the confused state of architectural education. That is the concern of teachers. But what if the academy mirrors the state of architecture in the outside world?

To answer this question, let me describe my own outside world, the campus of McGill University, with its rich heritage of late-nineteenth-century architecture. The first building—the original McGill College, now the Arts Building—with its Doric porch and central position on the main axis of the campus, is still the most recognizable McGill landmark; its cupola appears on the MasterCard I carry in my wallet. Built in 1865, it was for many years the only building on the campus.

Radiating from this center, and embracing the campus green like two extended arms, is a magnificent series of limestone buildings, most of which were built between 1890 and 1910. On the east side the styles are a mixture of Scottish Arts and Crafts and neo-Romanesque, the latter derived from the great American architect of the moment, H. H. Richardson, and his disciple Bruce Price, then active in Montreal building Windsor Station and McGill's Royal Victoria College. Like Price's work, the McGill buildings are picturesque compositions with arched windows, circular towers, and steep roofs topped with gables, dormers, and clusters of chimneys. They include Andrew Taylor's Chemistry Building (now housing the School of Architecture) and his Physics Building, and Percy Nobbs's Engineering Building. On the other side there is a greater variety of styles. The Redpath Museum is a classical shed with a pedimented front designed by Hitchinson and Steele. Then there is J. J. Browne's neo-Gothic Presbyterian College, followed by the medieval-looking Redpath Library—Taylor again—which contains the splendid hammer-beamed hall that now serves as the chief assembly space of the university.

Unlike Princeton, which is characterized by a consistent neo-Gothic style, McGill chose variety in the architecture of its buildings. Nevertheless, in hindsight it becomes clear that the diversity of styles did not represent a divergence of views about what constituted correct architecture. These architects chose different styles not out of personal willfulness but to suit different programs. The Presbyterian College, like all four Protestant theological colleges at McGill, is neo-Gothic because that style is appropriate to its use. The facade of the museum, as befits a repository of antiquities, exhibits an unusual mixture of Greek, Roman, and Egyptian motifs. Nobbs gave the Engineering Building a robust, masculine appearance, fitting its practical mission. His Student Union is a more elegant and urbane building, patterned on a London men's club, then an appropriate model for a student center.

Since the short period of their construction, much has been added. There are flat-faced stone-and-glass boxes from the fifties and busy precast-concrete compositions from the seventies. Most universities have at least one circular building; at McGill it houses the medical sciences. There are also student residences housed in three Corbusier-like slabs abutting Mount Royal. A recently completed bookstore incorporates trendy pinnacles and circular windows.

None of these newer buildings measures up to the more substantial products of the initial burst of building activity. The limestone blocks appear as solid as the mountain in the background; by contrast, the more recent additions seem flimsy, tentative, almost temporary. The older buildings also welcome the people who use them. The Victorian and Edwardian architects incorporated outdoor steps, which not only provide a special sense of entrance but also serve in summer as convenient lounging places. The new buildings, on the other hand, are entered without ceremony, through prosaic lobbies with suspended ceilings of acoustic tile. Taylor and Nobbs adorned their buildings with evocative figures and mottoes; the new architecture adheres to the abstract geometry of international modernism.

A curious footnote. My own department recently moved from a building constructed in 1958 to one completed in 1896. There had been a minimal amount of renovation in the mechanical and electrical systems, but the original building was little changed. Both staff and students agree that our new home is vastly superior to our old one—in spite of the fact that the bland 1958 building was designed expressly as a school of architecture and our present quarters were planned for the department of chemistry.

In *India: A Million Mutinies Now* (1990), V. S. Naipaul describes the country's architecture:

> Indians have been building in free India for 40 years, and what has been put up in that time makes it easier to look at what went before. In free India Indians have built like people without a tradition; they have for the most part done mechanical, surface imitations of the international style. What is not easy to understand is that, unlike the British, Indians have not really built for the Indian climate. They have been too obsessed with imitating the modern; and much of what has been done in this way—the dull, four-square towers of Bombay, packed far too close together; the concrete nonentity of Lucknow and Madras and the residential colonies of New Delhi—can only make hard tropical lives harder and hotter.
>
> Far from extending people's ideas of beauty and grandeur and human possibility—uplifting ideas which very poor people may need more than rich people—much of the architecture of free India has become part of the ugliness and crowd and increasing physical oppression of India. Bad architecture in a poor tropical city is more than an aesthetic matter. It spoils people's day-to-day lives; it wears down their nerves; it generates rages that can flow into many different channels.

This Indian architecture, more disdainful of the people it serves than British Indian architecture ever was, now makes the most matter-of-fact Public Works Department bungalow of the British time seem like a complete architectural thought. And if one goes on from there, and considers the range of British building in India, the time span, the varied styles of those two centuries, the developing functions (railway stations, the Victoria Memorial in Calcutta, the Gateway of India in Bombay, the legislative buildings of Lucknow and New Delhi), it becomes obvious that British Indian architecture—which can so easily be taken for granted—is the finest secular architecture in the sub-continent.

There is a curious parallel between Naipaul's observation that the buildings by British architects in India were superior to those the Indians would build themselves and the contrast between the first buildings at McGill and what followed. Despite their short acquaintance with Canada, the Scots Andrew Taylor and Percy Nobbs produced better work than their native-born descendants. By better I mean not only more appealing, more comfortable, and more humane buildings but structures that paradoxically are more at home—more characteristically Canadian.

I am not arguing here that the British Victorians in Canada or India had an innate architectural talent that their colonial subjects lacked. Rather, their approach was responsive to their new environment and produced successful architecture.

The architectural successes and failures at McGill could stand as a model of our cities and towns. I have always thought that the present strength of the heritage movement across the continent is at least partly due to the public's disaffection with contemporary architecture. The unspoken argument of many conservationists is that all new building should be resisted on the ground that the new inevitably will be a poor substitute for the old.

I believe that this skepticism is related to another issue. One of the greatest architectural shortcomings of our cities today is the apparent inability of contemporary architects to produce large numbers of unassuming but satisfying buildings to form the backdrop for the occasional important monument. We need good background buildings, but who wants to design them? (Judging by the high-flying final projects, not the current generation of students.) Everybody wants to be a star. Is this a product of the Me Decade? A result of the celebrity that some architects now enjoy? Or is it the result of the way in which architects—and their clients—think about buildings?

The leading American journal *Progressive Architecture* publishes an annual issue featuring outstanding houses. It's interesting to see how the houses are presented. In many cases the rooms are empty, photographed before the owners have moved in and spoiled the architect's design. In other illustrations the furniture is so studiously arranged that the effect is even more bizarre. The absence of the slightest sign of the owners' personalities makes these interiors appear uninhabited. In a house designed by Richard Meier for a couple with an extensive collection of art and craft objects, the caption notes that because the architect did not approve every artifact in the collection, some pieces were temporarily removed when the photographs were taken. Le Corbusier's famous statement that "life always has the last word" appears quaint and old-fashioned in this context.

In the same issue (1990) of the magazine is an interview with the noted Italian architect and industrial designer Ettore Sottsass, best known as one of the founders of the Memphis group. Sottsass describes a resort village he is designing in Colorado. The houses were to be sold, he says, "not as speculation houses, but the way you buy a painting, or a sculpture."

Leaving aside the issue of whether or not paintings and sculptures aren't bought precisely for speculation, Sottsass's characterization is a reminder that architecture is now commonly considered as one of the plastic arts. According to this view, buildings are aesthetic objects whose purpose is not only to house human activities but also—and perhaps chiefly—to celebrate the individual expression of the designer. Hence the emphasis on originality.

To explain how this concept infiltrated architectural thought, it is necessary to underline the influence of art history on architecture. Art history was traditionally the study of all important art. In the case of architecture it was easy enough to identify the important buildings: they were those built by the important institutions, the Church and the nobility. Hence the history of architecture was the history of religious buildings and palaces.

The number of such buildings was relatively small, as was the number of architects. In the late eighteenth century, growing prosperity made architecture accessible to many more clients, and the range of buildings that architects designed expanded with the size of the profession. Beyond churches and grand houses, architects were being commissioned for public buildings, such as hospitals, prisons, libraries, and museums. They were also designing factories, speculative housing, even farm buildings. That is to say, the work of architects now included buildings whose monumental and symbolic role was often secondary, or even nonexistent.

This was all very well for the profession, but it complicated the work of the art historians. Not only was the sheer quantity of buildings increased, but aesthetic and theoretical concerns were often superseded by engineering and commercial considerations. It was no longer clear which buildings were important, and the art historian's role changed accordingly: he was required to be not only an observer and a chronicler of the past but also a critic.

As in the plastic arts, the identity of the artist who created the work determined the canon. The study of architecture could now be described not as the study of all important buildings but as the study of the work of a relatively small number of important architects. Who were the important architects? Naturally, those whose work accorded with the art historian's values. Hence the modernist historians' disdain for the work of eclectic architects like John Russell Pope, who designed the National Gallery of Art in Washington, D.C.; Thomas Hastings, the architect of the New York Public Library; and Charles McKim, who built Pennsylvania Station in New York. I mention these particular buildings because all three housed important institutions and became major urban landmarks, much beloved by the people who frequented them and successful in their function. But none was considered a work of art in the modernist sense, and consequently all were ignored by modern art historians.

Here begins the disparity between the buildings that made the greatest impression on the public and those that were recognized as "serious" architecture by historians and critics. The Ottawa City Hall, for example, was acclaimed because it adhered to the modernist dictum; the nearby Château Laurier, a much better example of sensitive and clever urban design, was dismissed as unimportant because it was in a historical style.

The nineteenth-century art historian described the past as a succession of styles (Romanesque, Gothic, Renaissance), and modern architectural criticism adapted that approach. Hence we have modernism followed by late modernism, postmodernism, deconstructivism, and so on. Since the identification of styles is based chiefly on the visual attributes of buildings, it follows that buildings are studied as isolated objects. Not surprisingly, the three buildings identified as masterpieces of modernist architecture—Le Corbusier's Villa Savoye, Wright's Fallingwater, and Mies van der Rohe's Farnsworth House—are all isolated houses in country settings. Each can be appreciated without reference to anything except the surrounding landscape.

Art historians have had a significant influence on contemporary architectural theory because they played an important role in the evolution of architecture. Nikolaus Pevsner, Henry-Russell Hitchcock, and Siegfried Giedion were the advance men of the modern movement. They became propagandists, establishing the historical and intellectual pedigree of the new ideas in architecture. Books such as Pevsner's *Pioneers of Modern Design* (1936) and Giedion's *Space, Time and Architecture* (1941) became de facto *Who's Whos* of the new architecture. The exhibition on the International Style organized by Hitchcock and Philip Johnson at the Museum of Modern Art in 1932 played a similar accrediting role.

Just as in contemporary painting and sculpture, critics were interested in the avant-garde. Hence the focus on originality, on the shocking and the new, the risqué and the unusual. Books and exhibitions also stressed the visual aspects of architecture at the expense of such issues as function, clients' needs, and the relationship of buildings to their surroundings.

More recently, architecture has been taken with its own glamour.

In an increasingly visual culture, it's not surprising that architecture should come to the fore. The discovery that architecture could play an important role in marketing was perhaps the chief influence on design in the 1980s.

Each architect now tries, within the limits of his budget and talent, to make an individual statement. Like the students in their final projects, professionals, too, are strutting their stuff, and the urban result—whatever the merits of the individual buildings—is chaotic and muddled. In contrast, the Victorian and Edwardian buildings at McGill exhibit a sense of compatibility. Their architects were respectful of the occupants, and also of the adjoining buildings. An architect would say that the buildings spoke the same language. This was not a question of talent. Taylor and Nobbs and their contemporaries certainly were gifted designers, but they were better architects because they were playing the game by better rules.

In April 1989 I was invited to talk about *The Most Beautiful House in the World* on a public television program hosted by Lewis Lapham, the editor of *Harper's* magazine. At one point Mr. Lapham turned to me and asked a blunt question: "Is architecture an art?" Most of my mumbled and inadequate answer was mercifully edited from the final program. Later, reflecting on what I'd said —or, rather, not said—I tried to understand why the straightforward question should have rattled me.

Webster defines "art" as creative work—which architecture certainly is—and distinguishes the "fine arts" from the merely useful on the basis of their aesthetic purpose; moreover, it specifically mentions architecture as an example of a fine art. Herbert Spencer listed architecture with sculpture, painting, music, and poetry as a mark of civilized life. And Goethe called architecture frozen music. Hence the simple answer to Lapham's question is: "Of course architecture is an art."

One of the oldest definitions of architecture was introduced to the English language by Sir Henry Wotton, a seventeenth-century English diplomat. Wotton, who is remembered as an angler and the subject of a biography by his friend Izaak Walton, was an architecture buff—an amateur in the best sense. He spent almost twenty years stationed in Venice and in 1624 published a short monograph on architecture, based on the work of Italian architects and writers such as Vasari, Palladio, and Alberti. Wotton called his book *The Elements of Architecture*, and he began it as follows: "In Architecture as in all other Operative Arts, the end must direct the Operation. The end is to build well. Well building has three conditions. Commoditie, Firmeness and Delight."

Though novel to an English-speaking reader, Wotton's description was hardly original. He was paraphrasing the famous triad of *utilitas*, *firmitas*, and *venustas*, coined by the Roman architect Vitruvius. A contemporary of the emperor Augustus, Vitruvius wrote a treatise on architecture that resurfaced in the fifteenth century—the only survivor of its kind. *Utilitas*, *firmitas*, and *venustas* showed up in the books of Alberti, written in the middle of the fifteenth century, and of Palladio, who published his influential work in 1570; Wotton wrote fifty-four years later. The great French architect and educator Jacques-François Blondel refers to "la commodité, la solidité, la beauté" in his 1752–56 treatise *Architecture Française*. By the time my professor, Peter Collins, taught me about *utilitas-firmitas-venustas*, the concept was almost two thousand years old.

I think two aspects of this definition of architecture explain its durability. The Vitruvian triad effectively describes the complex nature of architecture. *Venustas*—delight or beauty—deals with aesthetics and situates architecture with the fine arts. *Utilitas* and *firmitas*—commodity and firmness—concern practical issues and suggest that building might be, despite Webster's definition, described as one of the useful arts.

Another implication of the triad is often overlooked. Blondel writes that "good taste consists in joining together commodity, firmness, and delight." Palladio is equally adamant that the three attributes are inseparable. He does not say that beauty will follow automatically from functional design or economic structure, as many modernists claimed. Nor does he say that one can forgive beautiful buildings a lack of utility—or beautiful chairs a lack of comfort, as Philip Johnson once suggested. Palladio is unequivocal: perfection can be achieved only when a building combines all three elements of the Vitruvian triad.

One can surmise, although Palladio does not say this, that contradictions may arise between function and beauty, or between beauty and structure. By describing architecture as combining three very different qualities the Vitruvian definition suggests that the art of building, unlike the other fine arts, is always an art of compromise. The questions of judgment and balance become central.

Both Alberti and Palladio recognized that a building's function directly affects its design. This was not a question of form following function, but rather of form recognizing purpose. In the introduction to his eighth book, on ornament, Alberti noted: "It is quite clear that each building does not require the same ornament. With sacred works, especially public ones, every art and industry must be employed to render them as ornate as possible: sacred works must be furnished for the gods, secular ones only for man. The latter, being less dignified, should concede to the former, yet still be ennobled with their own details of ornament." Like Vitruvius, Alberti maintained that the purpose of a building should be visible in its design. Large public buildings, for example, required commodious interiors. "What a disagreeable and unseemly thing would it be," wrote Palladio, "if in a very large building there should be small halls and rooms; and, on the contrary, in a little one, there should be two or three rooms that took up the whole."

Decorum was essential to these Renaissance architects. A palace should look—and feel—like a palace; a church, like a church. A villa should not resemble a town hall. The one signified privacy and domesticity; the other, civic pride and monumentality.

The difficulty for an architect today who wishes to design grand civic buildings is that monumentality has lost its ability to impress; imposing facades are just as likely to appear on boutiques and weekend cottages as on courthouses. Blame for this goes to the client as well as to the architect. If you pay extra for a pair of Calvin Klein jeans, you want people to notice. If you pay extra—and you do—for a Richard Meier or a Arata Isozaki, you want a building that will stand out.

Firmness, Vitruvius's second attribute of architecture, calls for a great degree of skill. As Alberti observed: "The construction of a building does not just entail setting stone on stone, and aggregate upon aggregate, as the ignorant may imagine; for, because the parts are different, so too the materials and methods of construction vary quite radically." Alberti took it for granted that design and construction were inseparable. It is this merging of intentions and means that sets architecture apart from engineering, as well as from stage design.

Firmness derives both from the building materials—the richness of wood, the cold precision of metal, the hues and textures of stone—and from the way in which they all come together in a unified whole. Firmness also conveys a sense of permanence, which is one of the chief pleasures of architecture.

The form of a building is intimately concerned with construction. A good architect is above all a builder; a bad architect designs first and then asks, "How am I going to build this?" When the link between design and construction is broken, as it is in so many modern buildings, architecture is the loser, and architects are cast adrift, searching for inspiration in history, philosophy, sculpture, and painting.

The concern that the architect shares with the artist is beauty. There is no question that architecture can be sublime. My first sight of the Villa Rotonda, in the haze of an early morning, was a moment that I will never forget. But beauty is not reserved only for masterpieces. It is—or should be—present in all works of architecture. It manifests itself in many small ways: a framed view, the changing pattern of light and shadow on a stone wall, the pleasing shape of a roof silhouette. Architectural beauty—perhaps delight *is* a better word—often has an everyday quality that is undramatic but precious.

Decorum demands that the architect be master of many aesthetics: the tragedy of Maya Lin's Vietnam War Memorial in Washington, D.C.; the heroism of Lutyens's Viceroy's House in New Delhi; the chaste beauty of Labrouste's Bibliothèque Sainte-Geneviève in Paris; or the modest charm of a country house. A mastery of scale is also essential. A wonderful explanation of the relationship between beauty and scale is attributed to the Italian architect Carlo Scarpa: "If you are making a corridor that is twenty feet wide, you can make it out of concrete; if it is ten feet wide, you should use stone; if it is six feet wide, use fine wood; but if it is two feet wide, you should make it out of solid gold."

There is a final way in which the art of building differs from the fine arts. Buildings are always attached to particular places. They must respond to topography and climate, and also to their position in particular architectural settings. Photographs in architectural magazines and books may block out these settings, but it is only a temporary ruse. For the architect-builder, the context is always a challenge, and sometimes an inspiration. For the artist-builder it is a constraint, an inconvenience, or, at best, a mere backdrop. The reader can judge which approach is likely to produce a more satisfying environment.

Suggesting a return to the Vitruvian ideal could be described as reactionary. The historian John Lukacs, in his wonderful memoir *Confessions of an Original Sinner*, has provided a marvelous definition of the reactionary: "A reactionary considers character but distrusts publicity . . . he favors conservation rather than conservatism; he favors the ancient blessings of the land and is dubious about the results of technology; he believes in history, not in Evolution. . . . A reactionary will recognize how, contrary to Victor Hugo's hoary nineteenth-century cliché, An Idea Whose Time Has Come may not be any good."

The idea that architecture consists of the building of art has produced a multitude of idiosyncratic and startlingly original work; it has even made architecture glamorous. But the lifting of traditional constraints has also resulted in an ephemeral freedom that has not produced better architects, better buildings, or better cities. And we desperately need all three.

Index

Index

Index